Being Reflexive in Critical Educational and Social Research

Social Research and Educational Studies Series

Series Editor: Robert G Burgess, Professor of Sociology,
University of Warwick

Being Reflexive in Critical Educational and Social Research

Edited by

Geoffrey Shacklock and John Smyth

UK   Falmer Press, 1 Gunpowder Square, London, EC4A 3DE
USA   Falmer Press, Taylor & Francis Inc., 1900 Frost Road, Suite 101,
        Bristol, PA 19007

First published in 1998

A catalogue record for this book is available from the British Library

ISBN 0 7507 0776 3 cased
ISBN 0 7507 0775 5 paper

Library of Congress Cataloging-in-Publication Data are available on request

Jacket design by Caroline Archer

Typeset in 10/12 pt Times by
Graphicraft Typesetters Limited, Hong Kong

Printed in Great Britain by Biddles Ltd., Guildford and King's Lynn on paper which has a specified pH value on final paper manufacture of not less than 7.5 and is therefore 'acid free'.

Contents

Contents

Acknowledgments

We express our appreciation to Flinders University of South Australia for making available a research grant to make this book possible.

As always, Solveiga has had an indispensable role in the production of this book; ensuring that references were located, authors were hassled, and that it all came together in a timely fashion.

Chapter 2 originally appeared in *Qualitative Inquiry*, Volume 2, Number 3, 1996 pp. 251–74 and our appreciation is expressed for the permission to reproduce it here.

Series Editor's Preface

The purpose of the *Social Research and Educational Studies* series is to provide authoritative guides to key issues in educational research. The series includes overviews of fields, guidance on good practice and discussions of the practical implications of social and educational research. In particular, the series deals with a variety of approaches to conducting social and educational research. Contributors to this series review recent work, raise critical concerns that are particular to the field of education and reflect on the implications of research for educational policy and practice.

Each volume in the series draws on material that will be relevant for an international audience. The contributors to this series all have wide experience of teaching, conducting and using educational research. The volumes are written so that they will appeal to a wide audience of students, teachers and researchers. Altogether the volumes in the *Social Research and Educational Studies* series provide a comprehensive guide for anyone concerned with contemporary educational research.

In recent years there has been much debate about 'critical research' and 're-flexivity'. Geoffrey Shacklock and John Smyth have brought together an international group of researchers to write about the practice of such work. Writing in the autobiographical tradition the authors share new insights on the research process and the practice of critical social research. I am sure that the volume will be of great value to established and beginning researchers.

Robert G Burgess
University of Warwick

1   Behind the 'Cleansing' of Socially Critical Research Accounts

John Smyth and Geoffrey Shacklock

Why This Collection?

The idea for this collection on being reflexive about critical educational and social research, came from conversations we had on the personal struggle of doing research, and writing accounts of those struggles. In the first instance, these conversations were pedagogical because of their focus on researching the process of placing closure on a dissertation. Later, the conversations became more concerned about the absence of such commentaries. It became clear that it was often difficult to find an account of the complexities of doing critical research, written by a researcher who could construct the account out of a critical appraisal of their own work.

We saw a need for deeply personal and individual readings of 'the experience of critical research' in educational and social settings. We saw a need for individual researchers to present accounts of the experience of the critical research act using reflective postures that challenged why one course of action was taken from among a range of possibilities. Such accounts, we thought, should focus upon those issues and dilemmas which caused trouble and uncertainty in the research process. As we saw it, such accounts would tell the story about the intersection of the critical research perspective and the particular circumstances of the research context, as they occur in the actual experience of doing critically–oriented research.

This collection is therefore grounded in the primacy of the reflexive moment in critical forms of research. Each account develops through expressions, self–reflections about the researcher's struggle with the epistemological, methodological, and political issues that are always inherent in critical qualitative research in educational and social settings. We believe those accounts provide the 'personal' dimension that links the theoretical discourse of socially critical research and its methodological imperative, to the particular research act. These portrayals are an explicit recognition of the impact of the researcher on the intentions, processes and outcomes of the research.

We have tried to assemble a collection that fills a space in accounts of critical educational and social research; sometimes referred to as the phenomenon of the 'missing researcher'. The reflexive narratives of researcher's encounters with the intersections between the researcher's values and the research processes reintroduces the researcher as person into the account. Issues like: ethics, gender, race, validity, reciprocity, sexuality, voice, empowerment, authorship, and readership can be brought into the open and allowed to 'breathe' as important research matters.

We see these reflexive readings on critical research as important windows on the tensions between: epistemology and methodology, critical theory and post–modern thinking, and scientism and politicization, experienced by critical qualitative researchers. Many of the important issues that critical researchers face in their work are exposed in a way that says: 'I too know how it feels to do this kind of research'.

Contributors open up how they went about the task of dealing with the uncertainties of bringing a critical research project from conception to completion. These contributions are about the (in)/visibility of thickness–thinness between the two sides of the theory–practice coin. In other words, that aspect of the research process which usually has great volume but low surface area — its substance is always high for the researcher(s), but its visibility is often low for the research (product) audience.

What we have in the contributions to the book, is 'rendition–exposure' that allows others to experience something of the struggle and excitement of the research act. In Eisner's (1979, 1991) terms, the contributors have engaged in acts of research 'connoisseurship'; they have presented personal insights of the research act as part of an examination of their own research experience. They give expression to inner dialogue that generally exists only as a sub–text in parts of a research account. We believe that these reflexive accounts give valuable readings of researcher understanding of how complexity in research is understood by researchers themselves.

What Do *We* Mean by Critical Research?

There are some misconceptions as to what constitutes critical research; for example, that its emphasis is negative or carping, or that it is somehow committed to fault–finding. Readings like this are give–aways that those making them have not read themselves into the meaning of 'critical' as expressed in the sociological literature.

One of the more concise straightforward explanations of what it means to operate critically has been provided by Robert Cox (1980), when he said: '[To be critical is to] stand apart from the prevailing order of the world and ask how that order came about' (p. 129). Cox argues that the place of theory is neither incidental nor unimportant in this, and that theory can be regarded as serving two possible purposes. The first view of theory is that it is a guide to help solve problems posed within a particular perspective. This view of theory 'takes the world as it finds it . . . with the prevailing social and power relations and institutions into which they are organized, as the given framework for action' (ibid, p. 128). The second set of views about theory, is that its purpose is to 'open up the possibility of choosing a different valid perspective from which the problematic becomes one of creating an alternative world' (idid, p. 128). Depending upon which purpose we opt for, theory will have quite a different meaning. While for both approaches the starting point is some aspect or instance of human activity, the orientation to the relationship between the parts and the whole is quite different in each case. From a problem–solving perspective, the approach is one that 'leads to a further analytical sub–division and limitation of the issues to be dealt with . . .' (ibid, p. 129). In the case of critical theory, the approach is one which 'leads towards the construction of a larger picture

Figure 1.1:   Critical social research

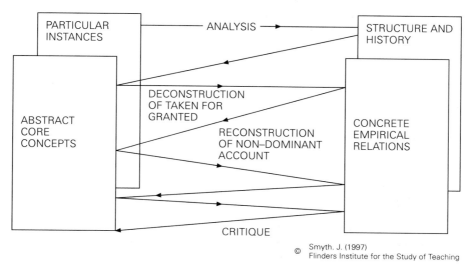

©   Smyth. J. (1997)
    Flinders Institute for the Study of Teaching

Source: Adapted from Harvey (1990)

of the whole of which the initially contemplated part is just one component, and seeks to understand the processes of change in which both parts and whole are involved' (ibid, p. 129). This is a distinction which is fundamental to the chapters contained in this book.

Another way of speaking about this is in terms of the dialectical relationship between particular instances, concrete empirical relations, abstract core concepts, and structure and history. Harvey (1990) speaks about critical research as cutting through 'surface appearances' (p. 19) by locating the issues being investigated in their historical and structural contexts. Critical research, as Harvey argues, continually engages in an ongoing conversation, analysis and critique of these elements, starting from the position that the object of study is not ' "objective" social appearances' (ibid). Phenomena, from a critical vantage point, are not considered to stand on their own but are implicated, embedded and located in wider contexts that are not entirely innocent. Furthermore, such structures are 'maintained through the exercise of political and economic power' which is 'legitimated through ideology' (ibid, p. 19). Research of this kind raises serious questions about 'who can speak?' (Roof and Weigman, 1995).

Critical research then, is centrally concerned with the simultaneous process of 'deconstruction' and 'reconstruction'. It works something like this. Within a piece of research, some core abstract concepts are located which are considered to be central; they are used repeatedly to interrogate situations of concrete lived reality in order to develop a new synthesis. In this sense, theory is not, therefore, simply 'abstract analysis' nor is it something merely to be tacked onto data at the end of some process of analysis; rather, what occurs is a theory–building process involving:

> . . . a constant shuttling backwards and forwards between abstract concept and concrete data; between social totalities and particular phenomena; between current structures and historical development; between surface appearance and essence; between reflection and practice. (Harvey, 1990, p. 29)

The intent is to engage in a constant questioning and building up of theory and interpretations through repeated ongoing analysis until a coherent alternative reconstruction of the account is created. As Harvey notes, the selection of a 'core' concept is not a final or a single instance; 'it only emerges in the course of the analysis . . . and it is only "correct" in the sense that it provides . . . the best focus [at that time]' (ibid, p. 30). In many respects, this genre of research is conversational in that there is constant dialogue between core concepts and data about fieldwork situations. It amounts to a kind of 'negotiating the question' (Roof and Weigman, 1995, p. x) in that what is worthwhile saying or pursuing can never be stated definitively, but only as a consequence of having commenced some inquiry, discussion or conversation. It is very much a case of 'conversation begins in response, not in a speaker's singular assertion' (ibid).

What Will This Book Add to the Field of Critical Research?

Engaging in critical research of the kind generally described above, and undertaken elsewhere by the contributors to this book, involves a number of what Lather (1992) calls 'critical frames'. These might be taken to include aspects like the following:

- studying marginalized or oppressed groups who are not given the authority to speak;

- approaching inquiry in ways that are interruptive of taken–for–granted social practices;

- locating meaning in broader social, cultural and political spheres;

- developing themes and categories from data, but treating them problematic-ally and as being open to interrogation;

- editing the researcher into the text, and not presuming that she/he is a neutral actor in the research;

- being reflexive of its own limitations, distortions and agenda;

- concerned about the impact of the research in producing more equitable and just social relationships (Smyth, 1994).

Given that much of the work that is the subject of reflection in this book comes from researchers who have undertaken some version of critical ethnography (although not all would describe it in that way), we would do well to attune ourselves to some of the difficulties articulated by ethnographers generally.

Pearson (1993) makes the point that: 'ethnography is a messy business, something you would not always gather from many of the "research methods" texts which deal with the subject' (p. vii). What *Being Reflexive* does, like Hobbs and May's (1993) book that engages authors in getting behind previously published interpretive ethnographic accounts, is to offer a variety of accounts (albeit from the socially critical domain) by researchers who have similarly described 'the difficulties which can (and do) arise when researchers attempt to "immerse" themselves in other people's lives' (Pearson, 1993, p. vii). Like Pearson we started from the vantage point that:

> Published accounts of fieldwork are invariably cleansed of the 'private' goings-on between researcher and researched. When the lid is taken off, however, this can be something of a shock. (ibid, p. vii)

Both Hobbs (1993) and May (1993) attest to their feelings about the changed relationship they experienced once the fieldwork was completed and the text 'concluded' — a point made by most of the authors in this volume. It is what occurs after the account has been 'sanitized' that can often be the most revealing, for, as Hobbs (1993) notes, the original pass at codifying the procedure by which the research was done invariably masks and conceals much:

> It seeks to neatly dissect the research process, packaging its various components into self-contained, hermetically sealed units bonded with a common epistemology. (p. 46)

Yet, the reality for many researchers is that 'changes . . . take . . . place outside the sanctified confines of the fieldwork' and that 'our experiential and interpretive faculties continue to function long after the gate to the field has been closed. Funding may have been turned off but intellectual work keeps flowing' (ibid, p. 48). For May (1993) the challenge here is to 'invert the hidden equation' where the equation is 'feelings = weakness' (ibid, p. 76). He says, the myth 'is perpetrated whereby personal feelings (read as "inaccurate" or "untrue") during ethnographic research are typically viewed as impediments to good practice and analysis' (ibid, p. 72). May concurs with Hammersley and Atkinson (1983) that: 'Rather than engaging in futile attempts to eliminate the effects of the researcher, we should set about understanding them' (1993, p. 75).

With this set of considerations in mind, we see the contribution of this book as building upon the work of writers like: Quantz (1992) and McLaren and Giarelli (1995) in education, and Morrow and Brown (1994), Harvey (1990), and Burawoy et al. (1991) in critical social science more generally. We also see the book, in part, as an indirect rejoinder to Hammersley (1995) who seems to be confused about whether there is such a tradition, who has contributed to it, the basis for its claims, and the manner in which socially critical research *can* make a contribution. While we certainly agree with Hammersley that there are a 'range of conceptions of the "critical"' (p. 35), we are much less inclined to be dismissive or to agree that 'there are no grounds for advocating a distinctively "critical" form of social research'. That Hammersley has been so insistent and diligent in his refusal, suggests that there is indeed something of substance that is the object of his critique.

What do we Mean by Reflexivity?

Reflexivity in research is built on an acknowledgment of the ideological and historical power dominant forms of inquiry exert over the researcher and the researched. Self–reflection upon the constraining conditions is the key to the empowerment 'capacities' of research and the fulfilment of its agenda. It would be fair to say that, what some call the 'ideal' position of researcher as found in the dominant position of the social sciences, based in the collection of neutral fact–like data, and the subsequent formulation of law–like propositional knowledge about social life, per-meates epistemological understandings and methodological groundings for all re-search. Realistically, researchers operating out of a critical perspective are not immune to the effects of technical cognitive interests which structure knowledge and understandings about ethics, power, politics, reliability, and validity in research. However, the emancipatory cognitive interest (Habermas, 1971) of the critical per-spective yields a medium for the exposure of ideological constraints on the research, through reflexivity. We believe that a researcher can, through the possession of critical knowledge about the research process, be placed in an empowered position to recognize and transform constraints implicit in the research process. It is this very positioning which the authors in this book report upon in their reflexive musings about their research.

Within the narratives of critical qualitative inquiry there are often strong reflexive tones. For instance, Simon and Dippo (1986) suggest that a critical ethno-graphy must 'reflexively address its own situated character' (p. 200) through an admission of how the research account is shaped by historical factors affecting the researcher, and is constrained by 'institutional forms' affecting the knowledge gen-eration process. In their view, reflexivity is about 'coming to grips with the recog-nition that most ethnographic data is "produced" and not "found"' (ibid, p. 200). Anderson (1989), too, has argued that reflexivity is crucial in keeping research findings openly creative in the generation of ideas, by preventing the research data from being poured into a given theoretical mould. This is important because the 'locking–in' of the research to dominant ideas and positions is a real prospect when there is no self–reflective problematizing of the taken–for–grantedness of research community attitudes to things like: the researcher's constructs; the informant's commonsense constructs; the research data; the researcher's ideological biases; the structural and historical forces that inform the social construction under study; and, the significance likely to be attached to the text by the reader of the account (ibid, pp. 254–5).

As we see it, the process of reflexivity is an attempt to identify, do something about, and acknowledge the limitations of the research: its location, its subjects, its process, its theoretical context, its data, its analysis, and how accounts recognize that the construction of knowledge takes place in the world and not apart from it. Indeed, reflexivity in 'critical' research work is important in honestly and openly addressing issues concerning the validation of research findings, as well as those ethical and political questions which arise from relations between the researcher and the researched that are implicit to the research agenda and the research methods.

We like Ruby's (1980) description of reflexivity as the conscious revelation of the role of the beliefs and values held by the researcher in the selection of a research methodology for knowledge generation and its production as a research account. He puts it like this:

> . . . being reflexive means that the producer deliberately, intentionally reveals to his (sic) audience the underlying epistemological assumptions which caused him (sic) to formulate a set of questions in a particular way, to seek answers to those questions in a particular way, and finally to present his (sic) findings in a particular way. (ibid, p. 157)

Being reflexive, therefore, is to acknowledge that 'we are always on some corner somewhere' (Richardson, 1992, p. 104) and that there are no privileged views on getting at the truth in the generation of research problems, processes, and accounts because these things are, like the researcher, socially situated.

Roman and Apple's (1990) exposure of 'the phenomenon of the missing researcher' (p. 50) and the denial of the subjectivity of the researcher in the pursuit of 'objective' and 'neutral' collection of empirical data in the 'natural' depiction of social life, is a strong case for the importance of the reflexive position. Their view of reflexivity, as being grounded in 'a self–critical stance toward the ethics and politics of the power relations between the researcher(s) and the researched in the constitution of social subjectivity' (ibid, p. 55), is one that we share. The authors in this collection give us deeply personal insights through their reflections on how they, as researchers, dealt with the issues of power and subjectivity connected to the role of researcher, as 'producer', in the generation of research findings in their own work.

For us, being reflexive in doing research is part of being honest and ethically mature in research practice that requires researchers to 'stop being "shamans" of objectivity' (Ruby, 1980, p. 154). To not acknowledge the interests implicit in a critical agenda for the research, or to assume value–free positions of neutrality, is to assume 'an obscene and dishonest position' (ibid). Part of the 'contract', for critically framed research, is an acceptance of the historically embedded roles of the researcher, research methodology, and research account and the disclosure of the interests, subjectivity, and non–neutral nature of the relations between producer, process, and product which exist in any research.

Why is this Collection Useful to Researchers?

The reflexive narratives of experienced educational and social researchers contained in this volume present an invaluable resource for experienced and novitiate researchers alike. While accounts of the research 'story' behind the published research account are more common now, than they were 10 years ago, they are not always easy to locate and even less easy to 'do' as the contributors to this volume have attested during the course of the project. Usually they appear some considerable time after official, rhetorically pure, accounts of the research have been reported in journals and books. Indeed, they turn up in quite different places. Fortunately this is beginning to change and we are pleased to be contributing to that through this collection.

A collection of reflexive narratives about doing critical research like the one in this book brings together a broad set of approaches to the reflexive positioning — and we don't believe there is any one single way. It gives a richly diverse perspective on the intersection of the methodological and the biographical in critical research as told by experienced researchers whose research accounts are already in the wider literature.

For the new, or inexperienced researcher striving to face the challenges of adopting a critical perspective in their work, accounts like these provide a window on how others have faced up to the challenges and dilemmas that occur as a result of the values and interests inherent of all forms of human inquiry. Accounts like these become revealing for the inexperienced researcher because they clearly show how the researcher, as an individual, cannot walk away from the difficulties of working relationally with other human beings in a research setting. Commitments to the research, and to other people, often cause dilemmas and relational tension for the researcher and the researched. How these are dealt with, in the act of the research itself, are research tales that novitiate researchers need to hear. It is our hope that this book can provide the beginnings of some insights.

Experienced researchers need such tales for the same reasons. They, too, need the sustaining and affirming nourishment that a reflexive account can provide. As Douglas Foley suggests in his contribution to this collection (chapter 7), the deeply personal reflections of the researcher who admits vulnerability, like Ruth Behar (1996) so compellingly does, brings a sense of common endeavour and community through the vicarious participation in the struggles of another researcher. Struggles that in detail are different, but in other ways are very much like your own. The experienced researcher should find this collection a doorway into the worlds of others doing similar kinds of critical work, in different places and in different ways. Being reflexive, and sharing vulnerability, is part of giving back to the community of researchers of which we are so much a part.

How, Then, is this Book Organized?

There are a number of consistent themes and patterns that keep appearing through the various chapters. There is the *temporal dimension* — it quite simply takes the passage of time, and an effort to engage through writing, to see the issues involved in doing critical research. The process of confronting the 'wrongs' of fieldwork and the dilemmas this brings with it, is brought out by Fine and Weis in chapter 2, in their focus upon representational issues in critical research. This takes particular form in the difficulty of being authentic and critical; the traps that come with being seen to be involved in social scientific voyeurism; how theorizing writes over the voices of the researched; the diversity of life narratives to be reported and respected simultaneously; and, the marginalization of critical researchers within their own communities.

David Tripp in chapter 3 struggles with the notions of the key ideas of the book, 'critical' and 'reflexive', and develops a set of working principles for himself which he uses to read off an example in which he recently acted as a facilitator. While somewhat different from other contributions to the book, in that it does not turn back upon the work of a *magnum opus* kind, the critical incident Tripp analyses is a nice working exemplification of critical reflexivity worked through in a bounded instance of action.

Many of the contributors struggled hard with the opportunity writing this piece presented them with to *position their work*. For example, Goodman in chapter 4, found that the process of self–disclosure as a researcher, while important, produced a high level of provisionality, tentativeness and uncertainty about his own positionality, leaving huge unanswered questions about what motivates us to read the world in a particular way.

For others, the task was no less agonizing but the opportunity for revisitation lead to a *renewal of reciprocity* established during the original research. Sparkes, in chapter 5, found that reestablishing contact with 'Jessica' and the story of her coming–out as a lesbian physical education teacher, enabled him to see all of the old complexities in a much more scoped fashion; for example, the motives of self–advancement in constructing research accounts, the skewed nature of the benefits, and of his own need to continually reaffirm and renegotiate the nature of the tensions he experienced in the original research, were major issues for him. There is a strong element of the 'unsettling' in Sparkes' account, shared by other contributors to the book as well.

Levinson in chapter 6 provides a 'window' on what it meant for him to revisit a study of a Mexican school and in particular the intersection between *social commitment and research practice* in the personal lives of all of the people involved. For him the period since completing the study has meant a continual monitoring of the kinds and levels of social commitment possible through research contexts, and how he might move in the future from his current enc0nsement in the self–confessedly 'interpretive camp' to one with a 'stronger action component'.

What kind of *narrative is best capable of representing the work* in a way that 'deconstructs the authority of the author' so that he/she becomes a situated, subjective, historical observer, is a major issue for Foley (chapter 7) in a cascading account of revisiting a number of his previously socially critical accounts. For Foley, the possibilities feel like 'living in an exciting era of crumbling discursive regimes', an opportunity he relishes and which he urges fellow anthropologists to embrace as a way of breaking politically with old scientific realist styles.

Noreen Garman (chapter 8) provides an example of *the role of the reflexive process in writing* research accounts. In an account about internationally funded development work for educational needs in Bosnia and Herzegovina, Garman draws on personal vignettes about her stay in a war ravaged country, in the form of email postcards, as a 'reflexive medium' for locating herself in her work for educational change. For her the postcards are a way of reflexively narrating, for the first time, the meanings given to those experiences. The account is conceptually organized around three 'research stances' for writing this experience of educational change: *exotic horror, alien dwelling* and *bitter wisdom*. Within this chapter there are valuable insights about the reflexive potential of personal revisitations for the facilitation of the act of writing.

A focus on *ethical dilemmas* pervades many of the chapters, but it comes out particularly in Street's (chapter 9) revisitation of her critically ethnographic doctoral study of nursing in a hospital ward. She found these issues to be particularly poignant in circumstances where the fieldwork demanded that she deal continually with institutional ethical standards, where academic ends skew what is possible/preferred, and where the dominant experimental discourses of medicine so pervasively invade official thinking, policy and practice. How to deal with this at a personal–professional level was a major challenge for her.

Writing a retrospective account provides an opportunity to *see things in a different light*, and even to be candid and honest in a way not possible first time around. Stephen May's (chapter 10) reflections on the question 'What can I see now, that I didn't before?', produces a freshness of perspective not that common in academic work. His preparedness: to confront whether he had adequately heeded the 'warning signals' in his original study of the Richmond Road School; how external demands (for validation) drive methodological choices; the fragility of the emancipatory possibilities; the commitment to a 'critical' agenda, and whether this was matched by an ability to 'deliver'; how different ways of 'crafting the tale' can give quite different stories — all contributed to a strong thread running through his account of the pain involved in the reflexive positioning of the researcher.

Carspecken and MacGillivray, in chapter 11, show us in a way unusual in academic writing, *what positioning actually means* through the conversation they have with one another and the reader about reflection, validity and meaning — as it emerged out of an instance taken from their fieldnotes. They liken their process to the vulnerability of the 'confessional' — a situation that positions them in relation to certain discourses. The movement between first, second and third person positions, enables them to show us something about validity claims and how they are related through reflection to position–taking.

Kanpol in chapter 12, revisits three of his previous research studies (as a critical ethnographer) both as an analyst of social structures, but also in the additional role of considering the relationship of the researcher to those wider structural elements of society. For Kanpol, it is the *ability of the researcher to describe who they are as a person*, expressed as a function of their life experiences, that powerfully shapes the capacity to be a socially critical researcher. In this, he provides an interesting account of his own reading of the relationship between 'cynicism' and 'joy' in critical research.

Grace's chapter (chapter 13) is a fitting finale to the book because of the way it systematically lays out the context of his own recent study of critical policy scholarship, and the personal struggle he had with voice, gender and race issues — concerns also advanced by other contributors to the book as to why reflexivity is such an important facet of the critical research agenda.

References

ANDERSON, G. (1989) 'Critical ethnography in education: Origins, current status, and new directions', *Review of Educational Research*, **59**, 3, pp. 249–70.

BEHAR, R. (1996) *The Vulnerable Observer: Anthropology That Breaks Your Heart*, Boston, MA: Beacon Press.

BURAWOY, M. et al. (1991) *Ethnography Unbound: Power and Resistance in the Modern Metropolis*, Berkeley, CA: University of California Press.

COX, R. (1980) 'Social forces, states and world orders' millenium', *Millenium: Journal of International Studies*, **10**, 2, pp. 126–55.

EISNER, E. (1979) *The Educational Imagination: On the Design and Evaluation of School Programs*, New York: Macmillan.

EISNER, E. (1991) *The Enlightened Eye: Qualitative Inquiry and the Enhancement of Educational Practice*, New York: Macmillan.

HABERMAS, J. (1971) *Knowledge and Human Interests*, Boston, MA: Beacon Press.

HAMMERSLEY, M. (1995) *The Politics of Social Research*, Thousand Oaks, CA: Sage.

HAMMERSLEY, M. and ATKINSON, P. (1983) *Ethnography: Principles in Practice*, London: Tavistock.

HARVEY, L. (1990) *Critical Social Research*, London: Allen and Unwin.

HOBBS, D. (1993) 'Peers, careers and academic fears: Writing as fieldwork', in HOBBS, D. and MAY, T. (Eds.) *Interpreting the Field: Accounts of Ethnography*, Oxford: Clarendon Press, pp. 45–66.

HOBBS, D. and MAY, T. (1993) *Interpreting the Field: Accounts of Ethnography*, Oxford: Clarendon Press.

LATHER, P. (1992) 'Critical frames in educational research: Feminist and post-structural perspectives', *Theory into Practice*, **31**, 2, pp. 1–13.

MAY, T. (1993) 'Feelings matter: Inverting the hidden equation', in HOBBS, D. and MAY, T. (Eds.) *Interpreting the Field: Accounts of Ethnography*, Oxford: Clarendon Press, pp. 69–98.

McLAREN, P. and GIARELLI, J. (1995) *Critical Theory and Educational Research*, Albany, NY: SUNY Press.

MORROW, R. and BROWN, D. (1994) *Critical Theory and Methodology*, Thousand Oaks, CA: Sage.

PEARSON, G. (1993) 'Talking a good fight? Authenticity and distance in the ethnographer's craft', in HOBBS, D. and MAY, T. (Eds.) *Interpreting the Field: Accounts of Ethnography*, Oxford: Clarendon Press, (pp. vii–xx).

QUANTZ, R. (1992) 'On critical ethnography (with some post–modern considerations)', in LeCOMPTE, M., MILROY, W. and PREISSLE, J. (Eds.) *The Handbook of Qualitative Research in Education*, San Diego, CA: Academic Press, pp. 447–505.

RICHARDSON, L. (1992) 'Trash on the corner: Ethics and technography', *Journal of Contemporary Ethnography*, **21**, 1, pp. 103–19.

ROMAN, L. and APPLE, M. (1990) 'Is naturalism a move away from positivism?: Materialist and feminist approaches to subjectivity in ethnographic research', in EISNER, E. and PESHKIN, A. (Eds.) *Qualitative Inquiry in Education: The Continuing Debate*, New York: Teachers College Press, pp. 38–73.

ROOF, J. and WIEGMAN, R. (Eds.) (1995) *Who Can Speak? Authority and Critical Identity*, Chicago and Urbana, IL: University of Illinois Press.

RUBY, J. (1980) 'Exposing yourself: Reflexivity, anthropology, and film', *Semiotica*, **30**, 1–2, pp. 153–79.

SIMON, R. and DIPPO, D. (1986) 'On critical ethnographic work', *Anthropology and Education Quarterly*, **17**, pp. 195–202.

SMYTH, J. (1994) 'Critical educational research for new educational times: The case of advanced skills teachers in Australia', *New Zealand Journal of Educational Administration*, **9**, pp. 2–12.

SMYTH, J. (1997) 'Political, ethical and epistemological issues in critical research', *Qualitative Inquiry*, in preparation.

2 Writing the 'Wrongs' of Fieldwork: Confronting Our Own Research/Writing Dilemmas in Urban Ethnographies

Michelle Fine and Lois Weis

Inspired by Laurel Richardson's (1995) call for 'writing stories', the authors of this essay struggle with how to produce scholarly texts drawn from narratives of over 150 poor and working–class men and women — white, African American, Latino, and Asian American. They unveil a set of knotty, emergent ethical and rhetorical dilemmas they have encountered in their attempt to write for, with, and about poor and working–class informants at a time when their lives and moralities are routinely maligned in the popular media; when the very problematic policies that may once have 'assisted' them are being abandoned; and when the leverage of and audience for progressive social researchers and policymakers has grown foggy, and weak in the knees. Writing with a desire to create a conversation about ethics, writing, and qualitative research, the authors worry about the contemporary role of qualitative social researchers.

As critical ethnographers, we have explored the perspectives that working class and poor adolescents hold about the relationships between the economy, education, families, and political action. Our major works, *Working Class Without Work* (Weis, 1990), *Between Two Worlds* (Weis, 1985), *Framing Dropouts* (Fine, 1991), *Disruptive Voices* (Fine, 1992), and *Beyond Silenced Voices* (Weis and Fine, 1993) all hold as central the social analyses narrated by low–income and working–class adolescents and young adults.

With the support of the Spencer Foundation, we are currently expanding our research to include the perspectives and practices of Latino, African American, and white young adults, ages 23 to 35, as they narrate their educational, familial, and economic biographies and project and enact their parental involvements within their communities, churches, and children's schools. Specifically, we have interviewed 150 individuals across racial and ethnic groups (men and women) in Buffalo and Jersey City, and have conducted focus group interviews with specified populations in each city to probe further their perspectives and practices, unearthing at once their despair about and envisioned opportunities for individual, community, and social change. We thus far have conducted group interviews with African American welfare– and non– welfare–receiving mothers; Latina mothers who are probing the meaning of workfare programs in Jersey City; African American men who see the church as a way of envisioning both self and community differently from what they see as the dominant society's definition; white women who, although caught in patriarchal working–class communities, both push and accept the limitations of their female bodies and selves; and white men who patrol the borders of white masculinity, desirous of keeping all others out of what they see as their rightful position. We have assembled a rich array of interview material that will enable us both to narrate the experiences of the poor and working class during the 1980s and 1990s and to press carefully into the policy realm given our findings. We have met with and are interviewing a broad range of policymakers in both cities to explore fully the situated nature of our findings, as well as to affect broader social policy. We have testified and written Op Ed pieces on local and State policies as they affect constituents (for example, vouchers and school takeover in Jersey City, welfare reform) and intend to do more (Weis and Fine, 1995).

Perhaps the most arrogant way to think about our project is that we aim to produce a biography of the Reagan–Bush years, as narrated by poor and working–class young adults in urban America; a more modest description would suggest that we are engaged in a two–city community study that, through the oral life histories of poor and working-class White, African American and Latino young adults, unravels the transformations in urban economic, racial, social, and domestic relations that have transpired over the past 20 years.

We are two Jewish white woman academics, trained well in the rigors of social psychology (Michelle) and sociology (Lois), experienced in the complexities of critical ethnography, who, with generous support from the Spencer Foundation and the assistance of extremely talented graduate students, are eager to traverse the borders of research, policy, activism, and theory, and are worried about what it means to do 'critical work' in our provincial urban backyards just when the Right has cannibalized public discourse and when the academy has fractured amid post–structuralism and identity politics. This article may be conceptualized as an early 'coming out' about some of the methodological, theoretical, and ethical issues that percolate from our fieldwork, keeping our e–mail bills high, our nights long, our essays delayed, and our commitments to social change *and* social theory swirling in ambivalence.

With this article we hope to pry open a conversation in need of public shaping. Many of the friends and colleagues with whom we have discussed some of these research/ethical dilemmas say they are relieved that someone is 'saying aloud' this next generation of methodological and conceptual troubles. And yet answers evade us. With this writing we wedge open this conversation that we presumably needed, hoping that colleagues working ethnographically 'in our own backyards' will engage with us in excavating the next generation of always tentative resolutions. As we write, we straddle the semi–fictions of empiricism and the intellectual spheres of critical theory, feminism, and post–structuralism; as we read and hear our friends (and ourselves) pleading for researchers to be critical and self–reflexive, we note that many of these same friends have long stopped collecting data; as we consume the critical literature on race and gender and ask our informants to talk about both, they keep responding, 'Really I'm black, why do you keep asking?' or, 'A woman — what do you think?' We write in that space between despair and hope because we hear much of the former from our informants and whispers of the latter from the same and because that is the space within which we can live. Yes, structures oppress, but we *must* have hope that things can be better.

We speak now because we worry that many of us are simply studying the apocalypse to cope with it, as one more piece of the sky falls. This chapter represents a concrete analysis in the midst of what Michelle has called 'working the hyphen'.

> Much of qualitative research has reproduced, if contradiction–filled, a colonizing discourse of the 'other'. This essay is an attempt to review how qualitative research projects have *Othered* and to examine an emergent set of activist and/or post–modern texts that interrupt *Othering*. First, I examine the hyphen at which self–other join in the politics of everyday life, that is, the hyphen that both separates and merges personal identities with our inventions of others. I then take up how qualitative researchers work this hyphen . . . through a messy series of questions about methods, ethics, and epistemologies as we rethink how researchers have spoken 'of' and 'for' others while occluding ourselves and our own investments, burying the contradictions that percolate at the self–other hyphen. (Fine, 1994, p. 70)

This chapter, then, offers up our questions/dilemmas/concerns as we grapple with what it means to be in the midst of a study that attempts to work across many borders, always searching for ways to 'work the hyphen'. We take our cue from Richardson (1995), who invites what she calls 'writing-stories':

> With the post–structural understanding that the social context affects what we write, we have an opportunity — perhaps even an ethical duty — to extend our reflexivity to the study of our writing practices. We can reflect on and share with other researchers what I think of as writing–stories, or stories about how we came to construct the particular texts we did. These might be of the verification kind, or they might be more subjective — accounts of how contexts, social interactions, critiques, review processes, friendships, academic settings, departmental politics, embodiedness, and so on have affected the construction of the text. Rather than hiding the struggle, concealing the very human labor that creates the text, writing–stories would reveal emotional, social, physical, and political bases of the labor. (p. 191)

Echoes (and Aches) In Our Head

On Community

Perhaps our most vexing dilemma at the moment concerns the question 'What constitutes community?' How do we write about communities in which we find little sense of shared biography or vision? We write 'as if' the contours of geography or a standard metropolitan statistical area adequately define the boundaries of these two 'communities'. Coherence organizes life within, whereas difference defines life between.

And yet we recognize from our theoretical interests, confirmed by the narratives we've collected, that piercing fractures define life within communities and some pronounced similarities emerge across the two cities. Internal geographic coherence seems a naive fiction, whereas blunt cross–community contrasts seem deceptively polarized.

Simple demographic fractures, by race/ethnicity, gender, class, generation, and sexuality marble inside each city. Within local neighborhoods or racial/ethnic groups, gender, sexuality, and generational divisions boldly sever what may appear at first glance to be internal continuities.

For instance, within presumably the same community, African Americans will refer to local police with stories of harassment and fear, whereas whites are far more likely to complain about a rise in crime and brag about a brother–in–law who's a cop. Parallel dynamics can be found in both Jersey City and Buffalo.

Likewise, from within the same households we hear white working–class women describe growing up in families with much childhood exposure to alcohol and abuse, whereas comparably situated white men — raised in the very same homes and neighborhoods — are virtually silent on these topics. Again, the parallels across the two cities have been striking.

Jersey City whites describe 'good old days' of economic security and pine for the day when they'll be moving to Bayonne, whereas African Americans harbor few wistful memories of good old days and try to avoid 'getting stopped at red lights' in Bayonne, lest their stay be extended beyond what they expected.

At historic moments of job security and economic hard times, the presumed harmony of working-class/poor communities is ravaged by interior splits, finger pointing, blame, and suspicion. Coalitions are few, even if moments of interdependence for survival are frequent. Within homes, differences and conflicts explode across gender and generations. A full sense of community is fictional and fragile, ever vulnerable to external threats and internal fissures. A sense of coherence prevails only if our methods fail to interrogate difference. And at the same time, commonalities *across* cities — by demography and biography — are all the more striking.

So, for the moment in our writing, we script a story in which we float a semi–fictional portrait of each community, layered over with an analytic matrix of differences 'within'. For our analysis — within and between cities — we delicately move between coherence and difference, fixed boundaries and porous borders, neighborhoods of shared values and homes of contentious interpretations.

On Race

As with community, race emerges in our data as both an unstable and an enduring aspect of biography. Gates (1985) has written beautifully about race, always using quotes; Dyson (1993) argues against narrow nationalistic or essentialist definitions for either skin color or language; Hall (1981) narrates the contextual instability of racial identities. Like these theorists, our informants are sometimes quite muddy, other times quite clear, about race. Indeed, some of our informants, like the one below, suggest that race constitutes inherently undefinable territory. This is not a narrative of denial as much as it is one of complexity.

Question: Your dad?

Answer: Yes, my dad was the craziest Puerto Rican you had ever seen in the 70s. Oh my Lord.

Q: What is your mom's background?

A: Mom, Mom was raised Catholic, but in my mother's days, when an Irish and German woman went with a Chinese guy, in those days that was like, oh no, no that cannot happen. My grandfather had to drop his whole family for my grandmother, so they could be together. Everybody disowned him in this family.

Q: Because he married a —

A: Yeah, he married my grandmother.

Q: What about your mom's side?

A: That is my mom's side.

Q: What about your grandfather's side?

A: My grandfather, he was in Vietnam, World War II, oh, I forgot the name. It was a very big war, that I know.

Q: Korean War?

A: Yeah, something like that, I just can't remember what it was. Yeah, he had honors and everything my mother told me.

Q: So you looked very different?

A: Yeah, I'm a mixture.

Q: You have Chinese blood?

A: Right. I got Irish and German, I got Puerto Rican and Italian, I have a lot. I'm a mixed breed.

Q: I was wondering. The first time I saw you I thought you were from the Middle East.

A: From the Middle East?

Q: Yeah.

A: Oh, golly gee, no. I'm, like, really mixed. I'm like everything. I got all these different personalities that just come out all the time. I swear to God. No lie. No lie.

When we began our interviews in Jersey City and Buffalo, we were well influenced by post–structural thinking on questions of race. With Hall (ibid) particularly in mind, and willing to acknowledge the artificiality, the performances, and, indeed, the racist roots of the notion of race (1/32nd drop of blood, etc.), we constructed an interview protocol that generously invited our informants to 'play' with race as we had. So we asked them, in many clever ways, to describe time–/ context–specific racial identifications — when they fill out census forms, walk through supermarkets, when alone or among friends. By the third hour, informants of color, trying to be polite, grew exasperated with these questions. White folks were sure we were calling them racist, or they went on about being Irish, Italian, human — never white. Needless to say, the 'playfulness' of the questions didn't work.

We don't mean to retreat now to a simplistic formulation by which we declare that race is more 'real' than critical race theory suggests. Indeed, our data give much support for reasserting a floating sense of race — one always braided with gender, generation, biography, and class. Yet, reading the narratives, it's hard to miss entrenched, raced patterns of daily life. Most white respondents *say* they don't think much about race; most people of color wish they weren't reminded of their race — via harassment, discrimination, and on–the–street stares — quite so often. Many argue that race *shouldn't* make much of a difference. Yet the life stories as narrated are so thoroughly raced that readers of the transcript can't not know even an 'anonymous' informant's racial group. Personal stories of violence and family structure, narrative style, one's history with money, willingness to trash (and leave) men and marriages, access to material resources, relations with kin and the State, and descriptions of interactions with the police are all profoundly narrated through race, fluid though it is.

Race is a place in which post–structuralism and lived realities need to talk. Race is a social construction, indeed. But race in a racist society bears profound consequence for daily life, identity, social movements, and the ways in which most groups 'other'. DuBois noted that race was the dividing line for the twentieth century. He may have been a two–century prophet.

But how we write about race in our work worries us. Do we take the category for granted, as if it were unproblematic? Do we problematize it theoretically, well knowing its full-bodied impact on daily life? Reflecting on our writings thus far, we seem to lean toward theorizing for and about whites who deny they have a race, whereas we offer much more open latitude around the voices of people of color who articulate their thoroughly embodied experiences within race. We try to construct theoretical structures of racial formations, borrowing from Omi and Winant (1986), recognizing that whiteness requires — indeed, creates — blackness in order to see the self as moral, hard working, family–oriented, a good citizen. We give lots of room to those who define themselves with multiple roots and at varied hyphens. We envy and resent colleagues who have stopped collecting data because they have done such a marvelous job of complicating that which actually doesn't feel so complicated to our informants. Yes, race *is* a social construction, but it's so deeply confounded with racism that it has enormous power in people's lives. We can't simply problematize it away as if it does not really exist. To the informants with whom we spoke, race does exist — it saturates every pore of their lives. How can we destabilize the notion theoretically, while recognizing the lived presence of race?

Here are some trivial but telling examples. One problem that may appear, at face value, to be a 'sampling problem' related to race, involves our struggle to find 'equally poor' and 'equally working–class' African American, Latino, and white young adults in both cities, so that comparisons by race/ethnicity would not be compounded by class. Guess what? The world is lousy with confounds. Although we found poor and working–class whites, the breadth and depth of their cross–generational poverty was nowhere near as severe as in the African American sample.

White informants were sometimes as well off as, but were more often slightly worse off than, their parents. But — and here's the *unacknowledged* impact of 1940s' and 1950s' US federal subsidies for the white working class/middle class — these young adults often had access to a small house or apartment that their parents were able to buy, a small nest egg of cash the family had squirreled away, or a union–based pension that Dad had saved up. In contrast, our African American and Latino informants are in very tough financial straits but are not, for the most part, worse off than their parents. Their parents rarely had a home, a small stash of monies, or pensions that they could pass on. Further, some of our African American and Latino informants who have amassed small amounts of capital over time lost it at some point when someone in the extended family had a health crisis, a housing crisis, or a problem with the law.

Despite our meticulous combing of raced neighborhoods, our ambitious search for sampling comparability lost, hands down, to the profound 'lived realities' of multi-generational poverty disproportionately affecting poor and working–class families of color. What may appear to be a methodological problem has been revealed as constitutive of the very fabric of society. Problematizing race alone does not help us confront the very real costs and privileges of racial categorization.

Bad Data

Moving from worries of epistemology to worries about data, we excavate more headaches:

Q: Do you feel that your word is not trusted, that you need someone else to say, you need a lawyer or psychiatrist to say everything is okay now?

A: Because of DYFS [Division for Youth and Family Services], yes.

Q: But you can't have . . .

A: They won't, yeah. They won't just take you for your word, no. You need to have . . .

Q: You need to have somebody else say that for you?

A: Yes. DYFS, yes.

Q: How would DYFS treat your kids, though?

A: Because when you get child, they say I put their life in danger, because I did, but I was . . . I was in jail, I was in the psychiatric ward. They had to do the best interest for the children, I couldn't take care of them at the time.

Q: Oh, so DYFS took your kids?

A: Yeah, so DYFS gave them to their father. I'm in court now.

Q: At least it's not foster care, though.

A: That's what I said. They're with family. They might hate it there, they can't stand it. My kids say that they're treated worse.

Q: They hate their father?

A: No, they don't hate their father, they hate their grandmother, they hate the mother-in-law, they hate their grandmother. They don't like their grandmother.

Q: George's mother?

A: Yeah, they don't like their aunts, their uncles.

Q: They are a lot of Puerto Ricans?

A: They're all Puerto Ricans, but my kids were always like the outcasts because they didn't like me so my kids, my kids, I mean, George was 7 years old, seven years of George's life, George had to have seen his grandmother six times. Nicole, in the three years of her life, never seen them. You know, my kids got dumped into a family that they know nothing about.

What does it mean to uncover some of what we have uncovered? How do we handle 'hot' information, especially in times when poor and working–class women and men are being demonized by the Right and by Congress? How do we connect troubling social/familial patterns with macrostructural shifts when our inform- ants *expressly don't* make the connections? The hegemony of autonomous indi- vidualism forces a self–conscious theorizing of data — especially 'bad data' — well beyond the consciousness expressed by most of our informants. So, for in- stance, what do we do with information about the ways in which women on welfare virtually have to become welfare cheats ('Sure he comes once a month and gives me some money. I may have to take a beating, but the kids need the money.') to survive? A few use more drugs than we wish to know; most are wonderful parents but some underattend to their children well beyond neglect. These are the dramatic consequences, and perhaps also the 'facilitators', of hard economic times. To ignore the data is to deny the effects. To report the data is to risk their likely misinterpretation.

In a moment in history when there are few audiences willing to reflect on the complex social roots of community and domestic violence and the impossibility of sole reliance on welfare, or even to appreciate the complexity, love, hope, and pain that fills the poor and working class, how do we display the voyeuristic dirty laundry that litters our database? At the same time, how can we risk romanticizing or denying the devastating impact of the current assault on poor and working–class families launched by the State, the economy, neighbors, and sometimes kin?

Because of our early questions about both perspectives and representations, the interview schedule was originally created using input from a group of activists and policymakers of varying racial and ethnic backgrounds from Jersey City and Buffalo who were working with the research teams. Many questions were inserted to satisfy local concerns, for example, questions about police harassment, welfare reform and its effects on children born to women on welfare, state takeover of school, and so on. Nevertheless, with data collection over and analysis now under way, we continue to struggle with how best to represent treacherous data — data that may do more damage than good, depending on who consumes/exploits them, data about the adult consequences of child physical and sexual abuse, data suggest- ing that it is almost impossible to live exclusively on welfare payments (encourag- ing many to lie about their incomes so that they feel they are welfare cheats), data in which white respondents, in particular, portray people of color in gross and dehumanizing ways, and data on the depth of violence in women's lives across race/ethnicity.

We spend much time reading through the *Handbook of Qualitative Research* (Denizen and Lincoln, 1994), Gregory's (1993) ethnographies of Queens, Scheper–Hughes's (1992) analysis of mothering in poverty–stricken communities of Brazil, Connell's (1994) representations of white male identity formation in Australia, M. E. Dyson's *Reflecting Black* (1993), and rereading Gwaltney's *Drylongso* (1980) and Ladner's *Tomorrow's Tomorrow* (1971) to reflect on how to best write authentically and critically about the narratives offered, in ways that serve communities, theory, and public policy. We present these as dilemmas with which all fieldworkers must currently struggle. There is nothing straightforward or objective about reporting *or* withholding these data. Each strategic decision of scholarship bears theoretical, ethical, and political consequences.

On the Mundane

Sticking with dilemmas of data, we turn now to questions about mundane details of daily life.

> Well, I take . . . I get $424 a month, okay? And I get $270 in food stamps, so I take . . . there's four weeks to a month, so I take . . . I take the $270 and I divide it by four. And that's what I spend on food. It's just me and my daughters. And my oldest don't eat that much and I don't eat . . . I only eat once a day. I only eat dinner. I'm not hungry in the morning and I don't have breakfast. I have a cup of coffee or hot chocolate. My little one is the one that eats a lot. And whatever I don't . . . like I spend $65 a week in food. I go and I buy meat every day and I buy their breakfast, their lunch, her snacks for school. And whenever I can . . . I work at night . . . I work . . . if I get a call I go and clean somebody's house. I do that. Their father gives me money, you know. So I do whatever I . . . you know, whatever it takes, you know? Shovel your snow . . . [laughs] I don't care. You know, to me money's money, as long as your kids got what they need. But basically their father helps me the most. You know, he'll come in . . . oh, my dad does this, too, and I get really pissed off at him. He'll come in and he'll start looking through my cabinets and in my refrigerator, and my closet. 'Well, what do you have here?' And it's like, 'I'm fine. Johnny's coming over later.' 'No! Blah, blah, blah.' And he'll go out and he'll come back with food, and their father's always coming in looking through the refrigerator, and things like that, you know? I always . . . my kids have food, so that's good, you know? They never go hungry. You know, I . . . I hate to say this, but if I had . . . I mean, if it came to where my kids were gonna go hungry, I'd sell my body. To hell with that! My kids ain't gonna starve, you know? I'd do what it takes. I would give two shits. People could . . . my friends could tell me whatever they wanted. I have a . . . I have two friends that sell their bodies for money for their kids. And thank God, I have to knock on wood, I never had to do that. But I mean, if I had to, I would. If that's what it took to feed my kids . . . I mean, if their father . . . a lot of people that are on welfare have husbands worth shit. They don't care. If they had a father, but I guess that's, if that's what it took . . . I would try every aspect before doing that. But if that's what it really took to feed my kids, that's what I would do. I would do whatever it takes

to feed and clothe my kids, you know, and put a roof over their head. I wouldn't care what the hell it was. I guess that's what I would do, you know?

These are the dull and spicy details of negotiating daily life in poverty. When we (researchers) listen to and read narratives, we tend (with embarrassment) to be drawn to — in fact, to *code for* — the exotic, the bizarre, the violent. As we reflect, though, we nevertheless feel obligated to explore meticulously the very tedious sections of the transcripts: those sections not very sexy, exciting, or eroticizing, like when the informants walk their kids to school, read the newspaper in horror, turn on the television for a break, look for a doctor they can trust, hope their children are safe on the way home from school. These rituals of daily living — obviously made much more difficult in the presence of poverty and discrimination, but mundane nonetheless — are typically left out of ethnographic descriptions of life in poverty. They don't make very good reading, and yet are the stuff of daily life. We recognize how carefully we need to *not* construct life narratives spiked only with the hot spots . . . like surfing our data for sex and violence.

On Safe Spaces

In contrast to bad — or even mundane — data, over time we have collected data on those contexts carved out by young adults in which they try to survive, with sanity, the depletion of the public sector. These are data on 'safe spaces' that young adults have created to make sense of the insane worlds in which they live. Some of these safe spaces don't actually appear (to us) to be so safe or legal. Others are private and serene, filled with the incense of spirituality, belief in God, the language of social movements and nationalism, the daily coalitions of cross–racial/ethnic people trying to keep their neighborhoods safe. These spaces are delicious and fragile, but not entirely open to surveillance. They seek to be private.

In our first Spencer study, we heard from young women and men who survived in the working–class and poor segments of our society, how they viewed economic opportunities, how they would spin images of their personal and collective futures, especially as related to the power of schooling, how they conceptualized the shrinking public sector, economy, labor, and the military, and how they reflected upon progressive social movements that have historically and dramatically affected their ancestors' and their own chances in life. With respect to policies allegedly written for the poor and working class, our data enable us for the first time to hear from them. We have discovered pockets of possibility excavated by these young men and women, pockets that we desperately need to explore further. Amid their despair lies hope, and hope is cultivated in these safe spaces.

It would be profoundly irresponsible to argue that these working–class and poor women and men are simply depressed, despairing, and isolated, with no sense of possibility. As much as our individual interviews did suggest this at times, our focus groups alerted us that much else is happening. These young women and men are 'homesteading' — finding unsuspected places within and across geographic communities, public institutions, and spiritual lives — to sculpt real and imaginary spaces for peace, struggle, and personal and collective identity work. These spaces offer recuperation, resistance, and the makings of 'home'. They are not just a set of geographic/spatial arrangements, but theoretical, analytical, and spatial displacements — a crack, a fissure in an organization or a community. Individual dreams, collective work, and critical thoughts are smuggled in and then reimagined. Not rigidly bounded by walls/fences, these spaces often are corralled by a series of (imaginary) borders where community intrusion and state surveillance are not permitted. These are spaces where trite social stereotypes are fiercely contested. That is, these young women and men — in constantly confronting harsh public representations of their race/ethnicity, class, gender, and sexuality — use these spaces to break down these public images for scrutiny and invent new ones.

These spaces include the corners of the African American church, where young men huddle over discussions of how to 'take back the streets' to 'save the young boys'; the Lesbian and Gay Center, carved out quietly by working–class late adolescents and young adults who are seeking identities and networks when their geographic and cultural contexts deny them sexual expression; the Headstart and Effective Parenting Information for Children (EPIC) programs in which poor mothers, and sometimes fathers, come together to talk over the delights and minefields of raising children in a culture permeated with racism and decimated by poverty; the cultural arts programs where men and women join self–consciously across racial and ethnic borders to create what is 'not yet', a space, a set of images, a series of aesthetic products that speak of a world that could be.

Spaces such as these spring from the passions and concerns of community members; they are rarely structured from 'above'. They may be a one–time fiction, transitory or quite stable. They can be designed to restore identities devastated by the larger culture or they may be opportunities to flirt with identities and communities rejected by both mainstream culture and local ethnic groups. These spaces provide rich and revealing data about the resilience of young adults without denying the oppression that threatens the borders and interiors of community life amid urban poverty.

These 'free spaces' (Boyte and Evans, 1992) are rarely studied by social scientists. We typically enter people's lives and communities and ask them the questions that titillate us, creating 'unfree spaces'. As Keith and Pile (1993) argue, by asking questions of 'arbitrary closure', social scientists fail to see the world as it unfolds and is reshaped by community members across 'spacialities' and time. Typically, social sciences fix (our) gaze on public (or private) programs that are offered to low–income adults. Then we collect evidence of their non–involvement — laziness, resistance, helplessness. But we now know, as Brice Heath and McLaughlin (1993) have documented, that there is a rich underground to community life that is vibrant and fundamentally self–created. These are spaces designed by and for community, into which we, after three years of interviewing in Buffalo and Jersey City, have been invited. They may be transitory, healing, and mobilizing. They may be official or absolutely ad hoc. They may be a way to reconstitute traditional culture, racial, gender, or sexual identities, or they may be contexts in which individuals cross borders of race, ethnicity, gender, and sexuality to find a small corner in which to breathe in peace. These free spaces, of which we have only glimmers, have raised questions that need attention. When should these data about private/free spaces float into public view? Does the public/private distinction need to be problematized, as Gubrium and Holstein (1995) have argued?

Foucault (1979) has written on the invasive stretch of surveillance, typically pointing at state institutions. Here we deploy the same notion to self–reflexively point at ourselves, social scientists, surveying the safe cubby–holes of community life. Legitimately one may ask (and some have) whether we have any business floating through, writing about these sequestered quarters. Do our whiteness, our femaleness, our class status, our staccato appearances adversely affect or interrupt the music of life within free spaces? Does our social scientific voyeurism shatter the sanctity of that which is presumably (although recognizably *not*) free?

We respond to this question, for the moment at least, by presenting two different incidents. One occurred in a basement office in which New Jersey community activists meet to discuss local politics. We were welcomed for the initial interview, but the notion of our sustained presence clearly provoked discomfort. Not asked to return, we left. Elsewhere, and surprisingly more typically, we have been invited into spaces in which members, directors, and others indicate they are eager for documentation, anxious for others to know who they really are, what functions the programs serve, how deeply spiritual and religious 'those teenage mothers' can be, how organized and supportive 'those gays and lesbians' are. In these latter cases, informants have welcomed us into their spaces to exploit our capacity and willingness to write and to testify to those aspects of community life that the straight media ignore, that trenchant stereotypes deny, that mainstream culture rarely gets to see. Our rights, responsibilities, and relationships influence how (and if) we have access to these spaces.

There is another version of social science surveillance that has recently haunted us, and that is the process by which social scientists — in this case, feminist social scientists — reframe private experiences as social troubles. Taking the lead from Mills (1959) and many since, we see it as our responsibility to move from narratives to theories of social dynamics that operate amid macrostructures, relationships, and communities to produce life as lived, even if this is not life as analysed in the narratives of our interviewees.

Take the case of domestic violence, particularly among white working–class women, those still in what are considered stable, intact marriages but who are nevertheless being beaten at rates comparable to the women more explicitly living in less stable home environments. We have accumulated substantial evidence to suggest that women in both kinds of environments experience extraordinarily high levels of domestic abuse, and yet women in the seemingly stable homes rarely talk about it, refuse to critique the violence, and rarely question the role of men or their actions. They wouldn't call it abuse — should we?

In this work, we have been collaborating with two students, Amira Proweller and Corrine Bertram, on a domestic violence paper centered on the voices of brutalized and silenced working–class white women. Now what? Is this just a theoretical exercise in which we report narrations of denial? Or do we theorize *over* their voices, giving us little reason for collecting their stories?

There are lots of academics writing about these things, but few are really grappling with trying to meld *writing about* and *working with* activists within these communities (for such work, see Austin, 1992; Lykes, 1989, 1994; Weiss and Greene, 1992). We try to work with communities and activists to figure out how to say what needs to be said without jeopardizing individuals or presenting a universal problem as though it were particular to this class. And yet, cracking their silence — especially among white working–class women who are exceedingly reluctant to discuss or reveal, lest the ideology of domestic family life crumble and their role as savior of the family be exposed — is a feminist and intellectual responsibility fraught with dilemmas.

On Self–reflexivity

We have certainly read much, and even written a fair amount, about researchers' subjectivities (Fine, 1994). Our obligation is to come clean 'at the hyphen', meaning that we interrogate in our writings who *we* are as we coproduce the narratives we presume to collect. It is now acknowledged that we, as critical ethnographers, have a responsibility to talk about our own identities, why we interrogate what we do, what we choose not to report, on whom we train our scholarly gaze, who is protected and *not* protected as we do our work. As part of this discussion, we want to try to explain how we, as researchers, (can) work *with* communities to capture and build upon community and social movements. In other words, we will put forward parts of our ever–evolving political agenda, sharing the kinds of scholarship/action upon which we are focusing. We draw from our past work to illuminate what's possible 'at the hyphens' of researcher and researched (ibid), and what feels impossible.

Thus far, in Jersey City and Buffalo, we have been able to document how state policies and local economic/social shifts have affected young women's and men's belief systems, world views, and social consciousness. Through individual interviews we have gathered much of these data. Through the focus groups (for example, in the Lesbian and Gay Club, the African American and white churches, the EPIC parenting group, the Latina homeless shelter, the Pre–Cap college prep program for young adolescents), we have been able to encourage settings in which our interviewees have begun to weave together analyses that weren't entirely formed, to begin to piece together their commitments, for instance, to the 'next generation of African American boys', or to 'practice the ways of grandmother' around Latina spiritual rituals. Sister Kristin from the York Street Project and Dolores Perry from Headstart have both invited us to work more closely with groups of women and men in their programs, running focus groups that would raise questions, press issues, and help the participants reshape programs. In the EPIC group, we were told that the engagement of several members increased due to our kind of individual and group work. Indeed, Lois Weis was asked to facilitate an EPIC group on a long–term basis. The group interviews offered these women a way of piecing together the strengths of their lives, encouraging forward movement as they were raising their families in the midst of poverty.

Further, throughout the course of our three years of research, we have moved across the researcher–researched hyphen to apply our work toward support of local policy and community efforts. Michelle Fine has testified at state hearings on the state takeover of the local schools, advocating with community groups that the state remain in control until local participation can be encouraged and sustained. Research assistant Mun Wong coordinated a project among women on welfare who were eager to document the differential supermarket prices of similar items at different points in the month and in different markets in the community. We have provided census and qualitative data to city council members from the Latino community. Lois Weis supplied testimony in support of continual funding for EPIC and will be trained as an EPIC facilitator. Across communities, numerous conversations have taken place with key policymakers on a number of issues arising from our data.

We take for granted that the purpose of social inquiry in the 1990s is not only to generate new knowledge but to inform critically public policies, existent social movements, and daily community life. A commitment to such application, however, should not be taken for granted. This is a(nother) critical moment in the life of the social sciences, one in which individual scholars are making moral decisions about the extent to which our work should aim to be useful. Distinct camps are lining up with arrows poised.

We have colleagues who embrace the commitment to application, as we do, even if some think it is naive to imagine being able to infiltrate current policy talk on life within poor and working–class communities. Other colleagues have long seen their own scholarship as explicitly aimed toward political and social change (see Gittell, 1990, 1994; Lykes, 1989, 1994; Mullings, 1984; Piven, Block, Cloward, and Ehrenreich, 1987; Piven and Cloward, 1971, 1977; Powell, 1994). And we hear a growing chorus of colleagues who presume that if you are interested in policy and/or social practice, your data are thereby less trustworthy. This latter position was in retreat for perhaps a moment in time, but it seems to be returning to the academy in well–orchestrated volume. We do, of course, reject this position, but would ask again that academics who see this work as deeply nested in community life (recognizing that the notion of community is up for grabs) come together to argue cogently our responses to the following questions: Is this science? Is *only* progressive work biased? Is this politics or policy? And, to probe fundamentally, where are the sites of intellectual leverage by which our work can begin to fissure public and political discourse? That said, we take our responsibilities to these communities seriously, and are educating our graduate students to work with — not on or despite — local community efforts.

Throughout the design, the doing, and the interpretation of our fieldwork, we talk and write about the anxieties (many of which are represented in this article), struggles, passions, and pains. But we ask now, *how much* of our relatively privileged lives do we insert into essays when we chronicle lives under assault from the economy, the state, and within communities and even homes? Yes, *we* write the stories, we determine the questions, we hide some of the data, and we cry over interviews. But self–conscious insertion of self remains an exhilarating, problematic, sometimes narcissistic task. What more can we say than that we are two white Jewish women deeply committed to a better world? The post–structuralist question of 'who are we?' is an important one indeed, but what does that mean as we weave together lives of passion, pain, and assault? A narcissistic look at self seems misplaced here. Whiting ourselves out seems equally wrong-headed.

So, In Whose Voice?

Mark, a white working–class informant, tells us:

> It goes into another subject where blacks, um, I have nothing against blacks. Um, whether you're black, white, you know, yellow, whatever color, whatever race. But I don't like the black movement where, I have black friends. I talk to them and they agree. You know, they consider themselves, you know, there's white trash and there's white, and there's black trash and there's blacks. And the same in any, you know, race. But as soon as they don't get a job, they right away call, you know, they yell discrimination.

In whose voice do we write? Well, of course, our own. But we also present long narratives, colorful with/from informants in our scholarly and more popular presentations, essays, and articles. Some of these narratives, particularly from *Angry White Men*, contain hostile or grotesque references to 'others' — people of color, police, men on the corner. As theorists, we refrain from the naive belief that these voices should stand on their own, or that voices should survive without theorizing. However, we also find ourselves *differentially theorizing and contextualizing* voices. That is, those voices that have been historically smothered — voices of white women, and men and women of color — we typically present on their own terms, perhaps reluctant, as white academic women, to surround them with much of our theory. And yet, when we present the voices of white men who seem eminently expert at blaming African American men for all their pain and plight, we theorize generously, contextualize wildly, rudely interrupting them to reframe them.

Is this an epistemological double standard in need of reform, or is it a form of narrative affirmative action, creating discursive spaces where few have been in the past? Hurtado and Stewart (in press), in a new and fascinating essay on whiteness and feminist methods, argue that feminist scholars should self–consciously *underplay* (i.e., not quote extensively) hegemonic voices in their essays and relentlessly create textual room for counter–hegemonic narratives. Although we agree, we also think it is vitally important to critically analyse what it is white men are saying about us, about themselves, about economic and social relations. To do this, we interpret their words, their stories, their assertions about others.

All of this raises what we have come to think of as the 'triple representational problem'. In our texts we ponder how we present (a) *ourselves* as researchers choreographing the narratives we have collected; (b) the *narrators*, many of whom are wonderful social critics, whereas some (from our perspective) are talented ventriloquists for a hateful status quo; and (c) the *others* who are graphically bad–mouthed by these narrators (for example, caseworkers blamed by women on welfare for stinginess; African American men held responsible for all social evils by white men; police held in contempt by communities of color that have survived much abuse at the hands of police). Do we have a responsibility to theorize the agency/innocence/collusion of these folks, too? When white men say awful things about women of color, do we need to represent women of color, denounce and replace these representations? If not, are we not merely contributing to the archival representations of disdain that the social science literature has so horrifically chronicled?

Because all of these groups deserve to be placed within historical and social contexts, and yet power differences and abuses proliferate, how do theorists respect the integrity of informants' consciousness and narratives, place them within social and historical context, and yet not collude or dignify this perverse denigration of people of color? In what seems like too shallow a resolution, we have diversified our research teams, hired local activists and community members when appropriate to consult with us on design and interpretation, and read endlessly in an effort to get out of these boxes. However, these issues are *not* being raised by those in the field. We notice, perhaps defensively, that many of our friends and colleagues who now write on critical ethnography are writing about theory and methods, but not through data. Critical work on representations, post–structuralism, and ethnography has taken many of our once–in–the–field colleagues up and out, looking down now (as we have been wont to do) on a set of dilemmas that have nasty colonial pasts and precarious futures. Those of us still in the field, on the ground, so to speak, worry through this set of issues in highly concrete ways. We worry with no immediate resolution and only rare conversations. We know, though, that these points must be considered.

There are no easy answers to these dilemmas. In each of the essays we have produced thus far, we have tried to contextualize the narratives as spoken within economic, social, and racial contexts so that no one narrator is left holding the bag for his/her demographic group, but there are moments within the narratives when 'others' — people of color, case workers, men, women, the neighbor next door — are portrayed in very disparaging ways. We also struggle with *representation*, working hard to figure out how to represent and contextualize our narrators, ourselves, and the people about whom they are ranting. Under the tutelage of historians Scott (1992) and Katz (1995) and psychologist Cross (1991), we try to understand how and why these categories of analysis, these 'others', and these accusations are being cast at this moment in history, and who is being protected by this 'scope of blame' (Opotow, 1990). At times, however, audiences have nevertheless been alarmed at the language in our texts, at the vivid descriptions and the portraits. We are working on these issues, and welcome help from others who are also struggling with both theory and empirical data.

When Method and Voice Meet

We have noticed in the midst of analysis that the data produced vary by method collected. Methods are not passive strategies. They differentially produce, reveal, and enable the display of different kinds of identities. To be more specific, if individual interviews produce the most despairing stories, evince the most minimal sense of possibility, present identities of victimization, and voice stances of hopelessness, in focus groups with the same people the despair begins to evaporate, a sense of possibility sneaks through, and identities multiply as informants move from worker to mother, to friend, to lover, to sister, to spiritual healer, to son, to fireman, to once–employed, to welfare recipient. In the context of relative safety, trust, comfort, and counter–hegemonic creativity offered by the few free spaces into which we have been invited, a far more textured and less judgmental sense of self is displayed. In these like–minded communities that come together to trade despair and build hope, we see and hear a cacophony of voices filled with spirit, possibility, and a sense of vitality absent in the individual data.

We make this point because we have stumbled again upon an issue that may appear to be methodological but is deeply substantive and ethical. Both psychology and education have depended religiously upon methods of individual surveys, interviews, observations, and so on, at the cost of not seeing or hearing collectives. If, as we postulate, collectives are more likely to generate stories of possibility and hope, then perhaps we have a social science, painted in despair, that is as much a methodological artefact as it is a condition of daily life in poor communities.

On a Disappearing Public Sphere

Tamara explains:

> I didn't want to be with the father of my children anymore. And at that time he really gave me a lot of headaches. 'If you don't stay with me, then I'm not gonna help you with the kids.' Which he really didn't do, which I'm thankful. But I just figured, 'Well, the hell with it. Then I'll work . . . get the welfare.' Because I pay $640 for this apartment. That's a lot of money for a two–bedroom apartment, you know? And the welfare only gives me $424, so I have to make up the difference. And plus I have a telephone, you know. I have cable for my daughters, you know. And it's just a lot of money. And I figure, you know, I figured, well, I couldn't make it on my own. I wasn't making enough to make it on my own back then, so I had to go on welfare. So I did it, and it was . . . I didn't like it. I didn't like sitting there. I didn't like the waiting. I didn't like the questions they asked me, you know?
>
> *Q*: What kind of questions did . . .
> *A*: Well, they asked me if I was sexually active, how many times I went to bed with him, you know? And I told the guy, 'I'm sorry, but that is none of your business' and I refuse to answer the questions. Because to me, well what, they

Q: ask you if you, he asked me if I slept with black men or white men, Puerto Rican men. What was my preference. And to me that was the questions . . .

Q: Was this on a form, or he . . .

A: No, he was just asking questions, you know? And I refused to answer them, you know. And he kind of like got upset. 'We have to ask you this.' I was like, 'bullshit'. You know, they just wanted to, they asked, he asked me how many times I had sex in a day, and just really, you know, if I douched, if I was clean, if I took a shower. I don't think these are any of your business, you know? I take a shower every night and every day, you know? I think those are stupid questions he asked. I was, he asked me how many men I had in my life that I had, you know, if I have more than one man. And I turned around and told him, 'I'm not your mother.' I never heard of questions like . . . [laughs]

Q: Neither have I. [laughs]

A: They asked the weird questions.

Q: So, how, what was the procedure like?

A: It was embarrassing. Like, with Medicaid, for kids it's good. For kids, you know, you can go anywhere you want with the Medicaid. You can go to the doctors for kids. You know, they pay for braces. When it comes to an adult, I was going to, I was hemorrhaging. I was going to a doctor. I'd been bleeding since December, okay, and they're telling me, I've been going to a gynae-cologist through the welfare. 'It's normal, it's normal. Don't worry about it. It's normal.' So last week I was getting ready, for the past week I was feeling really dizzy and really weak, and I said the hell with it. Let me go see a gynaecologist. And I paid her. Thank God, you know, the Medicaid took care of the hospital. But I had to pay her $700 for the procedure that I had to have done. [laughs] I had to do it. It was either that or bleed to death, you know. [laughs] But a lot of doctors, I asked her, because she used to take Medicaid. And I ask her, 'Why don't you, you know, take Medicaid anymore?' And a lot of doctors that don't, doctors tell you because they don't pay them. She said she's been waiting for people that were on Medicaid to get paid for two years, three years, bills that's how old the bills are and she's still waiting to get paid.

For the past three years we have collected data on communities, economic and racial relationships, and individual lives deeply affected by public policies and institutions that rotted many years before. And yet these very same public policies and institutions about which we have deeply incriminating data are today disappearing, yanked away from communities as we write. Public schools, welfare, social services, public housing — defunded. Positioning a critique of the public sphere as it evaporates or, more aptly, as it has disappeared, seems an academic waste of time; worse, it anticipates collusion with the Right.

Our responsibility in this work, as we see it (and if it is doable), is *not* to feed the dismantling of the State by posing a critique of the public sector as it has been, but instead to insist on a State that serves its citizenry well and equitably. That is, social researchers must create vision and imagination for what could be, and demand the resurrection of a public sphere that has a full and participatory citizenship at its heart. Then we can layer on the critiques of what has been. That said, it's not so easy when Speaker of the House Newt Gingrich is just waiting to use our narrative words to do away with welfare; when Brett Schundler, Mayor of Jersey City, is foaming at the mouth to get voucher legislation passed in a city in which public schools enjoy little or no positive reputation; when conservative theorists and writers George Gilder and Charles Murray will gleefully abduct our phrases as they paint poor women as lazy and irresponsible. Creating a safe space for intellectual, critical, and complicated discussion when the Right has shown such acute talent at extracting arguments that sustain the assault may be a naive, but worthwhile, wish.

Responsibilities for our Writing

We watch the apocalypse and write about it. What is the relationship between what we see, the outrage we gather and feel, the relatively tame texts we produce, and our audiences, many of whom are alternately too depressed or too cynical to be mobilized? We feel the weight of academics; that is, as public intellectuals, we need to tell the stories from the side of policy that is never asked to speak, to interrupt the hegemony of elite voices dictating what is good for this segment of the population. And yet we feel the need to document the pain and suffering in these communities and the incredible resilience and energy that percolates. It is important to note, therefore, another underground debate within community studies, the tension between representing historically oppressed groups as victimized and damaged *or* as resilient and strong. This may seem an artificial and dangerous dichotomy (we think it is), but we have encountered colleagues within feminism, critical race theory, poverty work, disability studies, and — most recently — queer theory arguing these intellectual stances, with these two 'choices' carved out as the (presumably only) appropriate alternatives.

We share the worries, but worry more about the fixed choices that are being offered. Simple stories of discrimination and victimization, with no evidence of resistance, resilience, or agency, are seriously flawed and deceptively partial, and they deny the rich subjectivities of persons surviving amid horrific social circumstances. Equally dreary, however, are the increasingly popular stories of individual heroes who thrive despite the obstacles, denying the burdens of surviving amid such circumstances.

We lean toward a way of writing that spirals around social injustice and resilience, that recognizes the endurance of structures of injustice and the powerful acts of agency, that appreciates the courage and the limits of individual acts of resistance but refuses to perpetuate the fantasy that victims are simply powerless and collusive. That these women and men are strong is not evidence that they have suffered no oppression. Individual and collective strength cannot be used against poor and working–class people as evidence that 'Aha! see, it's not been so bad!' We need to invent an intellectual stance in which structural oppression, passion, social movements, evidence of strength, health, and 'damage' can all be recognized without erasing essential features of the complex story that constitutes urban life in poverty.

We take solace in the words of many of our African American male informants, drawn from churches and spiritual communities, who testify, 'Only belief and hope will save our communities. We have come a long, long way . . . and we have much further to go. Only belief will get us through.' Amid the pain and despair, hope survives. This, too, is a big part of community life, rarely seen in the light of day. It is time to recognize the full nature of community life.

Full Circle

Coming full circle, we are still a couple of white women, a well–paid Thelma and Louise with laptops, out to see the world through poor and working–class eyes through the words and stories that we collect across and within communities. We work with activists, policymakers, church leaders, women's groups, and educators in these communities to try to figure out how best to collect data that will serve local struggles, rather than merely to document them. We are surrounded by wonderful students of all races/ethnicities, languages and sexualities, and come to few conclusions with any illusion of consensus. We draw upon community activists and policymakers to help us invent survey questions and interpret the data; we use our data to write up 'evaluations' for community programs surviving on shoestring budgets. We write through our own race and class blinders, and we try to deconstruct them in our multiracial and multiethnic coalitions. Decisions about design, sampling sets, interview schedule, interpretation, representation, and dissemination of findings have been developed, clumsily but broadly, through an open process among the members of the research team, with consultation from community members. Questions have been added and omitted by research assistants and community members. Phrasing of questions concerning social class, language, neighborhood violence, and childhood abuse have been best articulated by people who know community life, needs for privacy, and acceptable places for inquiry. Researchers can no longer afford to collect information on communities without that information benefiting those communities in their struggles for equity, participation, and representation. Although such collaborations are by no means easy (see Fine and Vanderslice, 1992), they are essential if social research is to serve the public good.

At base we are trying to work the hyphens of theory and research, policy and practice, Whitenesses and multiracial coalitions, and at this moment in history we find few friends who don't demand that we choose one side of each dichotomy and stake it out! Our commitments to 'floating across' satisfy few. Policymakers want clear (usually victim–blaming) descriptions of social problems. Communities would prefer that we keep dirty laundry to ourselves. Some academics think we should stay out of policy talk and remain 'uncontaminated' by local struggles. More than a few whites see us as race traitors, whereas a good number of people of color don't trust two white women academics to do them or their communities much good.

In lame response to colleagues and graduate students, we are trying to build theory, contextualize policy, pour much back into community work, and help to raise the next generation of progressive, multiracial/ethnic scholars. We try to position ourselves self–consciously and hope that our colleagues who are engaged in critical work and still plowing the fields for data will enter with us into this conversation about writing the wrongs and rights in the field. When ethnography came 'home', informants moved next door and read our books. Academics were reluctant, remiss, too arrogant to clear up some of these questions of ethics, methods, and theory. Many of our colleagues, on both the Right and Left, have retreated to arrogant theory or silly romance about heroic life on the ground. Others meticulously and persuasively deconstruct the very categories we find ourselves holding on to in order to write a simple sentence about community life. We toil on, looking for friends, writing for outrage, searching for a free space in which social research has a shot at producing both social theory and social change as the world turns rapidly to the Right.

Note

Author's Note: This article is an analysis based on data collected with the generous support of the Spencer Foundation. Address all correspondence to Michelle Fine, Ph. D. Program, Social-Personality Psychology, City University of New York Graduate School and University Center, 33 West 42nd Street, New York, NY 10036, telephone (212) 642–2509.

References

AUSTIN, R. (1992) 'The Black community, its lawbreakers, and a politics of identification', *Southern California Law Review*, **65**, pp. 1769–1817.

BOYTE, H.C. and EVANS, S.M. (1992) *Free Spaces: The Sources of Democratic Change in America*, Chicago, IL: University of Chicago Press.

BRICE HEATH, S. and MCLAUGHLIN, M. (Eds.) (1993) *Identity and Inner-city Youth: Beyond Ethnicity and Gender*, New York: Teacher's College Press.

CONNELL, R.W. (1994) 'Knowing about masculinity, teaching the boys'. Paper presented at the conference of the Pacific Sociological Association, San Diego.

CROSS, W.E., JR. (1991) *Shades of Black: Diversity in African-American Identity*, Philadelphia, PA: Temple University Press.

DENZIN, N.R. and LINCOLN, Y.S. (1994) *Handbook of Qualitative Research*, Thousand Oaks, CA: Sage.

DYSON, M.E. (1993) *Reflecting Black: African-American Cultural Criticism*, Minneapolis, MN: University of Minnesota Press.

FINE, M. (1991) *Framing Dropouts: Notes on the Politics of an Urban Public High School*, Albany, NY: State University of New York Press.

FINE, M. (1992) *Disruptive Voices: The Possibilities of Feminist Research*, Ann Arbor, MI: University of Michigan Press.

FINE, M. (1994) 'Working the hyphens: Reinventing self and other in qualitative research', in DENZIN, N.R. and LINCOLN, Y.S. (Eds.) *Handbook of Qualitative Research*, Thousand Oaks, CA: Sage, pp. 70–82.

FINE, M. and VANDERSLICE, V. (1992) 'Qualitative activist research: Reflections in methods and politics', in BRYANT, F.B., EDWARDS, J., TINDALE, R.S., POSAVAC, E.J., HEATH,

L., HENDERSON, E. and SUAREZ–BALCAZAR, Y. (Eds.) *Methodological Issues in Applied Social Psychology: Social Psychological Applications to Social Issues* (Vol. 2) New York: Plenum, pp. 199–218.

FOUCAULT, M. (1979) *Discipline and Punish*, New York: Random House.

GATES, H.L., JR. (1985) *'Race,' Writing, and Difference*, Chicago, IL: University of Chicago Press.

GITTELL, M.J. (1990) 'Women on foundation boards: The illusion of change', in *Women and Foundations/Corporate Philanthropy*, New York: CUNY.

GITTELL, M.J. (1994) 'School reform in New York and Chicago: Revisiting the ecology of local games', *Urban Affairs Quarterly*, pp. 136–51.

GREGORY, S. (1993) 'Race, rubbish, and resistance: Empowering difference in community politics', *Cultural Anthropology*, **8**, 1, pp. 24–48.

GUBRIUM, J.F. and HOLSTEIN, J.A. (1995) 'Qualitative inquiry and the deprivatization of experience', *Qualitative Inquiry*, **1**, 204–22.

GWALTNEY, J.L. (1980) *Drylongso: A Self-portrait of Black America*, New York: Random House.

HALL, S. (1981) 'Moving right', *The Socialist Review*, **55**, 1, pp. 113–37.

HURTADO, A. and STEWART, A.J. (1997) 'Through the looking glass: Implications of studying whiteness for feminist methods', in FINE, M. POWELL, L. WEIS, L. and WONG, M. (Eds.) *Off/White*, New York: Routledge, pp. 297–311.

KATZ, M. (1995) *Improving Poor People*, Princeton, NJ: Princeton University Press.

KEITH, M. and PILE, S. (Eds.) (1993) *Place and the Politics of Identity*, London: Routledge.

LADNER, J.A. (1971) *Tomorrow's Tomorrow: The Black Woman*, Garden, City, NY: Doubleday.

LYKES, M.B. (1989) 'Dialogue with Guatemalan Indian women: Critical perspectives on constructing collaborative research', in UNGER, R.K. (Ed.) *Representations: Social Constructions of Gender*, Amityville, NY: Baywood, pp. 167–85.

LYKES, M.B. (1994) 'Speaking against the silence: One Maya woman's exile and return', in FRANZ, C.E. and STEWART, A.J. (Eds.) *Women Creating Lives: Identities, Resilience, and Resistance*, Boulder, CO: Westview, pp. 97–114.

MILLS, C.W. (1959) *The Sociological Imagination*, New York: Oxford University Press.

MULLINGS, L. (1984) 'Minority women, work and health', in CHAVKIN, W. (Ed.) *Double Exposure: Women's Health Hazards on the Job and at Home*, New York: Monthly Review Press, pp. 84–106.

OMI, M. and WINANT, H. (1986) *Racial Formations in the United States*, New York: Routledge.

OPOTOW, S. (1990) 'Moral exclusion and injustice: An introduction', *Journal of Social Issues*, **46**, 1, pp. 1–20.

PIVEN, F.F., BLOCK, E., CLOWARD, R.A. and EHRENREICH, B. (1987) *The Mean Season*, New York: Pantheon.

PIVEN, F.F. and CLOWARD, R.A. (1971) *Regulating the Poor: The Functions of Public Welfare*, New York: Pantheon.

PIVEN, F.F. and CLOWARD, R.A. (1977) *Poor People's Movements: Why They Succeed, How They Fail*, New York: Pantheon.

POWELL, L. (1994) 'Interpreting social defenses: Family group in an urban setting', in FINE, M. (Ed.) *Chartering Urban School Reform: Reflections on Public High Schools in the Midst of Change*, New York: Teachers College Press, pp. 112–21.

RICHARDSON, L. (1995) 'Writing–stories: Co–authoring "The Sea Monster", a writing-story', *Qualitative Inquiry*, **1**, pp. 189–203.

SCHEPER-HUGHES, N. (1992) *Death Without Weeping: The Violence of Everyday Life in Brazil*, Berkeley, CA: University of California Press.

Scott, J.W. (1992) 'Experience', in Butler, J. and Scott, J.W. (Eds.) *Feminists Theorize the Political*, New York: Routledge, pp. 22–40.

Weis, L. (1985) *Between Two Worlds: Black Students in an Urban Community College*, New York: Routledge.

Weis, L. (1990) *Working Class Without Work: High School Students in a Deindustrializing Economy*, New York: Routledge.

Weis, L. and Fine, M. (Eds.) (1993) *Beyond Silenced Voices: Class, Race, and Gender in United States Schools*, Albany, NY: State University of New York Press.

Weis, L. and Fine, M. (1995) *Voices from Urban America: Sites of Immigration and Spaces of Possibility*. Spencer grant proposal; submitted to and funded by The Spencer Foundation, Chicago, IL.

Weiss, H.B. and Greene, J.C. (1992) 'An empowerment partnership for family support and education programs and evaluations', *Family Science Review*, **5**, 1,2.

3   Critical Incidents in Action Inquiry

David Tripp

... knowledge and competence in a mature science are transmitted in the course
of a dogmatic and highly structured training, which indicates an intense commitment to existing modes of perception, beliefs, paradigms or problem-solutions, and
procedures. (Barnes, 1974, p. 10)

Outline

This chapter has three main sections: first, I attempt to outline what the labels 'critical and reflexive' mean to me (and in so doing I have therefore not presented a summary of the literature on the subject); second, I illustrate these with a brief account
of a piece of facilitated socially critical action research (chosen because it illustrates
a process of research training appropriate to the method); third, I discuss how this
instance exemplifies some aspects of the method. However, I'll begin with a few
words about the purpose of this chapter.

Introduction

I understand that I was invited to contribute to this volume because I am seen as
someone who tries to research in a way that could be categorized as 'critical and
reflexive'. Such labels serve a very important role in enabling us to call a particular
method into existence. One of the dangers inherent in the power of such labels is
that they tend to metamorphose into rigid dogma to which neophyte researchers are
made to conform. As this chapter is a contribution to research training in a method
which is critical of the traditional approach to training described by Barnes (above),
in writing it I needed to keep this problem in mind, lest I exacerbate it. And as it is
relevant to the account of my approach to critical–reflexive research which follows,
by way of introduction I'll begin with a brief explanation of my stance on this important training issue.

Starting with the fact that as academics we are responsible for educating the
next generation of researchers, even though our approach may not be 'mature' and
perhaps hardly 'a science', we must recognize that in so doing we tend to set people
up to accept and maintain a view of the world that is based on our values; and
because they are valuable to us, very naturally we want those whom we teach to
make our values their own. This presents something of a contradiction peculiar to

us as 'critical researchers', because the essential and defining feature of our method is that we take a critical stance on all values.

In practical terms, the import of what I teach as methodology is therefore somewhat contradictory, *Be critical of everything except being critical.* All I can say to that for the moment, is that it proves that ultimately no one, not even a critical reflexive researcher, can escape making a stand on their values. But that does not mean that one cannot avoid turning one's own critical stance into the kind of single homogeneous entity that characterizes dogma. One can be critical of many other things in many different ways, such as *how* one critiques *what*, and I believe that should be a matter of one's own personal values and view of a situation. So throughout this chapter I want to emphasize the personal nature of the development of a research methodology.

In this I am also trying to avoid reproducing my own training and development as an educational researcher, for that was exactly what Barnes captured so clearly (above); it was actually my training in literary criticism that encouraged me to be critical of the methods of critique I was given, though in that too, no one called into question the need to be critical (that came later with the development of study of popular culture in schools (Tripp, 1987). It is that process of producing a critique that is based on and consonant with my view of the world and what's important in it, that has led to my methods for research in education. And it is my wish to promulgate my view that has led to this article in this collection.

Three Key Ideas

On Being Socially Critical

In the context of the title of this collection I take the term 'critical' to mean a relatively simple attitude towards research in which *nothing is taken as necessarily 'given'.* I see a 'socially critical' approach to research as a matter of *problematizing research content and procedures in terms of what I see to be the ideal of a socially just form of inquiry.* Bringing the issue of social justice into research means shifting from only asking questions about the quality and appropriateness of matters internal to the research, to also asking questions that problematize processes in terms of *whose interests are being served and how,* and that problematizes content in terms of *what substantive knowledge (of what and whom) used in and generated by the research, is accepted as true (by and for whom)?*

As it is neither necessary nor possible for anyone to newly problematize all concepts and procedures one uses, we have to take much as given for much of the time in order to proceed with any research at all. That may be rather an impure stance, but if one accepts as guiding principles that we should continue to see everything as open to critique at some point, and we should always be working at problematizing something, it seems to work eventually to produce new approaches.

Some aspects of research which I have found it necessary to critique in my work are the notions and associated practices of generalization, participation, authorship, and data collection. There's no way in which I could reproblematize even only these few aspects in all the research which I have subsequently undertaken, let alone adequately to critique many other notions such as subjectivity or narration which are also relevant to much of my work, but my ongoing critique has led to different practices and rationales for them.

One way of viewing what we might problematize, is to consider the nature and extent of social justice in both research content and process, within and beyond the project itself. This simple breakdown gives us four areas to consider:

Figure 3.1: Four areas of research to critique

	internal	external
knowledge		
procedures		

In terms of the content of my research, I believe that my stance is critical in the sense that I set out to examine the meaning of a practice with a view to improving it, usually in terms of both effectiveness and social justice. It is therefore a process which seems inevitably to lead into identifying and questioning the wider social implications of the practice in question.

In terms of the process used, I find I have tended to develop my methodological critique as follows:

    (i)   noticing or having my attention drawn to an issue;
    (ii) taking a position on it; and then
    (iii) developing some general principles to bear in mind when taking procedural decisions in my research.

I have then:

    (iv) used the principles to inform decisions;
    (v)   monitored and described their effects;
    (vi) reflected on how well they work in practice;
    (vii) used that experience to evaluate, clarify and improve the general principles, thus detailing them and building up clear guidelines to follow in subsequent projects.

The whole process is a typical ongoing action inquiry approach, the first three steps being an analytical methodological inquiry which forms the planning moment of the cycle.

Those four areas cannot be treated as discrete categories, however; one can see that content as knowledge (what is being researched), can contribute to increased social justice both within the research project and in the social world beyond it. Similarly, process can be critiqued not only in terms of the nature and extent of social justice amongst the participants created by the project's procedures, but also in terms of issues such as how the findings are used, how the project articulates with the researcher's and other's work and concerns, and how the research is funded. The external factors can be seen as aspects of the project's context, and content and process interact in many ways, of course.

To illustrate the content and process of this critique, it was in problematizing my personal (N = 1) experience of leaving teaching in order to do classroom research that I developed an ongoing concern with why teaching and research were such widely separated occupations within education (Tripp, 1980, 1990a); and having looked at some of the implications of this separation for the whole profession, I changed my practice in several important ways, particularly with regard to how I worked with whom (Tripp, 1993).

On Being Reflexive

This view of the more obvious aspects of critique, brings us to the idea of reflection, or rather the *ideas of reflex*, for reflection comes from a word which has several meanings. Most people use it in the sense of a mirror reflecting light, and this is one very common and specific use of the word; but the term *reflex* actually codifies the much more general idea of something being turned back upon itself, and this is why it has also come to refer to a mental process in which one thinks about things by going back over them. And in the realm of professional development in education, reflection has come to refer to a kind of debriefing process in which one (and *one* there usually also means *solo*) evaluates one's own practical performance.

Another use of the term reflex, however, is to describe a particular kind of verb, a reflexive verb being one where the actor is acting on themselves, and is thus directly and immediately affected by their own action (*she raised herself; he prided himself*). In research, this is a very relevant meaning of reflex, and I see the term *reflexivity* as defining a particular dialectic between the research project as a constructed entity, and how people participate in constructing it, especially the researchers.

Clearly that dialectic will involve knowledge and procedures within and outside the project, but reflexivity is a much more internal process than either research procedures or what one does with knowledge. Specifically, reflexivity involves a kind of circularity in understanding in which the person trying to understand the so-called 'objective' phenomenal world they are investigating, examines the way in which their developing understanding changes them and their relation, not only to both the phenomenal world they are observing and their knowledge of it, but also to how the are observing and understanding the phenomenal world.

This makes it much more than the simple kind of feedback system one traditionally associates with the term, 'reflex'. It is also more than what an unrecalled source[1] appears to be referring to when he/she delightfully wrote that,

> The typical eskimo family consists of a mother, a father, two children, and an anthropologist. When the anthropologist enters the igloo he learns a lot about himself . . .

Learning about oneself is a kind of reflexivity, but it is only one kind, a kind that often just 'happens to' one, perhaps something one cannot avoid. When one consciously and deliberately sets out to develop reflexivity in research, one tends to produce other kinds of learning about oneself. I'm not really sure what the possibilities are, but I do know that when one combines it with an overtly critical stance in one's research, reflexivity will lead one to question one's own values and practices, even one's right to be doing whatever research it is one is then engaged in.

What seems to me to be a kind of reflexivity in my work stems from a combination of two habitual practices — one is a disposition to reflect on professional practice in a continuous, ongoing fashion; the other is an orientation towards maximizing the inclusion of those who are variously involved in my practice. These can both be intimately bound into research, of course.

My investigation of my own action (whether praxis or action inquiry) is reflexive in that they are very much determined by what I know about a situation and how I am seeing it, and as these change all the time, I consciously have to check them out; in fact, as one has to move in response to a moving target, it is important also to monitor one's movement. It is difficult to see how such practices could not be reflexive.

In practical terms, this means, for instance, that in our view of a situation first, we are going to be affected by both the direct observations we make of the situation in question, and by what we already know from other sources, such as knowledge we generalize from our own previous experience of such situations, and from others, often through our reading of their published research. Clearly these can and should involve research processes because the fundamental aim of all research is the generation, improvement and increase of useful knowledge.

Then there are many kinds and levels of reflexion; again, I believe that this process is improved by the kind of system and method provided by research procedures — research provides sets of possibilities for how we can analyse which aspects from what point of view and with what aim in mind. Knowing these and how they work enables us to choose and use appropriate methods, rather than only to think about things in an entirely random fashion.[2]

On Participation

Our orientation to others brings together reflexion and matters of social justice because it is something which we enact with others in various ways. In a broad sense of the word, everyone who is affected by our work is thereby involved in it, so our decisions must be based on some normative notions about who should participate in our research, in what ways, and to what extent. But as our enactments always require decisions, when we are engaging in critical research we should not thoughtlessly follow a particular protocol but consciously and deliberatively use our professional judgment. In any case, our orientation to others is a part of our view of the situation, and issues of participation are therefore an important aspect of any research method.

The term 'participatory research' is generally reserved for research in which researchers are seeking to maximize participant involvement; one would expect any socially critical approach to be highly participatory, but not necessarily overtly reflexive. Participation becomes reflexive when one monitors one's relations with other participants and bases one's actions on what one is learning about oneself in relation to them, and vice versa. In an action inquiry project it does not seem sufficient merely to monitor those relations — one must also act on the information, and that requires deliberately building participation as a flexible and emerging process into the research.

Moving on to kinds of participation, then, the popular binary *participatory* and *non-participatory* is too simplistic to help much here. Deciding the kinds and degrees of involvement of various people requires drawing some further distinctions, and one set which I particularly like is that of Pretty (1994) who delineates seven kinds of participation (presented here as summarized by Attwater, 1996):

(i)   passive participation (participate by being told);

(ii)   participation in information giving (for example, extractive surveys, and interviews);

(iii)   participation by consultation (external agents still define problems and solutions);

(iv)   participation for material incentives (for example, on farm research, food for work);[3]

(v)   functional participation (form groups to meet pre–determined project objectives);

(vi)   interactive participation (joint analysis and action plans);

(vii)   self–mobilization (local initiative independent of external institutions).

Attwater comments that Pretty's experience in agriculture is that sustained development requires participation, and functional participation is the bare minimum; this is also being increasingly accepted as being true in education.

All of those kinds of participation imply different kinds of power relations, and I think that it's important to spell these out in critical research because they will determine the kind of reflexivity possible, and I have done that with regard to teachers' participation in action research projects (Tripp, 1996):

Figure 3.2: Six ways for teachers to participate in research

Type of relationship		Control of research	Teacher's role	Other's role
1	Consenting	other	researched subject	researcher
2a	Consulting	other (+ coopted teacher)	actor/informer (researched subject)	researcher
2b		teacher (+ coopted other)	research supervisor (actor/informer)	research assistant (consultant)
3a	Cooperative	other (+ teacher)	informer/reflector (actor)	research leader (facilitator)
3b		teacher (+ other)	research leader (actor)	consultant (research assistant)
4	Collaborative	shared	research colleague (actor/informer)	(facilitator/informer)

(Secondary roles in brackets)

This figure summarizes how one might define different kinds of research according to the level of participation in terms of how the roles of participants vary and who has the most power over (and in) it. Clearly consenting is the least close and voluntary,[4] with the participant being only passively involved, perhaps by being observed, for instance. The main difference I see between cooperation and collaboration is that in the former different parties do different things when working together, whereas in the latter all parties do the same things together.[5]

These categories are not really ways to classify whole projects, in any case; it is my experience that a project will vary and change between these types almost from moment to moment, and certainly at different stages. I have found that although I may have initiated a project with type 1 or 3 power relations, there will be points when the teacher makes some suggestions about how to proceed, or tells me what's possible, or does things entirely on their own initiative without reference to me. The last two types would seldom if ever occur if one had to characterize in a pure fashion a whole project by just one of these types. So rather than use a scheme such as this to characterize a whole project, it is more useful to use it to map power relations at particular points with a view to clarifying them in order to ascertain that everyone is comfortable about the levels and direction of control.

The last point I want to make about participation in socially critical research is that whatever else happens, one should deliberately set out to ensure that the situation and its outcomes are just for all participants. This is not simply a matter of seeing to it that no one is disadvantaged in or by the research (Tripp, 1997), though that is important; it is more a matter of sharing the work and its benefits, and for me that is a distinguishing feature of collaborative (as opposed to cooperative) research.

I use five major criteria to establish and maintain justice, all of which have been in the literature in one form or another for some time (Carr and Kemmis, 1983; Holly and Whitehead, 1986; Hord, 1986; Lieberman, 1986; Ruddock, 1982; Simons, 1987; Tripp, 1990b; Wadsworth, 1991). These can be summarized as follows:

(i)   that there is a shared commitment to the necessity for the research;
(ii) that the research agenda concerns topics of mutual concern;
(iii) that control over the research processes is also equally shared;
(iv) that outcomes are of equal value to all participants in professional terms;
(v)   that fairness informs matters of justice amongst participants.

These are, of course, ideals; seldom if ever would they all be fully achieved for everyone; their purpose is to clarify what to aim at, and they can form the basis of procedural ground rules.

Clearing House

Having explained some of the ways in which I see how the issues of critique and reflection concern me in my work, and having outlined some of the principles which I use to guide decisions about these issues, I'd like now to provide a brief account of a university BEd action research unit which I use to introduce students to the practice of socially critical action research. In it, all students perform their own project in which I act as a facilitator. The following excerpt is my rewrite of a student's account of a part of the unit where they choose a recognized research strategy and use it to help plan new action in their action research cycle.

Background

Greg was tutoring part-time in a labour market course aimed at improving the employability of longer term unemployed young people. Part of the course is called 'Clearing House', which is a time when students, the coordinator, staff and youth worker gather on a regular basis to discuss any issues of concern to the group.

Greg had been alerted to an issue with Clearing House by an early critical incident in which one of his students had become so incensed that, even after (because of?) a warning that he could be fined a week's wages for bad behaviour, he had smashed his chair and stormed out swearing. Greg had noticed a serious contradiction between the rhetoric of listening and negotiation offered by the course coordinator, and his refusal to acknowledge students' wishes or listen to their difficulties and complaints in Clearing House.

Greg had also found that a serious problem for some of his students was their real and sharply felt powerlessness: having been unable to find work for some time, and with their continued benefits depending on their completing this course; they felt that they were being treated as worthless and immature people both personally and directly by staff, and also by the fact that much of the course was irrelevant to their situation and needs.

Greg observed that the students' attitudes and behaviour became much worse during and immediately after a Clearing House session, so he decided to perform an ideology critique on it in order to discover how he could improve the situation for his students. The method he used was that outlined in Tripp (1993, p. 59). This is basically an analysis and critical evaluation of assumptions, rationales and actual practices.

What's Meant to Happen

Staff and students sit in a semi–circle with the coordinator at the front in the centre of the classroom and the youth support worker sitting to her side. The coordinator begins by inviting participants to raise any issues or problems. Everyone can then have their say, be heard and taken seriously, and matters are to be resolved democratically amongst all participants.

What Does Happen

In fact Clearing House has become a time which staff use to enforce their own authority, values, rules and regulations. Staff silence students through imposing their own values and interpretations of events as the one correct position; they do not acknowledge (and often contradict) the position and lived experiences of students. Students are encouraged to share their opinions, then they are treated as worthless by staff who make final decisions with little consideration of the views students have expressed. Often students express their frustration and anger with the 'system' by shouting, leaving the room, ignoring what is happening, or remaining silent. The effects are that problems with the course are transformed into 'problem students', and they are thus being increasingly alienated from the course, and resorting to abuse and violence.

Why the Difference

The senior staff's perception and treatment of some participants as deviant and lacking in rationality, is made all the more obvious and extreme by their use of parental and exclusionary discourse during Clearing House, which they present as a democratic environment in which the group can engage in genuine dialogue with each other: the more obvious the contradiction, the more deeply felt it will be.

Underlying this explanation, the following are features of the course:

1 **Context**: Clearing House is a practice connected to the maintenance of vested interests and structures of power in the wider society. In particular, the course is intended to socialize participants into the labour market, which is construed as producing a disciplined and skilled labour force for employers. The successful completion of the course by students indicates that a certain kind of learning has taken place and that relevant competencies have been achieved. One of those competencies is to accept abuse from those in authority without complaint.

2 **Interests**: These labour market programs are intended to meet the needs of job seekers, employers and the government, but these needs are often divergent. Apart from (1) above, due to limited provision and compulsion to attend a course, some students have been placed in courses they do not wish to do and which do not meet their needs. Whilst staff recognize this, there is nothing they can do about it, so they attempt to deliver their course regardless, because they are on contract, and want to ensure their own further employment.

3 **Process**: Although some staff informally acknowledge problems, they don't help students; senior staff do not appear to have conflict resolution skills; when students are difficult, they distance themselves from the participants and discipline them; the students react violently.

4 **Result**: These conflicts of interests and contradictions in the process of Clearing House exacerbate an atmosphere of 'them and us', and in so doing increases alienation and despair, rather than producing a dialogue which cultivates learning, respect and empowerment.

Why the Practice is Maintained

Clearing House serves to reproduce and legitimate the dominant social order by reaffirming the authority and values of the staff, and instilling attributes employers are thought to value. These are achieved through Clearing House because it is a way of bringing out the students' anger and frustration so it can be dealt with; it is then handled in such a way that the students either take themselves out of the course (confirming staff's judgments of them, and making their teaching easier), or they remain in the course (becoming more passive and accepting and therefore more suitable as employees). Either way senior staff see themselves winning.

Having thus used a research technique (ideology analysis) to understand the situation, because it was an action research project, Greg then went on to plan his next action step. I have included it here as it is a very clear articulation of his professional values.

Action Plan for Improving the Practice

Greg decided to try to shift power from 'the system' to the participants (Tripp, 1992, p. 45) because he wanted to help the learning environment to become 'vibrant' and 'alive' with possibilities for growth and change. To do this he planned to:

(i)   be less exclusionary and provide everyone with the opportunity to speak and be heard;

(ii) make his class into a safe place where students can engage in genuine dialogue with him and other students; and

(iii) enable students to rethink the way things are and to develop a sense of self and their connection to the world in which they live.

Greg's next action step was to begin this process through:

• acknowledging the different histories, locations and experiences of students;
• recognizing that the social use of language incorporates many discourses (Mitchell, 1991) and consequently acknowledging the different terms of reference and narrative styles of the students and allowing all participants and everyone concerned to be heard;
• repositioning the learner as a 'maker of meaning';
• encouraging students to subject his approach to continuous critique through shared conversations and written assignments.

To monitor the process of implementation and the results of this strategy, Greg then:

(i)   made a point of recording anything he saw as a critical incident;

(ii) worked with the above approaches, inviting the students to discuss anything he saw as a critical incident with him;

    (iii)   wrote up their responses and, still working with the above approaches, checked with them that he had understood and accurately reported their points of view;

    (iv)   then used this information to plan his next action step.

Thus he proceeded with a typical action research cycle.

Commentary

As I have already used my allotted space in this book, I will only make a few brief points about the extent to which my work with Greg is a paradigm of critical reflexive research in education.

First, to look at the symmetry of the power relations in the process, we need to ask questions such as, *Who's work is this?* and *Who benefits?* Although we may answer, *Both of ours*, and, *Both of us*, those are far too simple answers to very complex and debatable questions; also we need to be able to verify our answers. One way of doing that is to agree and articulate that the research procedure was broadly as follows:

- I suggested our roles initially, Greg accepted these, and then we both constructed and acted in them with reference to each other;
- I explained how I saw the way we were working, Greg clarified and verified my account;
- Greg was the actor in the field, I facilitated his work by suggesting a range of activities and helping him choose appropriately by teaching to the understanding necessary for him to make informed choices;
- Greg performed the activities he chose, I helped him to do so;
- Greg chose what to work on, I helped him clarify, limit and shape it;
- I journalized my methodological issues, Greg journalized his fieldwork;
- Greg recounted to me what was happening and how he saw and explained it, I developed his account with questions and produced some alternative hypotheses;
- Greg produced the first draft of the ideology critique, I further analysed and rewrote it, then Greg responded to my analysis, and I rewrote it again;
- Greg included it in his finished project, I extracted it, added contextual information and rewrote it again for this chapter;
- I wrote this chapter, Greg responded to it.

That account shows a typical mixture of cooperation and collaboration: we were both engaged in the same project though we performed some different tasks in it; we both gained rewards, and though these were different (Greg 4 points credit, I a publication) they were of similar value to us professionally; and of course, both of us were learning from each other, and about the same situation. In such ways we were reflexive in our working together, and together and individually with the emerging research situation.

Perhaps I should mention just one outstanding amongst the many issues of reality and who gets to construct it. The ideology analysis is actually partial in that it is just one view of a multifaceted situation. Our view, however, comes over as *the* view; although the students endorsed our account of what was happening for them, it was not a view they could have constructed for themselves, and in that sense they were accepting our explanation of their situation, not, as in most qualitative research, the other way about. Furthermore, we did not check out our account with the staff concerned; though anonymous, they are still victimized by not even being consenting participants, and also in terms of our conclusions, which were negative and they were not in a position to defend. Some of this was unavoidable, but it is important to note all of this is invisible in our account because one has to know what is not mentioned in order to see the partiality of our account. And in one sense it is the process of collaboration and reflexivity in generating our account that makes it so: we retuned to each other and our emerging analysis in order to develop it into the logically adequate explanation Greg used as the basis of his future action, and I have used as the basis of this chapter.

Next, in the introduction to this chapter I wrote about the need to produce a critique *that is based on and consonant with my view of the world and what's important in it.* Clearly that is premised on my having first identified and articulated my view. In this case, both Greg and I had to do this, and also put them together. Luckily this was very easy and rewarding: Greg liked my methodological position and the way of doing research that it produced; I liked and admired Greg's work, view of his learners, and professional ideals and methods. My articulation of my values was more up front as it was an ongoing process for me, Greg's was more emergent as we considered the professional judgments he made about what to do and how. Both are now very clearly contained in this account. Again, our inter-action with each other and the research was both critical and reflexive, though being Greg's tutor and more experienced in this kind of research, I was more critical of Greg's work than he was of mine. I did make more trouble for Greg than he did for me. I asked awkward questions such as, *If the aim of the course is to produce docile and accepting employees, is it ethical to undermine that by working towards empowering the students?*

That raises a third point: did this situation imply that we could not critique the asymmetry of power of the tutor–student relationship in what is supposed to be a joint enterprise between equals? Though there was no way we could avoid it altogether, there was in fact an ongoing critique of it which enabled us to take it into account and develop it in a way we were both happy with. Though we re-mained designated as tutor and student, we did not accept the usual inequality without question; we critiqued it and mitigated it through negotiation.

The point here is that a given asymmetrical power relationship does not neces-sarily constitute a problem as such, but what people do with and about it, can. Any-one in a position of power can choose not to exercise it, to limit or delegate it, and in this case I invited and Greg accepted negotiation. We recognized that we were both equally held by the constraints of the unit's prespecified aims and content, and I would be the judge of the quality of Greg's work; but my role during the research was that of a facilitator, not supervisor, judge or director. Part of the facilitator's role is to be a 'critical friend', that is to critique, challenge and provide alternatives as well as to assist and support. Greg had some control in this in that he could set limits by ignoring challenges, or asking for things other than critique. Also, we agreed that the field was his domain, and what he did there was entirely his choice and responsibility.

So to summarize this important point, the outcome of critique will sometimes be to accept the status quo having understood the situation and found ways of being comfortable with it. This can also be linked back to the introduction, because one need not limit critique only to the ways of critique as suggested, for a critique of the need for critique may result in a clearer justification of critique rather than leading one to abandon it. Given the values I've already developed, in my case I sense that the circularity remains, and the authenticity of such a critique must be in question. However, the more general point remains, that a common outcome of being socially critical in our research is that we have a better understanding of our own position and that of others, and we can accept these along with our critique. That position is thus strongly reflexive.

Conclusion

In this chapter I have tried to explain and demonstrate some of the processes of socially critical reflexive research, not only with the example I included, but through exemplifying a degree of critical reflexivity in the content of the chapter and the way I wrote it. In dealing with the issues I've raised I've emphasized the importance of keeping a developing method open by showing how it is a very personal exercise in understanding. Of course, others will have introduced one to many of the ideas one adopts and adapts, but the way to keep dogma at bay is to work through things for oneself, not simply following routines laid down by the others one has drawn on. This leads to much useful and enlightening debate. I also hope some readers will make some of the principles I have outlined here their own.

Acknowledgment

My thanks to Greg Martin for working so openly and cheerfully with me, and for allowing me to use his work here.

Notes

1 I believe I have read this somewhere, but cannot find a reference. But if there is a source, then I do apologize to the author.
2 Not that random freewheeling thought is not very useful and productive; just that it is seldom sufficient by itself as a strategy for developing a research method.

3   I see (iv) as being somewhat different in that it seems to be a reason for participating rather than a kind of participation, and it could operate in conjunction with any of the other six. If we want seven kinds, then perhaps we could add below (1) *participation as a victim*, a category which is significantly often overlooked.

4   Consenting is often called 'non-participatory', but this is a misnomer, for even being a victim involves a kind of (involuntary) participation.

5   This is not a widely agreed distinction; Heron (1997) for instance, uses them in the opposite way, seeing power relations as more symmetrical in cooperation than in collaboration.

References

ATTWATER, R. (1996) Post to the Qualrs discussion list (moderated by Judith Preissle) from listserv@uga.cc.uga.edu.

BARNES, B. (1974) *Scientific Knowledge and Sociological Theory*, London: Routledge and Kegan Paul.

CARR, W. and KEMMIS, S. (1983) *Becoming Critical: Knowing Through Action Research*, Geelong: Deakin University Press (also available through Falmer Press).

GIROUX, H. (1990) *Curriculum Discourse as Postmodernist Critical Practice*, Geelong: Deakin University.

GIROUX, H. (1994) *Disturbing Pleasures: Learning Popular Culture*, New York: Routledge.

HERON, J. (1996) *Co-operative Inquiry*, Newbury Park: Sage.

HOLLY, P. and WHITEHEAD, D. (Eds.) (1986) *Collaborative Action Research*, Cambridge: Cambridge Action Research Network #7.

HORD, S. (1986) 'A synthesis of research on organisational collaboration', *Educational Leadership*, **42**, 5, pp. 22–5.

LIEBERMAN, A. (1986) 'Collaborative work'. *Educational Leadership*, **43**, 5, pp. 4–7.

MITCHELL, C. (1991) 'Preface', In MITCHELL, C. and WEILER, K. (Eds.) *Rewriting Literacy: Culture and the Discourse of the Other*, New York: Bergin and Garvey.

PRETTY, J.N. (1994) 'Alternative systems of inquiry for a sustainable agriculture', *IDS Bulletin*, **25**, 2, pp. 37–48.

RUDUCK, J. (1982) *Teachers in Partnership: Four Studies of In–Service Collaboration*, London: Longman/Schools Council.

SIMONS, S. (1987) *Getting to Know Schools in a Democracy: The Politics and Process of Evaluation*, Lewes: Falmer Press.

TRIPP, D. (1980) 'Reflections on the nature of educational research', *Classroom Action Research Network Bulletin*, **4**, pp. 5–9.

TRIPP, D. (1987) 'Media studies: Towards a new curriculum'. Base paper for invited workshop at the Easter School of the British Film Institute, Canterbury, UK.

TRIPP, D. (1990a) 'The ideology of educational research', *Discourse: The Australian Journal of Educational Studies*, **10**, 2, pp. 51–74.

TRIPP, D. (1990b) 'Socially critical action research', *Theory Into Practice*, **24**, 3, pp. 158–66.

TRIPP, D. (1992) 'Socially critical educational research', *Issues in Educational Research*, **2**, 1, pp. 13–23.

TRIPP, D. (1993) *Critical Incidents in Teaching: The Development of Professional Judgement*, London and New York: Routledge.

TRIPP, D. (1997) *The SCOPE Program*, Perth: Education Department of Western Australia.

WADSWORTH, Y. (1991) *Everyday Evaluation on the Run*, Geelong: Deakin University Press.

4   Ideology and Critical Ethnography

Jesse Goodman

During the last two decades, the field of educational and social research has under-gone a great deal of intellectual and methodological turmoil. Putman (1981) alleged that we were beginning to see the 'demise of a theory [positivism] that lasted for over two thousand years' (p. 74). No longer would educational research be considered worthy simply because social scientists possessed a unitary method for discovering 'truth'. As Fiske and Shweder (1986) noted,

> There was once a time, not so long ago, when the very idea of rationality was equated with the results and findings of positive (i.e., objective) science. . . . [Today, there are a] wide range of alternative positions concerning science and the subjectivity/objectivity that one might credibly adopt in a post–positivist world. (pp. 16–17)

Lather (1988) draws attention to the fact that there has been an avalanche of new ideologies that researchers have used in their efforts to study, understand, and learn from social reality. Phenomenology, hermeneutics, neo–Marxist, feminist, construction-ist, and post–modernist are just a few 'frames of reference', currently being used in educational and social research. In rejecting the positivist view of social reality and methodology for examining this reality, educational researchers are faced with an expansive propagation of contending ideas that raise serious questions regarding the legitimacy and authority of scholarly practice (for example, Marcus and Fischer, 1986). Gone are the days when substantive issues of conducting research can be taken for granted due to the universal consensus imbedded within positivist methodology.

Today, scholars not only are faced with questions about how to generate pro-jects worthy of social inquiry, how to observe particular educational settings, and how to find good informants who work in these settings, but must also confront issues (just to name a few) related to the purpose of their work, the rationality that they use in developing their own presuppositions, their personal life histories, the power relationships between themselves and those people whom they observe, and the eventual reporting of their experiences. Doing educational research in a post–positivist era has been 'dizzying' (Lather, 1988, p. 1), especially for those such as myself whose primary interests do not fall within the field of philosophy of science.

Although the evolution of these frames of reference has produced a lively and growing body of epistemological and theoretical work within the field of research methodology, there are relatively few researchers (for example, Lenzo, 1995; Sparkes, 1994) who address these previously mentioned concerns within a context of their own work. As Anderson (1989) noted some time ago, there is a significant need to share the way in which post–positivist educational researchers address a number of issues and dilemmas brought into focus as a result of the transformation that has taken place within the field of educational research. In an effort to contribute to this small but growing body of literature, this chapter will explore the way in which I confronted the issue of ideology while conducting a recent critical ethnography (Goodman, 1992). However, prior to addressing this issue, it is important to briefly describe the nature of critical ethnography and the study to which I will refer throughout this chapter.

Critical Ethnography

As Anderson (1989) noted a few years ago, 'the current situation [doing educational research], although chaotic, is also full of opportunity' (p. 250). In particular, it has provided researchers with what Geertz (1983) referred to as 'blurred genres' in which social inquirers are free to borrow ideas from across disciplines and utilize various frames of reference in their work.

One hybrid that emerged from these blurred genres is an approach to educational research that some have referred to as critical ethnography (Anderson, 1989). As its name implies, its roots can be traced to the 1970s interpretivist field studies (for example, Cusick, 1973; Ogbu, 1974; Rist, 1973; Smith and Keith, 1971; Wolcott, 1973) and critical/feminist analyses of schooling and society (for example, Apple, 1979; Deem, 1978; Freire, 1973; Gilligan, 1982; Grumet, 1981; Whitty and Young, 1976). Interpretivist efforts emphasized the importance of symbolic interaction. Research findings represent the researcher's interpretation of informants' interpretations of and negotiations with (through words, symbols, and actions) their experiences. The interpretivists' emphasis on human agency and localized experience appealed to many critical educational scholars who were searching for an alternative to the over determinism of conventional, structural social research (for example, Bowles and Gintis, 1976). Early efforts at merging ethnography and critical scholarship (for example, Sharp and Green, 1975; Willis, 1977) showed potential for gaining insight into the complex relationship between human agency and social structures.

Despite its contributions, critical ethnography seems to be an oxymoron. After all, many critical scholars in education view ethnography as too atheoretical in their approach to research while ethnographers see critical scholars as too ideological and thus overly biased in their research. As Anderson (1989) notes,

> This uneasy alliance raised serious questions about the compatibility of theory–driven social agendas on the one hand and phenomenological research methods on the other. To many, their marriage seemed, at once, both an epistemological contradiction and an inevitability. (p. 252)

This opposition and synthesis of ideas underlies every aspect of doing critical ethnographies of schooling, and thus makes this work particularly unwieldy.

For those who have not read, *Elementary Schooling for Critical Democracy* (Goodman, 1992), this research project began due, as the title suggests, to my interest in democracy and education. I was particularly curious about the way a school with an overt democratic ethos educates its students. Harmony, an independent school, located in Bloomington, Indiana, had as one of its written goals to 'foster the skills necessary for active and constructive participation in our country's democratic process'. Once located, I spent 12 months reviewing documents and observing and interviewing the administrators, teachers, students, and several parents associated with the school. During this year, I was immersed in the daily routines and special functions of the school, including the hiring of new faculty and various social gatherings held outside the building.

Issues of Ideology

There are numerous issues that we faced during this study. Issues of power, legitimacy of our work, relationships between us and informants, style of writing, assumptions of social reality, and substance of our analysis were deeply interwoven into all of our activities. Unfortunately, due to space and time restrictions, it is not possible to address every point of contention as a result of the previously mentioned 'marriage' between ethnography and critical scholarship. Therefore, this discussion will be limited to a few cardinal issues related to the role of ideology in critical ethnography. These issues include: (i) issues of purpose; (ii) difficulties of identifying one's ideology; (iii) concerns related to being reflexive about one's work; and (iv) charges of relativism related to this type of scholarship.

The issue of ideology is of little concern to positivist researchers. Indeed, the core assumption of positivist social research is that its findings are free from value ladened influences of the researcher. As a result, ideology plays no role in the conceptualization of what is to be studied or how data is collected. Once the data has been carefully analyzed, it may help support the development of a new or pre–existing theory, which from a positivist perspective is defined as a special category of knowledge that is supported by the results of numerous controlled experiments. The ultimate purpose of this work is to generate knowledge that will 'stand up' to this ongoing testing and eventually become 'truth'. Today, many scholars have come to accept Namenwirth's (1986) suggestion that ignoring the way in which one's own ideology (for example, theories, frames of reference, world views, a priori cognition) impacts upon one's research is naive and misleading.

> Scientists are no more protected from political and cultural influence than other citizens. By draping their scientific activities in claims of neutrality, detachment, and objectivity, scientists augment the perceived importance of their views, absolve themselves of social responsibility for the applications of their work, and leave their (unconscious) minds wide open to political and cultural assumptions. Such hidden influences and biases are particularly insidious in science because the cultural heritage of the practitioners is so uniform as to make these influences very

difficult to detect and unlikely to be brought to light or counter–balanced by the work of other scientists with different attitudes. Instead, the biases themselves become part of a stifling science–culture, while scientists firmly believe that as long as they are not *conscious* [her emphasis] of any bias or political agenda, they are neutral and objective, when in fact they are only unconscious. (p. 29)

No observance of 'scientific protocol', however precise and meticulous, can protect one from his/her own ideology. From a post-positivist perspective, one's ideology or pre–conceived theory is intimately and deeply embedded in every aspect of the research endeavor. It influences the type of phenomena we choose to study, what we notice during the collection of data, and the way in which we analyse the findings. As a result, a distinctive characteristic of critical educational ethnography is its 'openly ideological' nature (Lather, 1986). That is, critical researchers make a commitment to become aware of, reflect upon, and articulate their ideological convictions within the context of their work. As Alcoff (1991) states,

The desire to find an absolute means [methodology] to avoid making errors comes perhaps . . . from a desire to . . . establish a privileged discursive position wherein one cannot be undermined or challenged. . . . From such a position one's own location and positionality would not require constant interrogation and critical reflection; one would not have to constantly engage in this emotionally troublesome endeavor and would be immune from the interrogation of others. Such a desire for mastery and immunity must be resisted. (p. 22)

Although being openly ideological is a viable alternative to 'value neutral' research, there is much confusion associated with this effort.

Purpose

The first issue to be examined concerns the purpose of research. That is, questions of ideology are perhaps best examined within the context of articulating the purpose of scholarship. As Homans (1967) stated in his classic commentary, the purpose of positivist social research is to discover the natural laws that govern human behavior. Once these laws are proven to exist, society can then be constructed in accordance with them. Thus, social research had the same purpose as the natural sciences, namely, to discover knowledge that could be proven and identified as 'truth'. As previously mentioned, I, along with many other scholars, have rejected this positivist perspective and purpose of educational research. However, while it is one thing to reject the traditional purpose of social research, it is another to generate a viable alternative. If the educational research is no longer about 'truth making', what is its function?

The purpose of a given activity is intimately connected to one's perception of the nature of that activity. In my deliberations, I came to the conclusion that research is a unique form of social discourse (Rorty, 1979, 1982). Put within a larger context, social reality can be understood, in part, as a complex tapestry of interconnected conversations. Underlying each of these discourses is a set of conventions that give it a sense of identity and thus purpose. These conventions include such items as: social location (i.e., where this discourse takes place), attributes of participants (for example, class, race, gender, education, occupation, age, life experiences), style of communication (for example, verbal, written, visual, behavioral), and topics of communication. Some discourses have conventions about even 'little' things such as the type of clothes one can wear (for example, uniforms) while participating in it, the accent or diction of speech one can use, or the use of particular terminology. Each of us participate in several overlapping discourses throughout any given day. Take for instance, the discourse one has with parents, children, students, friends, clients, or co-workers. Within a given culture, there are numerous unique discourses that represent different groups and interest within that society. For example, consider the discourses of street prostitutes, military generals, 'popular' girls in a wealthy suburban high school, ballet dancers, homeless families living in shelters, black gang members in Los Angles, estate lawyers, members of a fundamentalist religion, and professional politicians, just to name a few.

As scholars, we have come to recognize the importance of understanding social reality through discourse analysis (Luke, 1995). As Foucault (1972) notes, systems of discourse represent systems of power within a given society. These discourses are connected to social conditions that define what is 'true' at any given moment in history. Although scholars have come to recognize the value of investigating the social discourse of others, we have largely failed to recognize that our own scholarship as just another unique discourse that takes place in society. While in education, this academic discourse (i.e. scholarship, research) is no longer dominated by the protocols that result in 'truth making', many of its conventions exist. This discourse is still chiefly located in doctoral seminars and professional conferences, journals, and books; it is still primarily a written and verbal form of communication; it still largely expects writing to follow the editorial practices of expository prose; and it is still dominated by people who have advanced degrees. Perhaps most importantly, it is an *informed* discourse. It is assumed that the contribution of a given scholar is the result of fairly extensive study of what others have contributed to relevant lines of thought, as well as any additional experiences (for example, field research, teaching, consulting, social activism) that have provided insights into the topic under consideration. It is also largely a *reviewed* discourse. Rarely is a given contribution to it made without prior review and subsequent commentary by one's colleagues. In the majority of cases, these reviews are conducted without knowing the contributor's identity. Finally, the majority of academic discourse is *public*. Articles, books, and conference papers are available to anyone who cares to seek them out. In most cases, academic discourse is not conducted in secrecy or only available to those who work for certain institutions (for example, the military, private corporations). Although the content and linguistic complexity of academic discourse makes it inaccessible to many individuals in our society, it exists in the public domain and is thus open for anyone to read and criticize.

The implications of this orientation are fairly significant. Positivist research was justified largely on the premise that it would provide 'truths' about human behavior that the society could then confidently utilize. For example, in education there was, at one time, a plethora of studies which identified numerous teaching skills or behaviors 'proven' to be effective (for example, Dunkin and Biddle, 1974). If educational research can no longer claim to provide these types of 'truths', then what is the rationale for having this academic discourse? As I will explore below, this discourse does not need to provide 'truths' in order to be of benefit to the culture within which it exists (see p. 53).

Given the perspective of research as discourse, my purpose in writing *Elementary Schooling for Critical Democracy*, was not 'to prove some rigid thesis, but simply to *say* [quoted emphasis] something clearly enough, intelligibly enough, so that it can be understood and thought about' (Frye, 1983, p. 173). In this sense, I see the purpose of my research as pedagogical. Similar to other forms of teaching, my goal is to share information in ways that stimulate others to reflect, to think, and to generate and share their own knowledge. As a result, post–positivist scholarship is ultimately, as Rorty (1982) articulately argues, pragmatic in the tradition of William James and John Dewey. Scholarship is most useful when it helps its readers to gain insight into the human condition in ways that are personally and socially meaningful.

However, in addition to this more general purpose, I had two specific intentions, namely to portray social reality and critically examine this reality within broad social and cultural contexts. In particular, I sought to understand social reality in ways that would provide insights towards the creation of a more emancipatory society (Fay, 1987). As Lenzo (1995) states,

> Critical inquiry assumes, first of all, that we live in a world of unequal distribution of resources and power; and further, that if people understood they were oppressed, how that oppression operated, and how they might begin to work against it, they could achieve greater self–determination and, consequently, work toward a more just social order. (p. 17)

This perspective raises the question of what it means to study social reality in an unjust and often uncaring world. Popkewitz (1984) calls for research that is

> concerned with how forms of domination and power are maintained and renewed in society. The intent of the research is not just to describe and interpret the dynamics of society, but to consider the ways in which the processes of social formation can be modified. Finally, it posited the social world as one of flux, with complexity, contradiction and human agency. (p. 50)

The goal of my study was not to simply report 'what's out there', but was to analyse this reality in ways that work against those social, economic, and psychological constraints and ideologies that keep us from creating a more just and humane reality. However, I had difficulty in locating other studies that accomplished this delicate balancing act, and thus serve as exemplars for my efforts.

Although the emancipatory ideology of the researcher is an essential aspect of critical ethnography, my review of the literature suggests that it has too often replaced portrayal as the central purpose of the research. The lives of the actors being observed have been largely glossed over as critical researchers 'race' to develop their own critical theorizing (Christian, 1987). Bowers (1982) argues that critical observers of social reality frequently become overly concerned with developing abstruse ideological systems of thought in deriving their understanding of the social world which has 'prevented them from testing their theory against the phenomenological world of people involved in concrete social and cultural relationships' (p. 546).

Situating oneself, as a researcher, who wants to conduct emancipatory research has its dangers. One example of this potential hazard can be found in the Marxist notion of 'false consciousness'. False consciousness suggests that actors in a given social context have been so completely socialized by dominant, ruling–class ideology that they, unlike emancipatory researchers, are unable to recognize their own oppression, let alone the oppression of others. It suggests that people who do not understand reality as Marx did suffer from *deficient* thinking, rather than merely having an alternative understanding of life's experiences. Berger (1975) argues that the concept of false consciousness lays claim to a cognitively privileged status which allows 'intellectuals' to designate reality. He and others (for example, Hall, 1985; Lenzo, 1995; Rorty, 1988) go on to suggest that no one (including academics) can claim to possess 'true consciousness'. All of us are simply trying as best we can to make sense of this experience of living.

In addition, what is emancipatory in one historical and social location is oppressive in another. For example, many social scholars view positivism as overly deterministic, narrow, and rooted in a social control mentality. Its oppressive nature is most easily seen in fields of research such as eugenics (Gould, 1981); however, it is not difficult to see its oppressive impact in many social sciences. Nevertheless, in the eighteenth and nineteenth century, positivism was experienced by social scholars as an emancipatory ideology, and is worth exploring is some detail.

It is important to remember that positivism grew out of Europe's *Age of Enlightenment*. As the time implies, intellectuals of this time noted Europe's emergence from what was believed to be centuries of ignorance and the beginning of a new age — enlightened by reason, science, and respect for humanity. If humans can unlock the laws of the universe, such as Sir Isaac Newton had done with gravity, intellectuals during the *Enlightenment* believed that all underlying laws of nature including human behavior could eventually be discovered through reason and scientific procedures. No longer would people have to summon supernatural powers or participate in mystical rituals to overcome illness or grow crops. Tremendous value was placed upon the discovery of knowledge through observation and controlled experimentation of nature and society, rather than through the study of authoritative sources, such as the Greek philosophers or the *Bible*. Religion in particular was singled out for criticism due to its wealth, power, and suppression of reason. Never again would church officials be in a position to suppress the knowledge of scholars as it had done to Copernicus and Galileo. Kant's motto, 'dare to know', exemplified the openness and emancipatory spirit of the times. Although the *Age of Enlightenment* came to an abrupt end with the excessive brutalities of the 1789 French Revolution, it served as the foundation for nineteenth and twentieth century positivism.

The positivist idea that society could be purposefully constructed according to the 'laws of nature' held tremendous appeal to scholars and much of the general public. Once discovered, these laws could be applied to any number of human endeavors in order to find the 'right way' to accomplish specific tasks (for example, educate children, run the economy, manufacture goods). Culture would no longer be passively reproduced through the acceptance of mere custom, religious dogma, or superstition. Positivism offered humanity the hope that society could be constructed on a solid foundation of logic, reason, and scientific study. Given its historical context, it is not difficult to understand why scholars viewed positivism as an emancipatory ideology.

The story of positivism suggests that it is difficult to identify a given frame of reference of social theory as emancipatory. For researchers (or anyone else) to place their own framework for understanding the world in which we live in a privileged position is perhaps morally unjustified and socially dangerous. Although critical theories of culture provided many insights into the way in which I approached my research of Harmony, I struggled to remind myself that I was not on a 'rescue mission' to save society from its ignorance.

As a result, I made a concerted effort to situate my critically informed commentary within a rich portrayal of the informants. Throughout my study, I was reminded of Wolcott's (1975) insight that,

> The ethnographer's unique contribution is his commitment to understand and convey how it is to 'walk in someone else's shoes. . . .' However, he must also attend to how the participants themselves say it *ought to be* [his emphasis], typically investigating actions and beliefs in a number of categories of human behavior. (p. 113)

I took as my guide the rather old fashioned view that at the heart of good research lies good description and that clear, authentic ethnographic portrayal will likely be more educative than the ideological insights of the researcher who made the observations in the first place.

The value of portrayal or 'thick description' is not, as some (for example, LeCompte and Goetz, 1982; Lincoln and Guba, 1985; Miles and Huberman, 1984) have suggested, an answer to questions of validity. Based upon comments I have received from those who have read my study, the most important value of portrayal lies in its ability to provide the reader with a vicarious experience. Perhaps one of the most unique cognitive talents that we, humans, possess is our ability to go beyond immediate and direct experience as a source for learning. Our facility to vicariously experience life from secondary sources is a powerful tool in understanding our own lives and culture. From this perspective, the power and perhaps ultimate contribution of my study is to provide readers with an opportunity to envision the lives of informants and then apply what they vicariously observe to their own unique situations. In addition, I have also been told that readers of my study appreciate the way my analysis was interwoven into this portrayal in that it provided a scaffolding upon which they reacted and generated their own ideas on a particular finding. Although the purpose of this academic discourse is not to proclaim 'truth', I am convinced that it can provide, as previously mentioned, a rich pedagogical experience. Perhaps most importantly, having a group of well informed individuals engage in thoughtful and public discourse on a wide variety of topics without fear of retribution is vital for the creation and continual renewal of a democratic culture, even if it no longer lays claim to truth making.[1]

If the purpose of research is pedagogical rather than truth making, then I realized that my ideology needed to be 'open'. Similar to good teachers, I needed to be candid about 'where I am coming from'. As previously mentioned, researchers can no longer hide behind an aura of objectivity and neutrality. However, being 'openly ideological' raised as many concerns for me as it potentially addressed.

Construction and Identification

First, there is the question of what ideology the researcher should identify as his/her own. Perhaps it is more accurate to refer to ideologies since in all likelihood most individuals view life through a complex web of different and at times contradictory value and information systems. For example, I recognize and can articulate several ideologies (for example, pedagogical, social, political, psychological, and spiritual) through which I understand life. Although my core values such as a commitment to social justice, compassion, and democracy have remained fairly constant, the details of my ideologies are in a continual state of flux. During these years as a researcher, my ideologies have been informed by a wide diversity of intellectual traditions such as: existentialism, hermeneutics, neo–Marxism, liberalism, feminism, post–modernism, humanistic and Jungian psychology, symbolic interactionism, paleoanthropology, and metaphysics. Recently, I have come to appreciate some ideas that have emerged out of conservative educational ideologies in the United States. For example, I am intrigued by Chubb and Moe's (1990) call for funding schools through a market–place voucher system in which poor children are provided with larger sums than wealthy children. If the differences of these vouchers were substantial, this 'free market' concept comes very close to the socialist ideal of income redistribution.

Obviously, there are several contradictions embedded within these ideological systems of thought, and at the time of my study, I had not reconciled these internal disputes. As a result, I was unable to label myself with any one or two ideologies. In addition, I have little desire to remove this ambiguity from my consciousness. I voluntarily accept my ideological confusion. During my study at Harmony, I did not know exactly which ideological orientations were at work in my collection and analysis of the data. Does this inability to locate or isolate my own ideological orientation imply that I and other ideologically ambiguous scholars like me are not suitable candidates for conducting openly ideological research?

In addition, many post–postivist researchers suggests that our class, gender, race, as well as our physical condition, sexual orientation, and perhaps even eating habits influence the way in which we conduct research and thus must be addressed as part of what it means to be openly ideological. Our autobiographies do have much to do with our ideologies. Although we might like to think that our ideologies are, as previously stated, informed by multiple value and information systems with the selection of one's ideals coming only after careful study, the reality is probably more complex. For example, I can trace many of my ideological principles to my childhood, and at the same time my formative years would suggest a vastly different ideological orientation than I currently have. I grew up with wealth and privilege in a traditional, patriarchal family. Like many of his peers, my father started a small business during the post World War II economic boom just when many social and economic restrictions against Jewish people were eliminated due to the shock of the German holocaust. As a result, I lived most of my childhood in an upper middle class suburb of Chicago and went to New Trier High School, one of the 'best' public high schools in the United States. Given this background, my more radical colleagues are surprised at my interest in economic and social justice and my choice of occupations. After all, most of my childhood friends became doctors, lawyers, stockbrokers, investment bankers, and business people. Unlike myself, they are not particularly interested in issues of poverty, racism, or other social problems that do not directly impact themselves. On the other hand, these same colleagues are wary of my unwillingness (which they associate with my privileged background) to condemn all forms of capitalism as inherently more evil than twentieth century communist alternatives.

Perhaps my progressive ideologies cannot be accurately associated with my class background. Even though I did not personally experience anti–semitism directly until high school and them only in a relatively mild form (a little name calling), I identified with my ethnic heritage and the oppression my forbearers suffered throughout most of European history. This identification may be the reason why in third grade (1956) I wrote an essay in which I identified my future occupation as a 'freedom rider', an individual who rode integrated public buses through the southern region of the United States as a strategy to end segregation. Another possible origin for my ideologies could have come during the late 1960s. Like many others, I became deeply involved in the counter–culture and anti–war movements of this decade (Keniston, 1968; Roszak, 1969). I wonder if I would be teaching courses and writing academic papers critical of our schools and society if I had not been swept up in the radicalism of those times.

Does being 'openly ideological' mean that, as a researcher, I need to engage in some form of psychoanalysis to determine and articulate exactly the way in which each of my ideologies and autobiography influence my observations and analysis of the social world? If so, I clearly failed to do so in my study of Harmony's elementary school. For me, being openly ideological meant being aware of my basic value commitments and personal history, and recognizing that this value system and background influenced the way in which I perceived and understood the social life at Harmony. Perhaps the primary burden of openly ideological research falls upon the reader. That is, s/he should read the findings of a given study with the knowledge that they cannot be disassociated from the life of the researcher. As a result, the researcher is under the obligation to at least briefly identify his/her ideological commitments and aspects of his/her biography so that the reader can take this information into account when interpreting the study's findings and analysis. If more information from the researcher than that is required, I may have to rethink the way in which I approach the study of schools.

Strategies of Reflection

This being said, I contend (or am under the delusion) that researchers are not trapped by their ideologies; and therefore, need to make every effort to reflectively situate his/her ideology during data collection and analysis. We would be wise in constructing our methodologies to consciously alter our views of the social world in an effort break free from our own preconceptions. As Lather (1986) suggests, 'Data must be allowed to generate propositions in a dialectical manner that permits use of *a priori* theoretical frameworks, but which keeps a particular framework from becoming the container into which the data must be poured.' (p. 267). I initiated several strategies for this purpose at Harmony. First, I selected research assistants with diverse backgrounds. As I mentioned in my book (Goodman, 1992), Jeff Kuzmic was a former public school teacher who grew up in a conservative, mid–size town in the mid–Western part of the United States. Xiaoyang Wu was from mainland China who spent much of her adolescence as a 'barefoot doctor' in the countryside, separated from her parents who had been denounced as 'Westernized' intellectuals during the Cultural Revolution. A significant aspect of our debriefing sessions was devoted to exploring our unique and often very different perceptions of similar events taking place in the school. Second, I made a decision to avoid reading too much prior to our fieldwork. Although I was interested in the relation-ship between democracy and schooling, I purposefully did not read much political theory prior to conducting the fieldwork. Only after spending seven months at the school and generating several conceptual themes from the data did I begin to study various discourses related to democratic theory. Perhaps the highlight of the study came from recognizing the dialectical relationship between individuality and community at Harmony and then discovering that these ideals were the subject of extensive commentary among political theorists. Third, I and my colleagues made a conscious effort to do as the cultural anthropologist does and put our pre–conceived ideals and values 'on hold', that is, to empathically 'take on' the percep-tions, attitudes, feelings, behaviors, goals, dreams, and meanings that our informants shared with us as if they were our own. While it was impossible to conduct this research with a blank mind, this ability to vicariously experience informants' lives is at the heart of the ethnographic adventure. As Bloom (1997) points out, develop-ing this empathy with informants is not always easy, but without it, doing any type of ethnography would be nearly impossible. Through this awareness, we were able to temporarily put aside our own *a priori* perceptions and 'see' life from the per-spective of our informants. Fourth, we made specific efforts to look beyond the obvious, that is, to pay attention to the irrelevant and irreverent happenings at the school. Perhaps most importantly, we paid special attention to data that seemed to challenge our initial observations, conceptions, and life experiences. We also regularly tested our emerging analysis by trying to locate data that would force us to reconsider our perceptions and analysis (Erickson, 1986). Although we did not conduct value neutral research, we did take concrete actions to avoid having our research become a mere confirmation of our previously conceived ideology.

Relativism

Finally, conducting openly ideological research raises the issue of relativism. Although I recognized the vulnerability of our analysis in our study of Harmony, I was not ignorant of those (for example, Bloom, 1987; D'Amico, 1986; Phillips, 1987) who suggest this type of openly ideological research eventually leads to intellectual and moral relativism. For example, Lyotard's (1984) notion of the 'post–modern condition' suggests an era in which we 'wage war on totality' (p. 82). Fixed philosophical and moral foundations are merely an illusion and thus cannot be utilized in our efforts to understand social reality. He argues that knowledge and the meaning people give to this knowledge can no longer be securely connected to broad sociological or historical ideologies. As D'Amico (1986) states, for some individuals, 'the central continuing post–modernist theme is a radical relativism [which encourages] . . . irrationalism, antipathy to science, and nihilism' (p. 136). For some scholars the loss of authoritative theorizing suggests that if we cannot know anything with certainty, then we can know nothing. Bloom (1987), in his now famous assessment of higher education and the social sciences, castigates post–modernism as

> the last, predictable stage in the suppression of reason and the denial of the possibility of truth in the name of philosophy . . . there is not text, only . . . cheapened interpretation [which] . . . liberates us from the objective imperatives of the texts which might have liberated us from our . . . narrow horizon. (p. 379)

From Bloom's perspective, questioning the legitimacy of authoritative knowledge has significantly undermined our efforts to intellectually progress as a culture and species.

However, framing the post–modern antipathy for teleological theorizing as crude relativism is misleading. As Eisner (1983) points out, discrediting the notion of absolute knowledge does not result in the loss of reasoned analysis.

> Because different theories provide different views of the world, it does not follow that there is no way of appraising the value or credibility of a view. First, we can ask what a particular theoretical view enables us to do, that is, we can determine its instrumental utility. Second, we can appraise the consistency of its conclusions with the theoretical premises on which they are based. Third, even if those conclusions are logically consistent with their premises, we may reject the premises. Fourth, we can determine whether there are more economical interpretations of the data than those provided by any particular theoretical view. Fifth, we can judge the

degree to which it hangs together. And sixth, we can assess the view on aesthetic grounds: How elegant is the view? How strongly do we respond to it? (p. 2)

In addition to Eisner's criteria, ideological orientations can be examined in light of their ethical and moral foundations. The fact that grand ideologies are inherently problematic does not mean that all thoughts are equally arbitrary.

Ideology in itself is not the problem as long as it maintains its essential vulnerability. My analysis of Harmony gives an impression of certainty, and I act upon my understanding of life *as* if it was 'true', but in my heart I always remember (and so should my readers) that I know nothing 'for sure' (Rorty, 1982). The value of any given ideology and the analysis that emerges from it must be contextualized within a specific sociohistorical time and place. As Lather (1988) states, 'What is destroyed by the post–structuralist suspicion of the lust for authoritative accounts is not meaning, but claims to the unequivocal dominance of any one meaning.' (p. 7). In rejecting the supremacy of grand theories we are not obliterating our ability to make rational and moral judgments.

Perhaps the concern over relativism is an expression of power relations within academic settings. Some scholars (for example, Harding, 1987, Lather, 1988b; Yeatman, 1987) have suggested that relativism is an overriding concern only within an intellectual context in which academics search for a privileged position as the grantors of certainty. For example, Harding (1987) expresses the perspective of many feminist researchers.

Historically, relativism appears as an intellectual possibility, and as a 'problem' only for dominating groups at the point where the hegemony of their views is being challenged . . . the point here is that relativism in not a problem originating in, or justifiable in terms of, women's experiences or feminist agendas. It is fundamentally a sexist response that attempts to preserve the legitimacy of androcentric claims in the face of contrary evidence. (p. 10)

If there is some truth to Harding's assessment that conventional social science reflects a masculine, Western cultural ethos, then it is likely that charges of relativism do not illuminate the weaknesses of post–modernist perspectives, but merely serve as a weapon to maintain this patriarchal hegemony.

Although charges of relativism should be seen as problematic, it is important to emphasize that in rejecting 'grand' ideologies of social reality, it is not being suggested that scholars' work must remain trapped in theoretical minutia that has no value outside of a highly specific time and cultural setting. Postmodernists' rejection of all foundational thinking can lead, unimpeded, to a glorification of novelty for its own sake or what Hall (1986) refers to as 'the tyranny of the New' (p. 47). Manthorpe (1990) raises an important point regarding this issue in her analysis of feminist science, 'This [relativism] would not simply be an epistemological problem, but a political one, for, in the absence of any criteria of validity which had been mutually agreed, it would only be the most powerful social groups who could successfully defend their interpretation of truth.' (p. 117). Giroux (1988) suggests that we view ideologies as a heuristic device rather than an ontological category. In this way, researchers can examine particularistic phenomena in light of larger contexts, 'in which it is possible to make visible those mediations, interrelations, and interdependencies that give shape and power to larger political and social systems' (p. 16). This perspective allows scholars to examine their relationship between micro and macro 'worlds' within a social and historical context while at the same time maintaining their subjective and intellectual vulnerability. Kellner (1988, p. 253) makes an important distinction between grand theories and grand narratives. Whereas the former is likely to subsume and distort reality into a totality of thought, the latter facilitates scholars' efforts to tell a 'Big Story, such as the rise of capital, patriarchy, or the colonial subject'. If we completely discard the role of ideology in our work, then we run a significant risk of not being able to adequately examine social reality in its full complexity, thus weakening the pedagogical power of educational research.

Conclusion

Conducting openly ideological research is filled with pitfalls, but the alternative of conducting 'value neutral' research is spurious. Although we can never 'get away from' our ideology and biography, we are not enslaved by these aspects of our lives. The issue of ideology is one of self–reflection and much speculation. Disclosure of ourselves as researchers is important, but the comprehensiveness of this disclosure is uncertain. My background as a male, Jewish, second generation citizen of the United States who has been attracted to progressive social, psychological, political, and pedagogical values and ideas has certainly influenced my work as a researcher; however, identifying the way precise elements of who I am exactly motivate me to 'read the world' in the way I do continues to be beyond my reach.

In addition, it is difficult for me to situate my ideological orientation with a single adjective (for example, phenomenologist, feminist, Marxist). Lather (1988a) notes that, given the current discourse, the ideologies themselves are better off referred to in the plural (for example, feminisms, Marxisms, post–modernisms). In carving out an ideological stance in my study of Harmony, it was necessary to draw from several traditions. Each contributed to my selection of what was observed and the manner in which my analysis was eventually written. What makes these deliberations more difficult is the lack of time I can reasonably devote to them. Given the tentative nature of my thoughts, it is perhaps useful to conclude this essay with a quote from Maxine Greene (1995):

> My interpretations are provisional. I have partaken in the post–modern rejection of inclusive rational frameworks in which all problems, all uncertainties can be resolved. All we can do, I believe, is cultivate multiple ways of seeing and multiple dialogues in a world where nothing stays the same. All I can do is to provoke my readers to come together in making pathways through that world with their students, leaving thumbprints as they pass. (p. 16)

Jesse Goodman

Note

1 Although the importance of this discourse being free and open has been and is an essential aspect of academic life, I do not mean to imply that it can be taken for granted. First, until an individual has tenure, s/he might not feel as if his/her contribution is free from petty criticism that might reuslt in the loss of his/her position. The denial of tenure to Henry Giroux by the President of Boston University is a good contemporary example. There have also been times when the political climate in a given culture destroys the open and free nature of this discourse as during the McCarthy era in the United States (for example, Holmes, 1989).

References

ALCOFF, L. (1991) 'The problem of speaking for others', *Cultural Critique*, **20**, pp. 5–32.

ANDERSON, G. (1989) 'Critical ethnography in education: Origins, current status, and new directions', *Review of Educational Research*, **59**, 3, pp. 249–70.

APPLE, M. (1979) *Ideology and Curriculum*, London: Routledge and Kegan Paul.

BERGER, P. (1975) *Pyramids of Sacrifice: Political Ethics and Social Change*, New York: Anchor.

BLOOM, A. (1987) *The Closing of the American Mind: How Higher Education has Failed Democracy and Impoverished the Souls of Today's Students*, New York: Simon and Schuster.

BLOOM, L. (1997) 'Locked in uneasy sisterhood: Reflections on feminist methodology and research relations', *Anthropology and Education Quarterly*, **28**, 1, pp. 111–22.

BOWERS, C. (1982) 'The reproduction of technological consciousness: Locating the ideological foundation of a radical pedagogy', *Teachers College Record*, **83**, 4, pp. 529–57.

BOWLES, S. and GINTIS, H. (1976) *Schooling in Capitalist America*. New York: Basic Books.

CHRISTIAN, B. (1987) 'The race for theory', *Cultural Critique*, **6**, 1, pp. 51–63.

CHUBB, J. and MOE, T. (1990) *Politics, Markets, and America's Schools*, Washington, D.C.: Brookings Institution.

CUSICK, P. (1973) *Inside High School: The Student's World*, New York: Holt, Rinehart and Winston.

D'AMICO, R. (1986) 'Going relativist', *Telos*, **67**, pp. 135–45.

DEEM, R. (1978) *Women and Schooling*, Boston, MA: Routledge and Kegan Paul.

DELAMONT, S. (1980) *Sex Roles and the School*, London: Methuen.

DUNKIN, M. and BIDDLE, B. (1974) *The Study of Teaching*, New York: Holt, Rinehart and Winston.

EISNER, E. (1983) 'Anastasia might still be alive, but the monarch is dead', *Educational Researcher*, **12**, 4, pp. 13–24.

ERICKSON, F. (1986) 'Qualitative research on teaching', In WITTROCK, M. (Ed.) *Handbook of Research on Teaching*, New York: Macmillan pp. 119–61.

FAY, B. (1987) *Critical Social Science: Liberation and its Limits*, Ithaca, NY: Cornell University Press.

FISKE, D. and SHWEDER, R. (1986) *Methodology in Social Science: Pluralisms and Subjectivities*, Chicago, IL: University of Chicago Press.

FOUCAULT, M. (1972) *The Archeology of Knowledge and the Discourse of Language*, New York: Harper and Row.

FREIRE, P. (1973) *Education for Critical Consciousness*, New York: Seabury Press.

FRYE, M. (1983) *The Politics of Reality: Essays in Feminist Theory*, Trumansburg, NY: Crossing Press.

GEERTZ, C. (1983) *Local Knowledge*, New York: Basic Books.

GILLIGAN, C. (1982) *In a Different Voice*, Cambridge, MA: Harvard University Press.

GIROUX, H. (1988) 'Post–modernism and the discourse of educational criticism', *Journal of Education*, **170**, 3, pp. 5–30.

GOODMAN, J. (1992) *Elementary Schooling for Critical Democracy*, Albany, NY: State University of New York Press.

GOULD, S. (1981) *The Mismeasure of Man*, New York: W.W. Norton and Co.

GREENE, M. (1995) *Releasing the Imagination: Essays on Education, the Arts, and Social Change*, San Francisco, CA: Jossey-Bass.

GRUMET, M. (1981) 'Pedagogy for patriarchy: The feminization of teaching', *Interchange*, **12**, 2/3, pp. 165–84.

HALL, S. (1985) 'Signification, representation, ideology: Althusser and the post–structuralist debates', *Critical Studies in Mass Communication*, **2**, 2, pp. 91–114.

HALL, S. (1986) 'On post–modernism and articulation', *Journal of Communication Inquiry*, **10**, 2, pp. 45–60.

HARDING, S. (1987) 'Introduction: Is there a feminist method?', In HARDING, S. (Ed.), *Feminism and Methodology*, Bloomington, IN: Indiana University Press, pp. 1–14.

HOLMES, D. (1989) *Stalking the Academic Communist: Intellectual Freedom and the Firing of Alex Novikoff*, Hanover: University of New England Press.

HOMANS, G. (1967) *The Nature of Social Science*, New York: Harbinger Books.

KELLNER, D. (1988) 'Post–modernism as social theory: Some challenges and problems', *Theory, Culture, and Society*, **5**, 2/3, pp. 239–70.

KENISTON, K. (1968) *Young Radicals: Notes on Committed Youth*, New York: Harcourt, Brace and World.

LATHER, P. (1986) 'Research as praxis', *Harvard Educational Review*, **56**, 3, pp. 257–77.

LATHER, P. (1988a) 'Ideology and methodological attitude'. Paper presented at the annual meeting of the American Educational Research Association, New Orleans, April.

LATHER, P. (1988b) 'Educational research and practice in a post–modern era.', Paper presented at the annual meeting of the American Educational Research Association, New Orleans, April.

LeCOMPTE, M. and GOETZ, J. (1982) 'Problems of reliability and validity in ethnographic research', *Review of Educational Research*, **52**, 1, pp. 31–60.

LENZO, K. (1995) 'Validity and self–reflexivity meet post–structuralism: Scientific ethos and the transgressive self', *Educational Researcher*, **24**, 4, pp. 17–23.

LINCOLN, Y. and GUBA, E. (1985) *Naturalistic Inquiry*, Beverly Hills, CA: Sage Publications.

LUKE, A. (1995) 'Text and discourse in education: An introduction to critical discourse analysis', In APPLE, M. (Ed.) *Review of Research in Education*, Washington, DC: American Educational Research Association.

LYOTARD, J. (1984) *The Post–modern Condition: A Report on Knowledge*, Minneapolis, MN: University of Minnesota Press.

MANTHORPE, C. (1990) 'Feminism and science: Toward a human science?', *Curriculum Inquiry*, **20**, 1, pp. 113–19.

MARCUS, G. and FISCHER, M. (1986) *Anthropology and Cultural Critique: An Experimental Moment in the Human Sciences*, Chicago, IL: University of Chicago Press.

MILES, M. and HUBERMAN, M. (1984) *Qualitative Data Analysis: A Sourcebook of New Methods*, Beverly Hills, CA: Sage Publications.

NAMENWIRTH, M. (1986) 'Science seen through a feminist prism', In BLEIR, R. (Ed.) *Feminist Approaches to Science*, New York: Pergamon, pp. 18–41.

OGBU, J. (1974) *The Next Generation: An Ethnography of Education in an Urban Neighborhood*, New York: Academic Press.

PHILLIPS, D. (1987) *Philosophy, Science, and Social Inquiry: Contemporary Methodological Controversies in Social Science and Related Applied Fields of Research*, New York: Pergamon.

POPKEWITZ, T. (1984) *Paradigm and Ideology in Educational Research*, New York: Falmer Press.

PUTMAN, H. (1981) *Reason, Truth, and History*, Cambridge, MA: Cambridge University Press.

RIST, R. (1973) *The Urban School: A Factory for Failure*. Cambridge, MA: MIT Press.

RORTY, R. (1979) *Philosophy and the Mirror or Nature*, Princeton, NJ: Princeton University Press.

RORTY, R. (1982) *Consequences of Pragmatism*, Minneapolis, MN: University of Minnesota Press.

RORTY, R. (1988) *Contingency, Irony and Solidarity*, New York: Cambridge University Press.

ROSZAK, T. (1969) *The Making of a Counter Culture: Reflections on the Technocratic Society and its Youthful Opposition*, Garden City, NY: Doubleday.

SHARP, R. and GREEN, A. (1975) *Education and Social Control: A Study in Progressive Primary Education*, London: Routledge and Kegan Paul.

SMITH, L. and KEITH, P. (1971) *Anatomy of Educational Innovation*, New York: John Wiley.

SPARKES, A. (1994) 'Life histories and the issue of voice: Reflections on an emerging relationship', *Qualitative Studies in Education*, **7**, 2, pp. 165–83.

WHITTY, G. and YOUNG, M. (1976) *Explorations in the Politics of School Knowledge*, Driffield: Nafferton Books.

WILLIS, P. (1977) *Learning to Labor*, New York: Columbia University Press.

WOLCOTT, H. (1973) *The Man in the Principal's Office: An Ethnography*, New York: Holt, Rinehart and Winston.

WOLCOTT, H. (1975) 'Criteria for an ethnographic approach to research in the schools', *Human Organization: Journal of the Society of Applied Anthropology*, **34**, 2, pp. 111–27.

YEATMAN, B. (1987) 'A feminist theory of social differentiation'. Paper presented at the annual meeting of the American Sociological Association, Chicago, August.

5   Reciprocity in Critical Research? Some Unsettling Thoughts

Andrew Sparkes

An Unsettling Introduction

reciprocal, *adj.* acting in return; mutual; complementary; inverse; alternating; inter-changeable; giving and receiving or given and received; expressing mutuality (*gram.*); . . . *v.t.* **reciprocate**, to give and receive mutually; to requite; to interchange; to alternate. — *v.i.* to move backward and forward; to make a return or interchange (*coll.*). (*Chambers 20th Century Dictionary*)

As I dwell on the notion of giving and receiving mutually, an unsettling comment by Wolcott (1995) on the darker side of fieldwork surfaces.

One cannot help but assume an air of self–righteousness in getting the word out . . . Perhaps I have become jaded after attending so many national and international meetings and hearing so many fieldworkers describe the plight of so many peoples for so many years — and I must admit to having indulged in such efforts myself — but I have begun to regard my own efforts as essentially self–serving and self–satisfying as well.

Engaging so wholeheartedly as we do in this 'rhetoric of reform' helps us to feel we have addressed critical issues and courageously spoken our piece. We make it *appear* that if we cannot make a difference in the case at hand, at least we do not dodge responsibility in bringing underlying issues before a wider audience. Pretty safe work, perhaps all the more satisfying for that: decrying the world's injustices from the safety of a podium to an audience of our (not their) peers in Grand Ballroom A of some major hotel in some major city, a pitcher of ice water comfortingly nearby, heads nodding with compassion at the circumstances we can but briefly outline in 900–second allotted time slots. It is nice to seem to be at the cutting edge without having to do any cutting and without being noticeably near the edge.

Where we derive satisfaction from believing that we are making the world a better place, we ignore the better place we make for ourselves in it. In that regard we prove to be all–too–human ourselves. Nothing particularly wrong in with that. It's just a bit awkward to have to own up to being our own beneficiaries. (p. 140)

I am further unsettled by the critical and feminist pedagogical insights provided by Gore (1992) when she raises the question of 'What can we do for you!' What *can* 'we' do for 'you'?

> When the agent of empowerment assumes to be already empowered, and so apart
> from those who are to be empowered, arrogance can underlie claims of 'what we
> can do for you'. This danger is apparent both in the work of the teacher who is to
> empower students, and in the work of the academic whose discourse is purportedly
> empowering for the teachers (and others). In the focus on others there is a danger
> of forgetting to examine one's own (or one's group's) implications in the con-
> ditions one seeks to affect . . . Rather than making pronouncements about what
> we can do, we need to ask 'what *can* we do for you?' . . . If empowerment is con-
> structed as the exercise of power in an attempt to help others exercise power
> (rather than as the giving of power), we confront the unforeseeable and contradic-
> tory effects of the exercise of power and must be more humble and reflexive in our
> claims. (pp. 61–2)

Dewar's (1991) thoughts on the problematic nature of 'giving' in relation to
power differentials in research relationships add to my angst.

> Notions of power and privilege must be addressed in order to understand what it
> means to 'have a voice' . . . the issue is not who has a voice; we all have voices
> and speak with them in very different ways. The problem arises when we define
> our strategy against oppression as one that enables us to 'give' certain groups of
> people a voice. What does it mean to give? What kinds of relationships does this
> imply? What kind of power and privilege is implied in the act of giving? What
> does this say about how voices are heard and interpreted. (p. 75)

And finally, as Manning (1997) reminds me.

> Although constructivist research assumes a subjective relationship between re-
> searcher and respondent, this relationship is not devoid of power differences.
> Negotiation of this power often fails or, at a minimum, remains problematic through-
> out the research. When the researcher publishes the research and gains privilege
> and advantages, such as recognition and tenure, from others' lives, it is impossible
> to fully resolve the inherent power differences. (pp. 94–5)

A Letter Arrives

With the unsettling thoughts of Wolcott, Gore, Dewar and Manning nagging at me,
I begin to reflect upon reciprocity, the seven–year relationship that I have had with
Jessica (a pseudonym), and two of the papers that I published about her life (Sparkes,
1994a, 1994b). Our first contact was framed within a student–lecturer relationship.
This relationship evolved as each of us revealed more of ourselves to the other and
Jessica 'came out' to me by telling me she was a lesbian. A brave move given her
previous experiences of white, male, 'middle class', heterosexual, lecturers like
myself, and the rampant homophobia and heterosexism that permeates the world of
physical education (PE) and sport.

Despite some initial misgivings, Jessica agreed to collaborate in a life history
project that I was conducting. Through a series of extended interviews over a

period of years we began to explore her experiences as a lesbian physical educator while at the same time extending my own understanding of issues relating to sexual identity. As a sense of trust developed over time, the nature of our relationship changed. We became good friends and our sharing went beyond the confines of the original research project. As a consequence, the nature of our relationship changed as the power dynamics shifted and reshaped themselves over time. Or so I thought.

At the end of August 1996, I telephoned Jessica to discuss the chapter on reciprocity I had been asked to write. The call ended with me requesting that Jessica put her ideas about the nature of reciprocity in our research relationship down on paper. Jessica was interested and agreed. However, for a variety of reasons that included a change of job, the following months were a stressful time for her and Jessica's response did not arrive until November 1996 after several more telephone 'prods' from me. The following are some extracts from her letter.

My starting point for looking at my views and experiences of reciprocity in the process had to be why it took me such a long time to sit myself down and write a response! . . . It wasn't as simple as putting it down to disinterest or laziness, or simply that I know I respond more positively when given clear deadlines. It was a little more involved than that, and no less relevant to the concept on which I was being requested to write.

The biggest stumbling block for me was confidence. Despite having successfully completed an MPhil earlier in the year, I felt out of practice, where do I start anyway? What does Andy want me to say? He's the expert, what can I possibly come up with that is going to be of any interest to him? I will never be able to think like he does, I'm just not that clever. I don't work alongside academics only PE teachers that have been in their jobs too long. It's Andy's job, he's an intellectual . . . I don't have philosophical conversations in the pub with my friends. Normally, all we talk about is the latest cinema release, holidays and how frustrated we all are in our respective jobs.

It's interesting that this response so clearly reveals the continuation of the power differential that I first experienced as one of Andy's students. It's scary really, I mean I've known Andy for seven years. He's been a friend longer than he was my university lecturer, and I've completed my MPhil. Why should I still feel so unworthy? Possibly, right now, in my life I do lack more confidence due to my job situation but I do believe that once again I have allowed my perception of 'researcher as expert' to effectively disempower me from feeling free to express what ever it was that came into my head. It was short sighted of me really because having been both researcher and participant I should have realised that as the researcher you simply want to encourage honest and open dialogue and responses. A response of 'I'm bored with this', or one that expresses a complete lack of understanding in the researcher's motives or questions is as equally valuable as 2000 computer processed words.

So, I acknowledge that I should have reminded myself of those important little things. But it no less impresses on me the power of conditioning. My unfaltering respect for your role as expert academic. It's the same mistake I made seven years ago. It's not that you are not an academic expert, it's that at times I would allow my impression of you as expert to transcend into your interpretation of me. When writing about my life and my experiences the only expert involved was me, I was the expert on me. I didn't see that at the time, it may sound incredulous but I was a student and I felt a mixture of curiosity, concern and extreme flattery that I was to be the topic of your next research project. So when I was sent early drafts of papers with invitations to comment, I would be hit first with a complete blind panic that I'd say something sensible on the phone, but my lack of confidence did prevent me from asking questions. A good example of this is when, very early on in the project, you came up with the central theme of 'being out and being me'. You asked me for a response and I remember very clearly being affirmative before I'd really thought about it. As it turned out, it was a relevant and pertinent theme. I didn't let anything go that would have changed either the sense or meaning of my experiences but I did find it hard to query things.

If the same research was taking place now, because I understand more about the research process, have known you for longer, have gained confidence through my own research, I would be more assertive and query everything. I would have a clear view, as I mentioned before, that it is accepted and perfectly acceptable that the expert on my life is me. Before, your endeavours to involve me in the research were often met with the unspoken response of 'You are the author, the academic (i.e. expert). What are you asking me for?' I was unaware of the part I could play, or of the necessity of playing a part of whatever stature.

During our phone call, one of the questions I asked Jessica to think about was 'Does reciprocity exist, or is it an idealistic, romantic ideal created to purge the researcher of any concerns about exploitation'? Her direct response in the letter was as follows.

What I Got: Then

The acknowledgment and validation that I had an important story to tell. This was no less than a revelation since my previous experience of college lecturers, especially straight, male, PE lecturers was diametrically opposed to this. Up until then it had always been my membership of the PE culture, a culture that would neither accept or acknowledge my existence, that was the problem. The reactions of lecturers in the past had always inferred that it was essentially my problem, something I and others like me had to deal with. Here was a lecturer who was not only positively acknowledging my sexuality but wanted to actively do something to change things. For the first time, it was the established PE culture that was being scrutinized and criticized as opposed to my membership of that culture.

My involvement with you led me to gain respect from my fellow students, and at times I felt flattered and proud to be able to contribute. I also felt nervous and curious until I could really understand and trust your motives. A great turning point in the establishment of this trust was when you chose to 'name' me after your own daughter, who had just been born.

Of great benefit to me at the time was the opportunity to talk to you at length about my concerns and fears of managing my sexuality in teaching. Since these were mostly tape recorded interview sessions they were mutually beneficial, but they were highly therapeutic for me at the time.

I also gained over the years the knowledge, understanding and confidence to embark on my own research project.

Now

The experience of being a research participant was extremely helpful when I began my own life history study, providing me with an insight into the nature of the researcher/participant relationship, and the potential problems of the power differentials and concerns about exploitation.

The research has enabled us to keep in touch and further establish our friendship. An excellent referee!

What Andy Got: Then

An area of research that practically nothing had been written on that also fitted with his previous work on aspects of marginality and the use of life histories. Here was the opportunity to build on an already extensive professional portfolio of published works.

The nature of the topic was perfect for one who is compelled to challenge the status quo and the hegemonic structures so as to incite reactions from colleagues and researchers ranging from positivists to feminists!

A willing research participant who had a lot to say and felt pleased, relieved and flattered to be given a chance to tell her story in the hope that it may create dialogue and ultimately change.

Now

The further development of ideas and issues raised during the initial research project. The opportunity to write references for me!

Missed Opportunities and Further Developments

In terms of future developments the ensuing years have provided me with a rich resource of experiences that enable me to tell you 'the story of a lesbian PE teacher in her early thirties'! So in that sense, whether it is written by you or me, there needn't be any missed opportunities.

Reflections on a Letter and Past Moments

In her letter, Jessica touches upon several issues that were raised in a confessional tale I wrote about our emerging relationship during its first three years (Sparkes, 1994a). Here, various issues were problematized such as biographical positioning, sharing stories and building trust, collaboration, researcher as therapist, friendship, the frozen text and the post–modern dilemma of voice, along with the impact of story telling and writing upon Jessica, myself and the reader. Aspects of Jessica's letter confirm and add to what I wrote about these past moments. Limitations of space do not allow me to explore connections between all of these in relation to Jessica's letter or to the insights generated by others who have provided reflexive accounts of researcher–participant relationships in educational settings (see Feldman, 1993; Fliesser and Goodson, 1992; Levin, 1993; Phtiaka, 1994; Zajano and Edelsberg, 1993). Therefore, I will limit myself to issues surrounding the potential of story telling/writing within life history work to act as a force for change and how this can form a vital trading point within critical research that simultaneously acknowledges, challenges and redefines power differentials and issues of difference over time.

Jessica's thoughts confirm those of Goodson (1991a) who pointed out that the life history approach as a possible route to collaboration does not suspend issues of ethics and exploitation. This is because the collaboration between the teacher and the external researcher is located in an occupational terrain that is itself inequitably structured. Her words also confirm how what might have been defined as an impediment (our differences in social positioning), in terms of the development of collaboration, ended up acting as a resource to enrich the collaborative nature of the enterprise. For example, in trying to locate Jessica's experiences in a wider context I had to delve into unfamiliar literature which, in turn, was passed on to Jessica for her own reading and interpretation. This literature provided her with insights into how I, in my researcher role, was attempting to make sense of her life from my own positioning, and how this position of relative privilege could be used in strategic ways to challenge homophobia and heterosexism. These insights provided a significant trading point in our relationship that, according to Goodson (1991b), rests upon the differential structural location of the research–taker who, as an 'academic', has the time and resources to collaborate with teachers in developing genealogies of context that can provide teachers with aspects of the 'complete picture'. This picture includes the structural constraints that shapes their lives. Goodson notes.

> Each see the world through a different prism of practice and thought. This valuable difference may provide the external researcher with the possibility to offer back goods in 'the trade'. The teacher/researcher offers data and insights; the external researcher, in pursuing glimpses of structure in different ways, may now also bring data and insights. The terms of trade, in short, look favourable. In such conditions collaboration may at last begin. (ibid, pp. 148–9)

This trading point has become more significant as the trusting and respectful relationship between Jessica and myself has developed over the years. In relation to this, as our commitment to facilitating dialogue and change increased, my privileged position as writer–researcher in the relationship, able to put Jessica's story in the public domain, became increasingly significant in the negotiation of a fair trade between us. For example, towards the end of 1991 both Jessica and I felt that, in order to stimulate debate about homophobia and heterosexism in schools, something needed to be written about her life for the consumption of others. We agreed that as the 'academic' in the relationship I would prepare the paper. This decision came about for several reasons. First, Jessica was too busy in her teaching job to undertake this task. I had access to the literature and more time than her to study our interview transcripts and actually write. Second, she felt that by giving me the task of constructing the text, the end product would be a useful stimulus and resource for her own reflections on her life. As I passed on drafts of the paper to Jessica for her comments this certainly proved to be the case.

The act of writing also made me reflect upon my life in relation to hers and, despite my many discussions with Jessica about the text and her support for my efforts, I could not escape the fact that I was responsible for the final version that would be published and that this responsibility was unavoidable (see Gorelick, 1991; Stacey, 1988). In particular, the 'frozen text' I produced raised the key issue of my authority to write about, and for, an individual who is a member of a group to which I do not belong. Commenting upon this dilemma, Richardson (1990) notes, 'For whom do we speak and to whom do we speak, with what voice, to what end, using what criteria? . . . How does our writing reproduce a system of domination, and how does it challenge that system? What right do we have to speak for others? to write their lives?' (p. 27).

Such questions were the focal point of many discussions between Jessica and myself. I was comforted by Richardson's view that there is no one 'right' answer to the problem of speaking for others and we are left having to realize that writing, as an intentional behaviour, is a site of moral responsibility and there is no way to avoid deploying one's power if one chooses to write in this world. As Richardson comments.

> Rather than decrying our sociohistorical limitations, then, we can use them specifically to ask relevant (useful, empowering, enlightening) questions. Consequently, the most pressing issue, as I see it, is a practical–ethical one: how should we use our skills and privileges . . . As qualitative researchers, we can more easily write as situated, positioned authors, giving up, if we choose, our *authority* over the people we study, but not the responsibility of *authorship* over our texts. (ibid, pp. 27–8)

As Jessica's letter indicates, whether those involved in the relationship in its early stages are able to give up the authority they have over each other, or are willing and able to allow the other to give up their authority over them, is another matter. These things are not easy and they take time and personal investment by those involved. That Jessica, seven years into our relationship, now feels confident enough to redefine the authority dynamics of our relationship supports the view of Fliesser and Goodson (1992) that cultivating collaborative relationships is incremental in nature. They suggest there is a need to, 'Negotiate and renegotiate roles at various times throughout the dynamic process of the research project, keeping in mind that participants' interests and needs change. Project members should be able to renegotiate their roles when they feel it necessary' (pp. 49–50). This, in turn, would impact upon how and what gets defined as relevant, useful, empowering, and enlightening questions within the relationship as well as shaping the interactions of those involved.

Andrew's Gains

As I listened to Jessica's story in the early years of our relationship I became increasingly aware of my involvement in it as a researcher by the telling of my own stories as we discussed ideas, explained things to each another, and sought clarification on issues. Connelly and Clandinin (1990) recognized this feature in their own narrative enquiry into teachers' experience and suggest that it is impossible not to become story tellers and story livers along with those we are involved with. They argued that, 'in our story telling, the stories of our participants merged with our own to create new stories, ones that we have labelled *collaborative stories*. The thing finally written on paper [is] . . . a mutually constructed story created out of the lives of both researcher and participant' (p. 12).

Being part of this mutually constructed story called for then, and still calls for now, much self–reflection on my part. As Sears (1992) points out, 'As we peer into the eyes of the other, we embark on a journey of the self: exploring our fears, celebrating our voices, challenging our assumptions, reconstructing our pasts' (p. 155). Similarly, as our interviews progressed I became increasingly aware of my own tacit involvement and entanglement in the strands of homophobia and heterosexism that continue to shape aspects of Jessica's life, and mine, in terms of the relations of oppression. On this issue Gorelick (1991) comments, 'The researcher is transformed in the process of research — influenced and taught by her respondent–participants as she influences them. Theory and practice emerge from their interaction' (p. 469).

For example, I became aware that although I taught an undergraduate module that focused critically upon a number of ideologies which pervade PE, exercise and sport, neither homophobia or heterosexism were included. My involvement in Jessica's story highlighted this as a significant silence on my part and led me to reshape this and other courses in order to explore how these ideologies act in relation to others to oppress specific groups of people. Indeed, to assist the students focus their attention on this issue, and implicate them in the process of oppression, the 'realist' tale of Jessica's life history is made available (Sparkes, 1994b). Of course, to the cynically minded this could be defined as mere tokenism. However, at least issues relating to sexual identity are now on the agenda for the students I work with, and the 'Jessica paper' as the students call it has been used as a resource on similar courses at other universities. In this sense, my involvement with Jessica has helped me to better understand the view of Harvey (1990) who argued:

> Knowledge does not reside in a cupboard or on a bookshelf to be taken out, dusted down and looked at. Knowledge exists in our everyday lives. We live our knowledge and constantly transform it through what we do, as much as it informs what we do. For critical social research this means that an analysis of oppressive structures is in itself a political act. Knowing cannot be shelved, it becomes part of our life, and informs our actions which engage these structures. (pp. 22–3)

My understanding that 'knowing cannot be shelved' has encouraged me to seek further ways of challenging and transforming my own, and others, connectedness within the strands of homophobia and heterosexism. Once again, the use of my privileged position as a writer–researcher has played its part in this process in terms of how I have integrated Jessica's story with those of other 'absent others' (Squires and Sparkes, 1996; Sparkes, 1996a), or created ethnographic fictions (Sparkes, 1997) with the intention of creating dialogue and change.

Writing about, for, and with others who belong to oppressed groups that I do not belong to, remains problematic for me (Sparkes, 1995). This is particularly so in relation to the notion of trading points. As Jessica hinted at in her letter, publishing my story about her in prestigious refereed journals has not done my curriculum vitae any harm, given that publishing in such journals is a valuable currency of the academic world. Indeed, since we began our collaboration I have received a promotion and it would be dishonest not to admit that the 'Jessica papers' were helpful in this process. Furthermore, some might argue that focusing upon issues of sexual identity and writing about the lives of silenced, marginalized and the oppressed other, serves as much to fuel my own identity construction as a 'critical' scholar within an academic world where territories have to be created and defended as part of any successful (usually male) career trajectory.

These are troubling issues. Were my academic intentions as altruistic as I would like to believe when I first entered into my relationship with Jessica? Is the cover story I provide about our developing relationship, and my writing in the services of a critical agenda, simply an elaborate fiction created by me to salve my own conscience about how, from the relatively safe vantage point of a male, heterosexual, academic, I might have exploited a friend to my own ends? I want to believe I acted with good intention throughout, and I want Jessica to believe me. However, the words of Manning (1997) and Wolcott (1995) that opened this chapter about power, self–serving, and self–satisfying efforts return to me again. All that I do know for sure is that I gained a great deal from Jessica in the trade between us and for that I am grateful.

Jessica's Gains

Questions about what Jessica gained from our relationship, from telling her story, reflecting upon her life, reading 'academic' papers, reading about herself through my writing, seeing the impact of her story on others, and eventually conducting her own research, are more difficult to answer. A useful starting point might be to consider the impact upon Jessica of telling her life story as part of a collaborative research process. As mentioned previously, at times, she described the process as therapeutic. Jessica also talked of feeling 'stronger' as part of a reflective process stimulated by the life history interviews.

> It's a whole process isn't it. Each time it is the process within itself of reflection, and of reconsideration and even that helps to put it into perspective, by the act of actually having to vocalize it. Even though I might have written stuff down myself or taken recordings myself. I sometimes find that if I'm going over stuff with you then different things come out or the conversation takes a different emphasis

sometimes. So me getting stronger is an ongoing thing, because it's sort of lasted over a period of years.

Part of this strengthening process involved the legitimation of Jessica's sense of injustice and an increasing awareness, via discussions and through reading some of the shared research literature, that other possibilities existed — that it didn't have to be this way. Jessica commented:

> Just the thought that you see it as a legitimate issue worthy of being written about makes me feel that what I'm going through is perhaps something that I shouldn't have to put up with, I can do things to change it, whether it's just changing my personal circumstances or expecting a different set of circumstances for myself . . . so by realizing that it's OK for me to *not* feel like I've got to do that [adopt passing or covering strategies] is important.

Of course, Jessica did not expect to achieve her ideal of 'being out and being me' without a prolonged struggle. However, at the time of the life history interviews, she felt more informed about this struggle and the part it would play in her own life. Her reflections on her life and the reading she had carried out then helped Jessica to develop short–term strategies to cope so that hopefully her long–term aims could be achieved, 'I feel it's really empowering in that I feel I'm arming myself constantly with the strategies to cope in the short–term but with an ultimate goal. So there is a reason for it all. I'm not just thinking that I've got to do this because I've got to do it just to survive'. In 1993 Jessica had a growing sense of direction that she hoped would enable her to create a situation that, in a socially just world, would enable her to be explicitly 'out' in any school she was working in, to be herself. As Jessica spoke then, 'to be me, because I think I've got just as much to offer kids as me being me as I have with this sort of facade of who they think I am'.

In this sense, it would seem that in the course of our interviews, Jessica has been able to use me as an audience for her verbal performance in a way that has helped her work out her thinking on a range of issues. In such circumstances, as Scheurich (1992) argues, individuals can often validate themselves in the process of telling their stories, an act which is potentially empowering in itself. Jessica's letter also acknowledges the issue of self–validation through the telling of her story. On this issue, Jago (1996) acknowledges that although the telling of self stories, as a way of making sense of experience, can be constraining, they also have the potential to reframe what are often oppressive surroundings. For her, when individuals study their own experience as a site for understanding the broader cultural context, using their own experience as primary data, the possibility for restorying arises that may delegitimate or contest dominant meaning systems (see also Sparkes, 1996b).

This would appear to be so for Jessica who, via writing about moments of her life, telling her story, reading transcripts of it, seeing it located theoretically through my interpretive lens, reading some of the papers that have shaped my interpretation, and then reacting to all of this, has been able to step back from the life as lived and the images created of it. In so doing, Jessica seems to have changed her relationship to specific experiences by occupying the paradoxical positions of author, teller, dramatic persona, and audience member. Like Jago (1996), Jessica has been a character in the story she has told/written as well as a witness to its telling. Consequently, the story she has told is simultaneously about her life and part of it. As a consequence, the significance of Jessica's story as told is found in the consequences it holds for future action and relationships. This is particularly so should the restorying reflect new found beliefs in personal agency and control that challenge the dominant cultural narratives. Talking of the three modest goals in relation to her own story telling, Jago comments.

> I want to illustrate the ways in which stories act as dwelling places, affecting expectations, beliefs and relationships. Second, I try to show that we each have the authority to change our lives by revising received stories. As authors of our life stories, we possess, in varying degrees, the capacity to reinvent them in new and more satisfying ways. Third, I become more firmly grounded within my revised story and invite others to share my experience. Storytelling not only allows me to appreciate the control I have over my life story but also enables others to see the process of story revision, that is, to experience my experience. (ibid, p. 511)

The Reader's Gains

Allowing others to experience her experiences of homophobia and heterosexism by putting her story in the public domain was a key trading point for Jessica in our relationship. As we moved towards this position we considered the impact of Jessica's story as a text open to multiple interpretations on readers who were not neutral and read from multiple positions. For the reader who was a lesbian PE teacher, or a lesbian teacher of another subject, we hoped that Jessica's story along with similar stories as they got told would become part of what Richardson (1990) calls a 'collective story'. While this form of narrative is about a category of people, the response at the individual level to a well–told collective story is, 'That's *my* story. I am not alone'. Jessica saw this as a very important reason for making her story available to others. The following were her comments when I gave her the first draft of the realist tale about herself (Sparkes, 1994b).

> The next thing I did on a sort of sub–conscious level was to read it as if it wasn't my story because I had to detach myself from it. I couldn't really get a feel for the whole thing without doing that. I really feel that it would have been very powerful for me to read that if it was somebody else's story, from somebody in my position. Like another lesbian PE teacher reading that might have a bit of an emotional experience I reckon. In fact, I really want to give it to somebody to read who I've spoken a bit about it to. I think that potentially it could move them . . . it gives their life as well. It's that collaborative experience. They can relate to it, it's association . . . I don't see it as a negative effect. If it moves somebody that's great. It means it is an association experience. Even though these individuals don't know each other then there is still that power of association and, you know, you cease to be on your

own then. That's the whole thing about the gay society, especially if you are born in the provinces or a small town, you go though this experience initially where you think you are the only one. That's what makes you so weak and vulnerable.

Such stories, as Richardson (1990) argues, can have transformative possibilities at the individual level in that they challenge the limitations of available narratives by providing new narratives that, on hearing them, legitimates the replotting of one's own life. Likewise, collective stories also have transformative possibilities at the socio-cultural level. Richardson comments:

> People who belong to a particular category can develop a consciousness of kind and can galvanize other category members through the telling of the collective story. People do not even have to know each other for the social identification to take hold. By emotionally binding together people who have had the same experiences, whether in touch with each other or not, the collective story overcomes some of the isolation and alienation of contemporary life. It provides a sociological community, the linking of separate individuals into a shared consciousness. Once linked, the possibility for social action on behalf of the collective is present, and, therewith, the possibility of societal transformation. (p. 26)

Therefore, the provision of theoretically framed stories has a part to play in bringing together individuals who, for the most part, stay separated from one another and do not develop a collective identity as an oppressed minority. For Woods (1992) this ensures that lesbian physical educators are unlikely to develop the collective strength to challenge their status and so they remain silent, fearful, isolated and powerless. In such circumstances Woods argues that more stories need to be heard and that stories like Jessica's represent a history, a present, and a future that should to be claimed with collective pride and not rejected with individual silence.

Jessica's story also has the potential to make connections with those who occupy different social categories. For example, early in 1992, Jessica gave the draft paper that I had constructed to the one person in her school that she had explicitly come out to.

> She was also very interested in my life history, my own story, and how I got to where I got to with it. Then it affected her on another level with her relating to the situation and the forms of oppression and to the covering strategies. She started identifying herself in that, in her own life. Then, on another level again, was how she felt for me in terms of me being at the school that she had been at and how, she almost felt responsible in a sense, as being part of the establishment and not having picked up on my misery or my concerns earlier than she had done. She actually felt a responsibility here as a colleague. But it definitely moved her emotionally in terms of relating her own life to mine.

Evoking feelings of responsibility and making emotional connections from one life to another means that heterosexuals can be implicated in various ways as part of her story. By making available a view of schooling from a particular standpoint that for the most part has been repressed, and by exploring Jessica's experiences of educational institutions, how she related these experiences to other moments in her life, and the strategies she adopted to cope with specific situations, important insights are provided into a reality that is oppositional to the taken–for–granted reality of the dominant and privileged sexual class in schools, that is, heterosexuals. In commenting upon the benefits of adopting a lesbian standpoint Harding (1991) comments.

> In identifying what one can see with the help of a lesbian standpoint, I do not point exclusively to insights about lesbians. The standpoint epistemologies have a different logic. Just as the research and scholarship that begin from the standpoint of women more generally is not exclusively about women, so these insights are not exclusively about lesbians. The point is that starting from the (many different) daily activities of lesbians enables us to see things that might otherwise have been invisible to us, not just about those lives but about heterosexual women's lives and men's lives, straight as well as gay. (p. 252)

From her position in the margins, Jessica's story provides a different vision of schooling. This vision can expand the unidimensional and partial story of those situated in the center by provoking a different understanding of their own situation as well as of the situation they create for others. Therefore, by presenting the struggles Jessica faced (and still faces) on a daily basis to construct her life, and maintain her sense of self, in the public spaces that the school provides, our intention was to provide insights into how schools, as a patriarchal institutions that are ideologically and culturally heterosexual, create and maintain a set of inequitable circumstances that exercise a level of control over the 'private' lives of lesbian students and teachers. Our intention was also to illustrate how these circumstances led these teachers to experience 'public' school life in ways that are hard to imagine for those (the majority) who are the beneficiaries of the privileges of heterosexuality. Finally, by focusing upon the enforced split Jessica had (and has still) to make between her public (professional) and private (personal) lives, along with the identity management strategies she was (and still is) compelled to draw upon to cope in specific situations, we hoped to illuminate how her experiences as a lesbian PE teacher were (and remain) structured and shaped by existing sets of social relationships that are oppressive.

This is an important issue given that the the majority who read stories like Jessica's will be positioned as heterosexuals. For this group, her story provides a stimulus for them to reflect on the tacit assumptions that guide their actions in daily life that may, or may not, reinforce homophobia and heterosexism in schools and other institutions. In relation to this Mattingley (1991) suggests, 'Since stories reveal the way ideas look in action, showing that experiences emerge when certain ideas are followed . . . analysing stories can allow a moral investigation of the practical consequences of beliefs and theories that are otherwise decontextualized abstractions' (p. 236). Likewise, Clandinin and Connelly (1991) comment:

> One purpose of narrative research is to have readers raise questions about their practices, their ways of knowing. Narrative inquiries are shared in ways that help

> readers question their own stories, raise their own questions about practices, and see in the narrative accounts stories of their own stories. The intent is to foster reflection, storying, and restorying for readers . . . Readers . . . need to be prepared to see the possible meanings there are in the story and, through this process, see other possibilities for telling their own stories. (pp. 277–88)

Stories, then, can provide powerful insights into the lived experiences of others in ways that can inform, awaken and disturb readers by illustrating their involvement in social processes that they may not be consciously aware of. Once aware, individuals may find the consequences of their involvement unacceptable and seek to change the situation. In such circumstances the potential for individual and collective restorying are enhanced.

Closing Comments

Clearly, the notion of reciprocity remains problematic for me and I will simply have to live with, and continue to work through, the tensions generated by the unsettling comments that opened this chapter. Like other contributions to this book, I have tried to highlight how for me the central feature of this endeavour will revolve around issues of process and not simple outcomes or products. Reciprocal relationships characterized by 'fair trade' are not static but dynamic and vibrant, they ebb and flow over time in their mutual giving and receiving. What this giving and receiving is, when it happens, who gives and who receives, on what terms, and under what circumstances, can only be negotiated and renegotiated by those involved as part of an ongoing commitment to a trusting, collaborative and equitable engagement that acknowledges and celebrates both difference and similarity along the way.

Another Letter Arrives

Having read the draft of this chapter in March 1997, Jessica wrote me another letter. It included the following and is a suitable note on which to end this chapter.

> So once again, I was affected at two levels. As 'Jessica', I delight in the fact that this was written. Not only does it indicate the continuation of our relationship, but it show vividly how important the relationship has been to both of us, and how it has and continues to change. I was really quite moved at times. Your need to problematize your position throughout, indicates very clearly that this is more than just another paper, more than an intellectual exercise. It's your lived experience just as my response to your work on me is mine.
>
> On a purely personal level, I also welcome the opportunity to continue to be involved in this way. I find it exciting and inspiring, and it makes me realize how caught up I've been in the logistics of my new job, the potential of another operation, and paying the mortgage! In a recent interview, I was asked to recount

a situation where I have found myself being 'passionate' about teaching PE. I guess I must have lied because it's being involved in this that really gets me going! And of course, it's pure self–indulgence isn't it, intellectualizing about one's own life.

It hasn't been very easy to read though another's eyes. Every point that comes to me emanates from the fact that you write largely about a relationship, and that relationship is with me. It's fascinating that you use the paper as a means of communicating your concerns and thoughts. It was bit like a personal letter at times, maybe we're well overdue for a night in the pub. I wonder if we saw each other more often, or I was a better correspondent, whether things would be different.

Acknowledgments

A special thanks to 'Jessica' for her reflections on this chapter and for allowing me to include extracts from her letters.

References

CLANDININ, D. and CONNELLY, F. (1991) 'Narrative and story in practice and research', in SCHON, D. (Ed.) *The Reflective Turn: Case Studies in and on Educational Practice*, New York: Teachers College Press, pp. 258–81.

CONNELLY, F. and CLANDININ, D. (1990) 'Stories of experience and narrative inquiry', *Educational Researcher*, **19**, 5, pp. 2–14.

DEWAR, A. (1991) 'Feminist pedagogy in physical education: Promises, possibilities and pitfalls, *Journal of Physical Education, Recreation and Dance*, August, pp. 68–77.

FELDMAN, A. (1993) 'Promoting equitable collaboration between university researchers and school teachers', *International Journal of Qualitative Studies in Education*, **6**, 4, pp. 341–57.

FLIESSER, C. and GOODSON, I. (1992) 'Negotiating fair trade: Towards collaborative relationships between researchers and teachers', in GOODSON, I. and MANGAN, J. MARSHALL (Eds.) *History, Context, and Qualitative Methods in the Study of Education*, Occasional Papers, Volume 3, Faculty of Education, University of Western Ontario, pp. 35–52.

GOODSON, I. (1991a) 'Sponsoring the teacher's voice: Teachers' lives and teacher development', *Cambridge Journal of Education*, **21**, 1, pp. 35–45.

GOODSON, I. (1991b) 'Teachers' lives and educational research', in GOODSON, I. and WALKER, R. (Eds.) *Biography, Identity and Schooling: Episodes in Educational Research*, London: Falmer Press, pp. 137–49.

GORE, J. (1992) 'What can we do for you! What *can* "we" do for "you"?: Struggling over empowerment in critical and feminist pedagogy', in LUKE, C. and GORE, G. (Eds.) *Feminisms and Critical Pedagogy*, London: Routledge, pp. 54–73.

GORELICK, S. (1991) 'Contradictions of feminist methodology', *Gender and Society*, **5**, 4, pp. 459–77.

HARDING, S. (1991) *Whose Science? Whose Knowledge?* Milton Keynes: Open University Press.

HARVEY, L. (1990) *Critical Social Research*, London: Unwin Hyman.

JAGO, B. (1996) 'Postcards, ghosts and fathers: Revising family stories', *Qualitative Inquiry*, **2**, 4, pp. 495–516.

LEVIN, B. (1993) 'Collaborative research in and with organizations', *International Journal of Qualitative Studies in Education*, **6**, 4, pp. 331–40.

MANNING, K. (1997) 'Authenticity in constructivist inquiry: Methodological considerations without prescription', *Qualitative Inquiry*, **3**, 1, pp. 93–115.

MATTINGLEY, C. (1991) 'Narrative reflections on practical actions: Two learning experiments in reflective storytelling', in SCHON, D. (Ed.) *The Reflective Turn: Case Studies in and on Educational Practice*, New York: Teachers College Press, pp. 235–57.

PHTIAKA, H. (1994) 'What's in it for us?', *International Journal of Qualitative Studies in Education*, **7**, 2, pp. 155–64.

RICHARDSON, L. (1990) *Writing Strategies: Reaching Diverse Audiences*, London: Sage.

SCHEURICH, J. (1992) 'A post–modernist review of interviewing: Dominance, resistance and chaos'. Paper presented at the annual meeting of the American Educational Research Association, San Francisco, April.

SEARS, J. (1992) 'Researching the other/searching for self: Qualitative research on [homo]sexuality in education', *Theory Into Practice*, **XXXI**, 2, pp. 147–56.

SPARKES, A. (1994a) 'Life histories and the issue of voice: Reflections on an emerging relationship', *International Journal of Qualitative Studies in Education*, **7**, 2, pp. 165–83.

SPARKES, A. (1994b) 'Self, silence and invisibility as a beginning teacher: A life history of lesbian experience', *British Journal of Sociology of Education*, **15**, 1, pp. 93–118.

SPARKES, A. (1995) 'Writing people: Reflections on the dual crises of representation and legitimation in qualitative inquiry', *Quest*, **47**, pp. 158–95.

SPARKES, A. (1996a) 'Physical education teachers and the search for self: Two cases of structured denial', in ARMSTRONG, N. (Ed.) *New Directions in Physical Education: Change and Innovation*, London: Cassell, pp. 157–78.

SPARKES, A. (1996b) 'The fatal flaw: A narrative of the fragile body-self', *Qualitative Inquiry*, **2**, 4, pp. 463–494.

SPARKES, A. (1997) 'Ethnographic fiction and representing the absent other', *Sport, Education and Society*, **2**, 1, pp. 25–40.

SQUIRES, S. and SPARKES, A. (1996) 'Circles of silence: Sexual identity in physical education and sport', *Sport, Education and Society*, **1**, 1, pp. 77–101.

STACEY, J. (1988) 'Can there be a feminist ethnography?', *Woman's Studies International Forum*, **11**, 1, pp. 21–7.

WOLCOTT, H. (1995) *The Art of Fieldwork*, London: Altamira Press.

WOODS, S. (1992) 'Describing the experience of lesbian physical educators: A phenomenological study', in SPARKES, A. (Ed.) *Research in Physical Education and Sport: Exploring Alternative Visions*, London: Falmer Press, pp. 90–118.

ZAJANO, N. and EDELSBERG, C. (1993) 'Living and writing the researcher–researched relationship', *International Journal of Qualitative Studies in Education*, **6**, 2, pp. 143–57.

6 The Social Commitment of the Educational Ethnographer: Notes on Fieldwork in Mexico and the Field of Work in the United States

Bradley A Levinson

Introduction

In June 1996, I had the extraordinary experience of sitting around a conference table and sharing stories with colleagues about the ways we had succeeded or failed in meeting our social commitments as educational ethnographers. The occasion was the Sixth Annual Interamerican Symposium on Ethnographic Educational Research. Students and teachers of educational ethnography from the US, Mexico, and other Latin American nations had gathered in Ciudad Juárez, Mexico (just across the border from El Paso, Texas) to learn from one another. After a day of formal presentations, symposium participants, representing a variety of social science and education disciplines, split up into workshops to discuss several themes of interest. I had been asked by the symposium organizer, Beatriz Calvo, to help moderate a discussion about the 'social commitment of the ethnographer'.[1] Over the next two days, and for several hours each day, participants worked earnestly to examine their own assumptions about ethnographic 'commitments', to elucidate the kinds of 'commitments' encouraged or discouraged by their own disciplinary frameworks and institutional arrangements, and to expose their own checkered experiences with ethnographic 'commitment'. The discussion was both emotionally cathartic and intellectually edifying. We crossed and expanded conceptual boundaries just as many of us had crossed and expanded geopolitical boundaries in arriving at the conference.

The focus on notions of 'commitment' proved particularly rich for discussion. Several scholars spoke pointedly of ethical dilemmas encountered when their professional commitment to maintaining research participants' anonymity contradicted their moral commitment to expose school practices of cruelty or harmful indifference. Some argued that interpretive research was exploitative and distant; for them, nothing less than concrete commitment to the improvement and empowerment of research participants' lives through action or collaborative research would fulfill

The research discussed in this chapter was initially supported by a Fulbright Grant from the Institute for International Education, and the writing was supported by a Spencer Dissertation Fellowship and a National Academy of Education Post–doctoral Fellowship. I thank Thomas Schwandt, Douglas Foley, Janise Hurtig, and Ann Nihlen for their comments, though the final product is fully my responsibility.

their felt professional mandate. Still others suggested that their primary commitment was to honor the norms of academic scholarship established by their colleagues and to advance the knowledge of educational processes in their field. Perhaps most dramatically of all, an Argentine colleague recounted the extreme strictures on research during the military regime of previous decades, and said that educational research now had to necessarily commit itself to the reconstruction of democratic practices in schools.

What I took from that discussion was a renewed appreciation of the heterogeneity of qualitative educational research practices, and a refined awareness of my own social commitments as an ethnographer.[2] Moreover, I came to a more expanded conception of reflexive research. Indeed, the notion of social commitment seems to me an especially rich way of expanding the question of reflexivity in educational research. Reflexivity, the process of critical self–reflection, has often been applied to the analysis and textualization of field data, as well as the formulation of research methodologies. Less often has reflexivity been invoked to consider the broader connections between fieldwork, self–knowledge, textual presentation, and the gamut of social relations involved in qualitative research.[3] The emphasis on *social* commitment, rather than a primarily personal commitment to the integrity of the data or analysis, highlights our inescapable imbrication in multiple social networks, and multiple relations of power. It situates the problematic of reflexive research more squarely in the often contradictory field of competing interests and social arrangements, and it reminds us that commitment has a political as well an ethical dimension. Finally, framing research in terms of social commitment also provides us with a means of overcoming the endless debates regarding objectivity and subjectivity in qualitative analysis. As Gorelick (1989), echoing Harding (1992) and Haraway (1991), puts it:

> There is a difference between social commitment and bias. Bias involves unacknowledged distortion. Social commitment means that you are seeking knowledge for a purpose — as a tool for opposing oppression — and are self–conscious about it. This purpose requires that you want to know reality with as little distortion as possible. (p. 351)

In this chapter I would like to ground this discussion of reflexivity and social commitment in an account of my own insights and dilemmas as a cultural anthropologist conducting long–term ethnographic fieldwork at a Mexican secondary school. I begin this account with an outline of implicit notions of 'social commitment' in two primary traditional forms of anthropological research: basic and applied. I then move on to examine the development of more radically reflexive research designs in the post–positivist environment of contemporary educational inquiry. After exploring some of the assumptions and debates which permeate these reflexive research designs, I advance a series of pointed questions which must serve as a touchstone for any critical researcher wishing to define his/her own reflexive social commitments. Finally, I develop the heart of the chapter, an examination of my own answers — or silences — to these questions in the context of my ongoing research in Mexico.

I highlight the special difficulties of carrying out cross–cultural and transnational research, as well as the institutional practices — what I call here the 'field of work' — which in large part govern the horizons of 'social commitment' it has been possible for me to make. I conclude with some reflections on where this research currently stands, and where it might still be headed.

Qualitative Research and Social Commitment: Theoretical and Historical Antecedents

Anthropological Traditions

The discipline of cultural anthropology extends across the traditional divisions between the humanities, social sciences, and natural sciences. Ethnographic fieldwork, the methodological heart of the discipline, has developed all along this spectrum, from deductive hypothesis testing to poetic evocation of cultural otherness. Still, cultural anthropology is most firmly rooted in the discourses and practices of the social sciences, with their functionalist legacy and their ameliorative intent. Historically, many anthropologists have entered the discipline with something more than mere scientific zeal or intellectual curiosity. Often enough, they have also intended to use social research to advance a commitment to political activism or enlightened social reform.[4] While many of us might now condemn some of the methods (somatic measurement, distancing language, and the like) or warped politics (support of colonial regimes as 'enlightened' administration, technocratic social engineering) of research in prior epochs, we cannot deny its sense of social commitment. Since the radical critiques of the 1960s (see below), however, more and more anthropologists have questioned the reigning conceptions of reform and commitment embodied in such research. Resurrecting some of the political ideals and commitments of an earlier generation, we have sought to develop a praxis more attentive and committed to the aspirations of oppressed groups, more willing to challenge dominant groups and their ideologies, more engaged as a mode of cultural critique (Behar and Gordon, 1995; Marcus and Fischer, 1986; Bodley, 1976; Weaver, 1973).

For most of the discipline's history, such social commitment has been enacted through the mandates of 'basic research'. Some of these mandates are expressed in the constitution and various bye–laws of the professional associations; others are more broadly and diffusely normative. Mandates of basic research stipulate above all the contribution to an ever growing, objective knowledge base which might advance theory and inform a rather variably conceived 'practice'. According to this model, the anthropological ethnographer draws on theoretical issues to determine the site of her fieldwork and the nature of her inquiry. The apparent distancing implied by this model has been amply critiqued by feminist methodologists (Mies, 1983; Fonow and Cook, 1991). Yet I would suggest that this distancing has been partially mitigated by the fact that basic research in anthropology has itself undergone important modifications in recent years, to wit: (i) the theoretical issues driving a study are now more likely than ever to explicitly reflect concerns with the distribution of power in societies and the contested politics of culture; and (ii) the fieldwork site is now more than ever as likely to be chosen because of its connection to the ethnographer's own personal history or identity, i.e., the anthropologist may be as much an 'insider' as an outsider.[5]

In one sense, the anthropologist's social commitment to the intellectual community still outweighs her commitment to the people she studies. Her research agenda is rarely set through a dialogue with these people. Rather, the dialogue only begins after the anthropologist has conceptualized the research project according to the dictates of theory. This is not to say anthropologists self–consciously exploit such research participants. On the contrary, basic researchers often fulfill important functions and take on important responsibilities among the people they study; they frequently move into advocacy roles vis–à–vis governments and dominant groups; and they must abide by ethical guidelines for research with 'human subjects', which stipulate that their ultimate responsibility is to the welfare and well–being of the people with whom they work.[6] These kinds of commitments often grow over the course of fieldwork, as anthropologists are likely to live with a group for a year or more, and often return continuously over a period of many years. Moreover, the paradigm of basic research carries its own, often implicit, norms of commitment. There is an understanding, perhaps we could call it a faith, that the knowledge produced by such research, a knowledge about the variety and integrity of cultural practices around the globe, will eventually be taken up by social actors in the service of enlightened reform. More recently, important leaders in the American Anthropological Association have been advocating an expanded role for anthropologists in the educational and policy dimensions of the public sphere.

Anthropologists of a more activist bent have often gravitated toward 'applied' research. Applied anthropology as a self–consciously interventionist research project has its conceptual origins earlier in the century. Propelled by the hegemony of US 'development' initiatives in the post–war era, by the 1940s applied anthropology had come into its own as a recognized sub–field, with its own journals, conferences, and theoretical debates. The mandates of applied anthropology stipulate research oriented toward the resolution of specific problems, or the improved 'functioning' of a community, program, or institution. Examples range from the spate of development assistance programs, in which anthropologists have aided the introduction of technological and organizational improvements with minimal cultural 'damage' and maximum 'empowerment', to the 'controlled social change' of early projects with the Fox Indians (see Foley, 1995; Gearing, 1970) and the Peruvian Indians of Vicos (Holmberg, 1958), to the improvement of business management (McCurdy, 1994).

In this model of social commitment, the justification for research does not derive solely from theoretical considerations; it derives from a perceived problem in need of solution, or an opportunity for humane intervention. To be sure, the anthropologist carrying out applied research may be beholden to the funding agency directing her research. This may or may not obligate her to accept the ideological point of view of such agencies. Often enough, the anthropologist allows the 'people' (community, institution) to determine the problem needing investigation, and designs the research accordingly, applying existing theory and fieldwork techniques toward its resolution. While this model appears to embody a greater and more immediate social commitment to the welfare of a group of people, it also begs a number of important questions regarding reflexivity and the politics of research, to wit: Who defines the 'problem(s)', funds the research, and maintains access to or control over research results? In a less than fully democratic society, can't dominant groups in institutions (bureaucrats, administrators) or the broader society (politicians, funding agencies, corporations, 'communities') determine the nature of the research according to their own interests? If this is so, how can the 'application' of such research be made more fully empowering for subordinate groups? Without close and conscientious attention to such questions, applied research can sometimes turn into a mere appendage of the dominant technocratic apparatus.[7]

Radical Critiques, Reflexivity, and the Collaborative Turn

As early as the 1970s, some anthropologists were already noting the speciousness of the distinction between basic and applied research (Weaver, 1973). Many anthropologists who had primarily seen themselves as 'basic' researchers had indeed carried out applied projects in their careers, while 'applied' anthropologists often used the insights of 'basic' research to recommend solutions and modifications of practice. Compelled to protect or justify the cultural beliefs and practices of groups with which they worked, some anthropologists have found their advocacy roles stretched into 'applied' areas.[8] Anthropologists of education give perhaps some of the best examples of work which straddles, and in some cases explodes, the conventional distinction between basic and applied research. Many of the founders and important figures of educational anthropology, such as George Spindler, Jules Henry, Eleanor Leacock, and Murray and Rosalie Wax, have combined original theoretical formulations and 'basic' fieldwork with passionate social commitment to educational improvements for concrete social groups.[9]

Such anthropologists, and many others like them, have long embodied a social commitment grounded in methodological and theoretical reflexivity. Indeed, unlike mainstream sociology, psychology, and the related behavioral sciences, the interpretive heart of cultural anthropology has implicitly challenged the hegemony of technocratic rationality in modern industrial societies. Not all anthropologists share this hermeneutic stance, but for those who do the interpretive method stands as a humane and holistic alternative to the objectifying data–mills of the positivistic sciences. To be sure, more recent internal critiques of anthropology's involvement with colonialism (Asad, 1973), its imperious assumption of ethnographic 'authority' (Clifford, 1983), its pernicious 'othering' of research subjects (Fabian, 1983), and its masculinist bias (di Leonardo, 1991; Behar and Gordon, 1995), among other tendencies, have created an even more reflexive and socially committed discipline. Yet, as I have noted, the roots of such reflexivity can be richly documented for earlier work in the discipline (Marcus and Fischer, 1986).

It is interesting to note, then, that many of the newer critical research designs in educational inquiry have formed in reaction to predominant models of social science research, among which anthropological fieldwork is often cited. Within schools and colleges of education, the effective challenge to the hegemony of positivist theory and method, led by the insights of feminism, critical social and race theory, hermeneutical constructivism, and post–structuralism, has spawned an array of research practices largely designed to develop greater social commitment to the empowerment of oppressed and subordinate groups. Among these research practices are those that increasingly go by the label of 'critical ethnography', though even this growing tradition houses many otherwise strange bedfellows (see Goodman, chapter 4 in this volume). Much critical ethnography continues to follow methodo-logical and interpretive conventions developed by anthropologists and qualitative sociologists (Levinson and Holland, 1996). Topics of study and descriptive ana-lyses are distinguished from other interpretive work by their commitment to structural transformation and social equality. It may seem, at times, as though such critical ethnographers and theorists define and enact their 'commitment' as much to ab-stract ideals of democracy and emancipation as to concrete persons or social groups. But other forms of critical ethnography have developed more self–consciously dialogical fieldwork techniques, which permit a greater participation and control by research subjects (or 'participants', as these researchers prefer to call them).[10] Much of this strand of critical ethnography has evolved through an engagement with the critical pedagogy of Paolo Freire (1973) or the intellectual production of second–wave feminism (Reinharz, 1992). Variably called 'action', 'participatory', or 'collaborative' research, this critical ethnography typically aims to empower the teacher as a researcher and activist within her own sphere of pedagogical influence (Miller, 1990). Through such empowerment, the teacher becomes in turn commit-ted to the empowerment and emancipation of her colleagues and students. Other forms of action–oriented critical ethnography work directly with students and, in 'openly ideological' fashion (Lather, 1986, 1991), invite them to become critically reflexive about their position in society and their possibilities for action as social agents.

As I noted in the introduction to this essay, few authors in the literature on critical educational research have sought to define and discuss reflexivity in rela-tion to notions of 'social commitment'.[11] Political and ethical dimensions of social commitment in research are often displaced into the textual realm or, as in Fine's (1994) recent discussion, manifest themselves in the 'stance' a researcher takes vis–à–vis the imagined community of research participants and the way this community collaborates to produce a text. Critical ethnographers and pedagogues in the action tradition are now more quick to condemn interpretive research which fails to mani-fest a commitment to immediate and local transformations, or which fails to enlist research participants as full 'collaborators' in defining and executing the research project (Van Galen and Eaker, 1995). One increasingly reads critiques like those made by Katherine Schultz in her review of Meredith Rogers Cherland's *Private Practices: Girls Reading Fiction and Constructing Identity*. Schultz (1996) says that most critical education research is long on critique and short on solutions . . . I worry about the value of the kind of research that positions the researcher as an inside observer, an outside critic, and someone who never brings the findings back to the community . . . my question concerns the ultimate value and ethics of a study that is not connected to change in the local context. (p. 455)

Yet Schultz admits at another point in the review that Cherland 'reaches interesting and potentially significant conclusions'. Importantly, Schultz does not define what kind of 'change in the local context' she might endorse. One assumes that she means a more intentional kind of progressive intervention, but this would be to overlook the inevitable changes introduced by virtually all ethnographic research, whether or not such research reflexively attends to such changes.

Given the currency of critiques like those made by Schultz, we must ask whether we can really have it both ways. Can we require an ethnographic study to be 'connected to change in the local context' and still reach 'interesting and potentially significant conclusions?' There are important models to follow, perhaps.[12] But we must also be careful not to condemn research which subordinates the goal of local change to the dissemination of its broader conclusions. After all, how can we fairly adjudicate a scholar's commitment to a local research community against her commitment to the broader human community? The model of 'basic research' described above has often been criticized as inherently exploitative, falsely objectivist, and irrelevant to the project of social reform or emancipation. Even critical ethnographers in the interpretive tradition, with their commitment to social transformation, come in for such criticism. Yet this critique is rather presumptuous in what it purports to know about the eventual benefits of research. For example, Clifford Geertz, a prime practitioner of basic research, has never conducted fieldwork with an applied or interventionist program. Yet his writings have been enormously influential in various projects of radical reform. His theoretical elaborations of ethnography and his elegant, insightful descriptions of cultural logics have been drawn on by numerous researchers to advance their own interpretive insights in arenas of policy and educational change.[13]

Moreover, we ought to be careful not to confuse *involvement* with a commitment to empowering change at the fieldwork site. Much of the radical critique of traditional ethnography suggests that anthropologists never had any emotional connections or personal commitments to the people they studied and worked with. Indeed, anthropologists' connections and commitments are often greater than those of self–consciously 'emancipatory researchers' who spend less time at a field site and develop fewer ongoing relationships.

If I have sounded a defensive note here, it is because anthropology increasingly has been depicted as the antithesis of truly 'critical' research. With Patai (1994), I worry about a new kind of orthodoxy in educational research, one which measures degrees of empowering collaboration at the research site to determine its value. It seems to me crucial to specify the many different kinds and levels of 'commitment' a more broadly conceived notion of critical research might entail. Why not support a variety of research practices attentive to local conditions and demands of both research sites and circuits of academic knowledge? Critical action research in the Freirean and feminist traditions holds great promise for 'neighborly' dialogue (Savage, 1988) between academics and educational actors. The commitment to collaboration and change in the local context of research is an admirable one, if it is executed in good faith and with sufficient attention to the contradictions of power. Yet such research does not exhaust the meanings or possibilities of critical or reflexive research. As Kelly (1993) notes, the 'hierarchically structured' context of schools may make participatory research and thoroughgoing collaboration nearly impossible (pp. 227–8). And especially in an era when so much theoretical attention has been focused on questions of power and social identity, interpretive research can still provide extremely trenchant and illuminating descriptions of educational processes. Rockwell (in press) argues that in Mexico, such descriptions themselves can play a radical role in rupturing official or 'common–sense' views of what happens in schools.

Critical Questions

Different approaches to critical research thus develop and embody different models of social commitment and reflexivity. Such approaches may have importantly overlapping features, and many researchers may consider themselves attempting to incorporate these features in the fashion of a theoretical 'bricoleur' (Denzin, 1996). Still, there are notable tensions between these research approaches. By way of transition to a discussion of my own attempts to navigate and resolve some of these tensions, I offer the following critical questions as a prolegomenon to any reflexive and socially committed research project:

- How do we negotiate conflicting interests at the field site itself? To whom is our greatest commitment if administrators, teachers, parents, and students have interests that are at odds with one another? How do we manifest a commitment to — or orchestrate a consensus among — such disparate actors?

- What kinds of responsibilities and commitments do we have as ethnographers to the individuals who take part in our research? How do we honor their trust and generosity? To what extent can or should we reciprocate their participation through means of material assistance (sending money, finding jobs, giving gifts, etc.), emotional connection (letters, phone calls, and visits; providing advice, etc.), or intellectual solidarity ('taking sides' in the representation of research results).

- Should we give 'veto power' to our research participants as part of a dialogical commitment? Do we grant them the right to modify or challenge what our texts might eventually say? If so, might this not vitiate the broader value of the research, to broader social questions and constituencies? Does this not abdicate the interpretive position and prerogative of the ethnographer

to 'see' and 'document' patterns of behavior that participants might not themselves see? Under what conditions should that interpretive prerogative be
abandoned?

• To whom and for whom do we write? Must our audiences (academic, popular, site–specific) be mutually exclusive? Must we develop separate documents
  and different languages for communicating to these audiences? If so, do the
  institutional conditions of our work presently encourage us to pursue these
  kinds of multiple representation?

Dilemmas of Commitment in the Transnational Field: A US Anthropologist in Mexico

Prior Experience and Institutional Context

As Francis (1996) has recently reminded us, the kinds of commitments we can
make in ethnographic research are often circumscribed — if not determined — by
the social context of academic knowledge production. Francis describes how her
own research on Papua New Guinean educational policymakers was transformed
as it became a PhD dissertation project. It was then that she felt the imperative
of joining an 'academic club' formed around 'identifiable empirical paradigms'
(p. 78). Despite the prevailing endorsement of dissertation research as a creative
and innovative production, as a student Francis was not empowered to challenge the
existing theoretical frameworks and empirical paradigms. She therefore struggled
to reformulate her research as a 'non–interventionist' interpretive project.

One area which thus needs closer examination is the ritual practice of academic licensing, i.e., the process of writing a dissertation in areas of qualitative
research, and the social norms which govern such practices. Much has already been
written in a critical, reflexive vein about assumptions governing academic writing
(Brodkey, 1987) and hiring practices (Rabinow, 1991). In anthropology, of course,
there is now an extensive literature on reflexive, dialogical approaches to fieldwork
(Crapanzano, 1980; Briggs, 1970; Tedlock, 1991). There are even recent volumes
which honestly explore the often painful intricacies of producing fieldnotes (Sanjek,
1990; Emerson et al., 1996). Yet if we are to examine the ways in which social
commitment of various sorts is encouraged and discouraged, we would do well to
consider that arena where we are most deliberately socialized as academics and
scholars: the dissertation process. In schools of education and related applied disciplines, dissertation research has been opening up. It is now common to find dissertation committees more frankly supportive of committed participatory research. Yet
in other cases, and especially in the traditional social sciences, experimentation is
less frequently encouraged. Even where textual innovations in reflexive representation are encouraged or accepted, there still exists an implied mandate to produce
something for the 'knowledge base' of scholars rather than for the edification or
emancipation of educational actors at the research site itself. And often enough, in

the absence of explicit sanctions, novice researchers internalize the expectations they have absorbed from departmental conversations and/or the disciplinary literature. This point cannot be overstated. Academic apprentices, caught up in a fundamentally conservative/conserving rite of passage, learn to make their primary social commitments to their immediate supervisors and the knowledge base of the discipline. Only some are lucky enough to have their apprenticeship coincide with periods of unusually intense academic ferment, or work with supervisors of unusually strong dedication to change and innovation at the site of research.

I suppose you could say I was one of the lucky ones. I was indeed 'lucky enough' to be encouraged to reflexively explore the kinds of commitments informing my research. I was encouraged to see my research as a kind of political intervention, though I can't say that this intervention was meant to include important change at the research site itself. When I entered graduate school in anthropology, I immediately gravitated toward critical accounts of education. At the time (1986), the field of education was in post–positivist ferment, and anthropologists of education were increasingly citing the work of Marxist critical ethnographers and cultural theorists like Paul Willis and Raymond Williams. I found much of this work exciting for its ability to analyse and describe the ways educational actors responded to the painful effects of dominant discourses and practices.

In retrospect, my attraction to this work lay in my conviction that it offered an analysis of how and why 'capitalist schools' contributed to suffering, inequality, and the reduction of human freedom (Liston, 1988). Yet I also found that in their zeal to establish a warrant for societal and educational transformation, such authors were ignoring or abandoning some of the best insights of earlier work in the anthropology and sociology of education (Levinson, 1992). I also felt that it was eurocentric in its conception of student culture and student agency. Not least because Mexican schools were only partly 'capitalist' in the sense such authors had assayed, I sensed that student culture would be different in Mexico, less flamboyant and less structured by the individualistic competitiveness of Euro–American schools. Thus, I formulated a research proposal for extended ethnographic study of a Mexican secondary school in a provincial city several hours outside of Mexico City. I intended to study the cultural meanings and forms students produced at this school (*Escuela Secundaria Federal*, or ESF) in response to the 'reproductive intent' of school structure and practice. What I eventually found would challenge the very notion of reproductive intent, for most discourses and practices at ESF served to equalize educational opportunities for boys and girls of different social classes. Patterns of student culture developed largely in response to these homogenizing and equalizing gestures, not in response to a hierarchical and differentiating school structure (Levinson, 1993a, 1996).

As part of my preparation for fieldwork, I also attempted to come to grips with my own political and ideological investments. This took the form of explicit biographical reflection. In late 1989 I wrote the following introduction to my 'statement of interests', a document requested by the Department of Anthropology of the University of North Carolina as an appendix to my dissertation proposal:

Growing up in a middle–class suburb of Los Angeles, it didn't take me long to discover that school meant different things to different students. My high school bussed in poorer kids from the city — some Latino, most African–American. The social world my own class had created within the school was complicated by the presence of these 'outsiders' who brought their own sets of understandings and practical strategies to what must have seemed a rather alien context. No longer was this 'just' a white, middle–class academic high school for any of us.

What strikes me most about my secondary years, in retrospect, is the power of the cultural forms we as students created. What we learned or aspired to in the classroom was only minimally related to our 'intelligence' or 'aptitude', as defined by the school. Rather, we often negotiated with teachers to produce the forms of knowledge we could appropriate to our own communicative ends. In a class on US government, for example, we shifted a discussion of election processes onto the terrain of school micropolitics that interested us most. We effected this shift through a combination of subtle sabotage and not–so–subtle complaint. Doubtless this kind of negotiation took on different aspects, with occasionally damaging consequences, between minority students and teachers in the school.

Throughout the course of my intellectual development, I have wondered about the schooling process. From a historical, cross–cultural perspective, the develop-ment of mass public schooling in the modern international context is both recent and disturbingly homogeneous. What does it mean that ever–increasing numbers of children worldwide are subject to enclosure and state–mandated pedagogical activities for at least 30 hours a week? What kinds of social relations develop in this complexly located institutional form? My anthropological background has given me a view of social relations in schools as informed by the wider sociocul-tural dynamics governing a site or social formation. Yet a universalizing discourse within the field of education attempts to neutralize these dynamics with a chorus of test scores and academic 'outcomes'. My professional research will in large part be dedicated to rescuing the fine–grained detail of these dynamics and elucidating their consequences for educational processes.

Over time, my interest in educational issues has converged with an interest in Mexican culture and society. My formative years in California put me into continuous contact with people of Mexican descent. By the time I had obtained my bachelor's degree, I wanted to learn more about Mexico. I traveled there and obtained a brief volunteer position at a rural elementary school, and my fascination with cultural issues in education was rekindled. Upon returning to California, I found a position as a teaching assistant at a middle school in a significantly Latino area. As a small–group instructor and yard supervisor, I was able to develop a rapport with students roughly the same age as those I intend to study in Mexico for my dissertation.

Three years later, in the dissertation itself, I reproduced this statement and added the following comments:

This document shows all the quirks of an intentional, institutional autobiography, the product of grantsmanship. For at the time, I was also writing applications for field research grants from Fulbright, Inter–American, and similar foundations. The occasion seemed to encourage the production of a seamless retrospective narrative, a projected biography showing the logical progression of personal experiences and interests culminating in the current research project. Absent from the narrative were the detours, the fits and starts, along the path of my intellectual journey: my involvement with Theravada Buddhism and South Asian culture as an undergraduate, my initial graduate interests in dream interpretation among the contemporary Maya, and my equally strong interests in popular culture sites such as Disneyland and MTV. According to the dominant institutional logic, though, including such detours in the narrative would have detracted from the appearance of continuity, of commitment, so important to researcher credentials.

It is only now that I can feel comfortable revealing this provisional, constructed nature of my personal narrative. Yet making this recognition allows me to perceive deeper continuities, deeper commitments, which inform my varied interests and activities. It allows me to see how the issues of domination and liberation, of suffering and freedom, had preoccupied me from a rather early age. It also allows me to see how my own engagement with these issues — meditational, psychotherapeutic, activist, and anthropological — betrayed a concern with the making of meaning in contexts of domination and liberation, and contexts of difference. This concern seems to me the leitmotif of those myriad activities which have comprised my adult (and in some respects my childhood) life. What's more, a kind of utopian idealism has provided the driving energy for many of these activities. My own life has been importantly structured by ideals of equality and solidarity. In many ways, my politics, spirituality, and intellectual work have been fused through this passionate search for social justice and community. While my idealism has been tempered along the way, it continues to inform my work by providing a 'language of hope and possibility', as Henry Giroux calls it. In writing this dissertation, I have had to remind myself that my own intimate biographical engagement with ideals of equality and solidarity is likely to influence my interpretation of the school–based social dynamics I describe. I remind the reader of this as well.

Here, in 1993, was a frank admission of the political and intellectual (even spiritual) commitments of my research. This was not so unusual, for textual reflexivity had already long been in fashion in cultural anthropology. Such reflexivity helped me to become clearer about my own investments in interpretation, and to 'remind the reader' of these investments as well. I revisited my initial enthusiasm for critical reproduction theory in education. Why had I eventually decided to formulate a research project in Mexico which attended to student agency in the context of domination? What were my commitments here? I could see now that my research was in some sense a transposition of my activist commitments of earlier years. Through my research, I hoped to add to the body of cultural critique, to advance radical theory in the hopes that such theory would provide a guide for political and social transformations of education in the years ahead. Mexico was to serve as a 'case study' for radical knowledge about educational processes. In this conception of ethnographic social science, there was little margin for considering a commitment in terms of 'action' at the field site itself. However, as time went by, my circle of commitments grew wider, and my increased engagement with Mexican colleagues and research participants enlarged the sense of possibility and responsibility surrounding the project.

Divided Loyalties and the Problem of Power

As I began writing my dissertation, I found this circle of commitments paralyzing. Different actors were implicitly making different claims on my work. I came to see myself as attempting to 'accommodate the voices' of these actors, and I wrote a prologue describing this attempt.[14] On the one hand, I was most immediately attempting to 'accommodate' the voices of my dissertation committee members, representatives of an intellectual discipline to whose knowledge I was contributing. Yet I was also hoping to contribute to knowledge, debate, policy formation, and transformative action in Mexico itself. I heard the voices of my Mexican colleagues caught in moments of struggle with a State threatening to curtail its own commitment to public education. And then, of course, there were the voices of the various research participants themselves. How could I honor my commitment to them, doing so in such a way that would recognize their distinct interests?

My reflection on this question in 1992 (see Levinson, 1993a) took the following form:

> This [conflict of interests] I think points to a major lacuna in the literature on critical ethnography and an engaged research praxis. Critical ethnographers in the action research mode posit the need for an impassioned, committed research dialogue at the field site itself: reflexivity; making our results available; allowing the disparate voices into the text. Yet this perspective is often presented as if the school were constituted by a common social interest, or as if that common interest could be orchestrated, produced, by the researcher him or herself: an interest which unites the school against a crazed society; against state or city bureaucracy; against drugs, crime, consumerism, and precocious sexuality. In fact, though, the school is internally diverse, conflictive. The meanings around what takes place in school are constantly contested and negotiated, between teachers, parents, and students, and of course within each of these categories as well. What may be good for one may not be good for another.
>
> Critical ethnographers recognize this structural conflict, but don't fully acknowledge its effects on the research process or its outcomes. To whom do we bring our research results? Into which circuits of actual or potential power do we insert our ethnographic knowledge? Power and conflict are a basic fact of life in schools, and an interpretive analysis, 'critical' or otherwise, lives or dies by it. If we see the school itself as a legitimate and necessary site for the circulation of critical ethnographic knowledge, then we must be less innocent about the way such knowledge is likely to be taken up in the school's ongoing struggles.
>
> So we find ourselves having to take sides. We can write a sympathetic account of school life, we can incorporate as many voices as possible, and we can show how people are not intrinsically mean, boring, or hurtful, but that social arrangements often impel them to act that way. But we do find ourselves taking sides. For example, Willis (1977), Everhart (1983), and Fine (1991) all take the side of the students, but they do so in a way which doesn't necessarily indict parents or teachers. As critical ethnographers, they are eager to give voice to students' experience, to valorize students' struggles within and against an often demeaning institution. They can show the lived contradictions of parents and teachers, but ultimately their

project lies with the students. This is underdog ethnography — committed, passionate, and partial.

I, too, saw my primary interpretive commitment to the students. Yet as a foreigner in Mexico, this commitment was made more problematic. Indeed, part of the lore of working as a foreign (especially US) national in Mexico involves the ever–present threat of sedition. I should qualify this by noting that Mexico is actually a very open and gracious country. It is especially remarkable for its openness to international research. Unlike most countries, it requires no special research clearance or visa application for extended study. Nevertheless, given a history of intervention and subordination, especially vis–à–vis their more powerful Northern neighbour, Mexicans also zealously guard their sovereign prerogatives. Only half–jokingly, many teachers threatened to '*aplicarme el treintaytres*' (charge me with the 33rd) if I overstepped the bounds of proper conduct. This meant they might report me and initiate deportation proceedings for violating the 33rd Article of the Mexican Constitution, which prohibits foreigners from unduly criticizing or threatening Mexican institutions. Other foreign researchers have reported similar statements. The effect of these statements, along with frequent requests to 'tell us what you're doing', was to highlight the proscriptive power of adult informants, and thus circumscribe my commitments to youth.

Allow me to illustrate how my interpretive commitment to, and understanding of, student experience was problematically mediated by adults: on one of my first visits to ESF, in the early summer of 1988, I found myself witnessing the Monday morning civic ceremony for the first time. For this ceremony, students line up with their groups around the main plaza. Girls escort the flag in disciplined fashion around the plaza, accompanied by the off–tune blaring of the school's all–boy military band. When the flag comes to a halt, students are led in the singing of the national anthem by one of the music teachers. Then the flag is escorted back away from the plaza and the band music comes to a merciful stop. Next, several members of one group each read short anniversary notes (*efemérides*), commemorating a great person or event in world or national history. Often one of the group's best speakers then takes the microphone for a short inspirational speech, and this is followed by yet another student's poetry recitation. Finally, the group's 'master of ceremonies' announces last week's awards and admonishments for punctuality, and hands the microphone over to the Principal or Vice–principal. The Principal then comments on the quality of the group's handling of the civic ceremony, commending them as an example or warning other groups to avoid the same pitfalls. He also announces any special business of the day or week, and exhorts the students to work well for group and country before dismissing them to first period classes.

I remember this first ceremony well because of the dilemma it presented for me. I was situated on the platform above the plaza, well in view of students and teachers alike. When the flag was passing by, I wondered whether to place my right hand in a kind of vertical salute over the heart, as the others were doing. If I complied in the gesture, would they think me a hypocrite for saluting a flag, and thus declaring an allegiance, that was clearly not my own? On the other hand, if I didn't salute the flag, would they take this as an insult, a sign of disrespect? I was probably visibly anguished. I hesitantly raised my arm, only to drop it definitively after just a few seconds. Nobody seemed to react one way or another.

That day at lunch my host and mentor, Mr. Solana, reproached me for having failed to salute the flag. I related to him the anguish I had felt in the situation, wondering whether the salute would have been perceived as hypocrisy. He assured me that nobody would have thought this; on the contrary, they would have applauded my show of solidarity. Mr. Solana was clearly irked by my disregard for their patriotic sensibilities. The next day I stopped in to see the Vice–principal, Mr. Alvarez, with whom I felt I could speak very openly. I presented my dilemma to him as well, and recounted Mr. Solana's scolding. He smiled and said that few besides Mr. Solana had probably even noticed. '*No todos somos tan nacionalistas*', ('not all of us are so nationalistic') he concluded coyly.

This anecdote illustrates one of the primary ways in which ethnographers come to achieve a knowledge of local dynamics: through the process of personally negotiating a controversial gesture, action, or practice. From that time on, I was even more sensitive to differences among teachers than I would have been otherwise. While I had presupposed that all Mexican schoolteachers were staunch and unremitting nationalists, now I began to see spontaneity, divergence, and variation. I began to see a fuller range of teaching styles and ideological orientations, a sea of conflicting interests (see Rockwell, 1995) I would eventually have to negotiate. My halting response to the flag ceremony, it turns out, had been commensurate with the actual complexity of the situation.

The anecdote also points to several other features of my life in the local setting which would determine the kind of research I could conduct, the kinds of truncated commitments I would have to make. First, I was always highly visible, primarily in the school, secondarily in the community at large. Second, and related, I came to understand in a more visceral fashion just what constant school discipline did to one's body and spirit. After this first civic ceremony, I made a point of always standing amongst the students themselves. On those mornings when I arrived at the same hour as the students, I took my place in line with the boys, kept my hands out of my pockets, listened attentively to instructions, and trotted off to class with the group which had invited me to stand in line with them. Ever mindful of the Principal's gracious — and revocable — permission to conduct the research, I took care to avoid teachers' accusations of fomenting disorder, and thus found myself often cutting short some 'rambunctious' interactions with students in line or during class.

When I observed classrooms, I took a seat among the students, often toward the left and rear. The seats were individual metal chairs with right–sided writing surfaces. Since I am left–handed, I positioned myself in this way in order to write and observe most of the class without having to constantly shift my body. The desks were rather uncomfortable. They barely accommodated my 5′7″ frame, and many of the students were bigger than me. On freezing days, moreover, the metal seats effectively transported the cold from cement floors to human bones. It was not uncommon to arrive at a class and find most of the students shivering or rubbing their hands for warmth. Aside from the physical discomfort, however, what also struck me was the oppressiveness of the arrangements. Teachers typically sat behind a full desk on a slightly elevated cement platform in front. Student desks were all arranged in rows facing the teacher and the chalkboard. This obviously facilitated teachers' visual control over student activity. But it also facilitated their control over my activity. Even as I covered the classroom with my social scientist's 'gaze', so too did the students and teachers keep track of me. The teachers' monitoring was more implicitly threatening. Although I probably would not have suffered the same consequences as students, I too had to conform to classroom rules, asking permission when entering and leaving, remaining seated during deskwork, and refraining from talking during formal lessons. Many of my classroom interactions with students took place via written notes or hushed exchanges which took on conspiratorial tones as we attempted to circumvent the ever–present censorship.

The third and final quality of my researcher's life which the flag anecdote illustrates is the centrality of adult figures like Mr. Solana and the Vice–principal, Mr. Alvarez, two of my best informants among the teachers. Teachers like these provided an important, sometimes problematic, mediation of student life, as their comments and practices forced me to constantly reevaluate the meanings I was ascribing to student action. Indeed, I lived with Mr. Solana and his family, and much of what I learned about life in San Pablo and ESF was mediated by the comings and goings in the Solana house. The Solana's youngest daughter, eventually my *ahijada* (ritual godchild), had been a student at ESF when I first arrived, though by 1990 she had moved on to one of the local high schools. Nevertheless, she and her five siblings, along with her parents themselves, provided an important window onto the relationship between schooling and family practice in San Pablo. In addition, Mr. Solana and his wife were forever explaining, recommending, admonishing. Both teachers for 30 years, they provided a vast wealth of knowledge on schools and school practices in San Pablo.

Allow me to present yet another example of my divided loyalties and the way in which local power relations circumscribed the extent and nature of my immediate social commitments. Over the course of the school year, I developed a particularly close relationship with Rosita and her family. At 14 years old, Rosita was the oldest of two daughters in a family of modest means, located in an established working–class neighborhood. Her father owned and operated a small cargo truck, and also supervised the operations of a small shop for the production of cotton napkins and tablecloths, which he owned in conjunction with his father and brothers. Her mother supervised domestic chores, cut and measured cloth, and sub–contracted embroidering and other detail work on the cloth to poorer neighborhood women. Rosita was one of those schoolgirls who said she came to consider me the big brother she never had. She often asked me for advice, and recounted arguments between her parents occasioned by her own insubordination to her father's wishes. In her father's eyes, Rosita's main fault was to seek the company of her friends (including boyfriends) in the afternoons, rather than staying home to study and work.

I became quite close with Rosita and her family, visiting often. If her father was home, I was invariably obliged to sit and chat with him, while Rosita and her mother sat on the margins of our conversation and listened, or went about their household chores. Rosita's mother often chipped in comments to the conversation, but did not otherwise take a leading role. Because of this, I relished the opportunities to speak with Rosita's mother at length, when her husband was outside the home. It was during these chats that I learned why she so adamantly defended her daughter's right to choose her own friends and leisure activities, even her career. She spoke with a sense of sadness and loss about her own lost opportunities, and about her too–early marriage to a man who turned out much like her own father. Rosita's mother was struggling in a marriage, and a web of affinal kin relations, which she regretted in many ways. Her solution, it seemed to me, was to invest in her own daughters' happiness and freedom. That is why she enjoined her husband to give Rosita more freedom, and that is why more overt household conflicts had begun to develop as Rosita matured.

I became enlisted in these two women's struggle against the patriarchal authority of the husband and father. I was an 'educated' person, an 'anthropologist' (Rosita's mother always called me '*maestro*', or teacher, despite my protests), and a man, who could perhaps convince their husband and father to loosen the reins on his daughter. Rosita and her mother never specifically requested my intervention, and of course there is little I could have done, anyway. What they did do, however, was to draw on my kind of authority to contest the authority of Rosita's father. They would invite me over frequently, and Rosita's mother sometimes would make a reference to the more 'liberal' practices of other families, hoping I would confirm her observation. For instance, when her husband refused to celebrate his daughter's birthday with a *quinceaño* party, Rosita's mother said, 'Everybody is doing it nowadays, right teacher?' This 'right teacher?' ('*¿verdad que sí, maestro?*'), directed at me, was a common intonation on my visits. It attempted to secure my agreement with causes and strategies being advanced by Rosita and her mother. It attempted to persuade the husband and father. I usually responded in agreement, carefully crafting my words to support the mother's contention while acknowledging the father's position as well. After I got to know the father well, and had earned his respect and trust, sometimes I even ventured to contradict him more emphatically.

Besides these oblique requests for intervention, Rosita and her mother both clearly enjoyed speaking with me. Each of them commented on several occasions that it was a relief and a benefit to be able to discuss their problems with someone who was outside the family and their immediate circle of friends and kin. I was one of the few people they knew who would probably never reveal their stories to other people in the school or community. Interviews and chats, it seemed, became an enormously reflexive and cathartic exercise, an opportunity to tackle dragons from the past and chart new courses for the future. In other words, these interviews, rather than revealing pre–formed identities, conflicts, or aspirations, became part of a process of intersubjective identity formation into which I had been drafted.

Some might argue that this research is exploitative. After all, the relationship was never fully symmetrical or reciprocal; neither Rosita nor her mother solicited my research project, and once engaged, neither could easily refuse my requests for interviews. From the beginning, I deigned to use their participation as another source of 'data' in an interpretive study, with no pretense of transformative praxis in the field. One could even say, most cynically, that I have eventually parlayed their cooperation into material and career gains. On the other hand, as I have tried to show, mutuality became an emergent quality of the relationship. Rosita and her mother expressed their gratitude to me on numerous occasions. I have continued to maintain my relationship with them, calling and writing, and visiting when possible. Though I retain ultimate control over the textual products of our collaborations, they have seen the transcriptions of some interviews and obtained copies of others, giving me their feedback about my interpretation (this is often made more problematic by distance and language differences).[15]

How can we reckon the outcome of this relationship? I must admit that my own role in these two women's empowerment was minimal. Yet my 'exploitation' of them for my own research ends must be balanced against its potential contribution to a praxis which would open up spaces for women's liberation in Mexico. My research with Rosita and her mother has allowed me to understand how some girls drew on school–based notions of student rights to contest their fathers' authority in the household, and how some mothers supported them in this struggle. It has also allowed me to fill in a larger argument about the way gender identities formed in the family affect the construction of aspirations and identities in the school (see Levinson, 1993b, 1997, in press). Do these research findings ring hollow in the lives of ESF students and families? Perhaps. The research will probably not have a major effect on Rosita's own struggle for freedom, at least not in any immediate sense. Rather, it will become part of a body of critical research, drawn on by feminists and pro–feminists to transform gender relations of power. In the particular context of Mexico, this will require translating the work and making it accessible to Mexican feminists working on similar issues. Perhaps the research might thus contribute to critically informed changes in schooling, law, or other everyday sites of gender oppression in Mexico which would eventually have some positive impact in the lives of Rosita and her mother.[16]

Conclusions in the Present Moment: Intercultural Dialogue, Power, and Social Commitment

As the years have gone by, I have indeed found myself acting more resolutely on my commitment to Mexican colleagues engaged in research on schools, class and gender, and student culture. As I have moved on from graduate school and found a place for myself in a school of education at a major research university, I have more room and more incentive for this kind of intercultural dialogue. A three–year stint teaching at a liberal arts college left me little time for translation and publication. Now I have begun to publish research in forums where Mexicans can read it. I have also taken a more active role in presenting my research results at various sites in Mexico, some academic, but some also directed toward practicing schoolteachers.

The work has taken on a longitudinal component as I have stayed in touch with many of the students who graduated in 1991. Soon I will return to interview them about changes in their lives since that year. I also hope to study changes in school structure and teacher perceptions after the major educational reform of 1993. My relations with many of the teachers and former students from ESF continue to be cordial. Two or three of the teachers have read portions of my dissertation, and we have discussed some of our conflicting interpretations. The Principal now wants me to stop in and hold a workshop with the current teachers, presenting some of my main findings from the research. This is a daunting prospect, for I must face the indifference or hostility of those teachers who never cared much about my research, who find it pointless or perhaps even threatening. I must also face the consequences of having taken the students' 'side' in most matters of interpretation.

Moreover, I must acknowledge the barriers of intercultural communication, and the way they implicate the different kinds and degrees of interest of the participants in my ethnographic research. Good interpretive research, of course, involves constant cross–checking of hunches and perceptions with the participants in the study. Such dialogue can come to take the form of 'member checks', where written interpretations are actually shared with participants. Yet in carrying out research transnationally, we cannot always expect this checking to proceed smoothly. I recall here a moment in my research when the Vice–principal of ESF came to reject an interpretation. I had come to him with my observation that the secondary school seemed to harbor a basic contradiction. One mission of the school was to train students for the job market and for assuming national citizenship under the assumption that students would not continue their schooling beyond the secondary level (in fact, only some 50 per cent of those who entered ESF did go on to study at the next educational level). Yet the mission of the school was also to prepare students for their next level of schooling, college preparatory studies. I often noticed that teachers of third–year students couched their lessons in terms of their value for future studies, and I wondered how those students who might not continue their schooling felt. I asked the Vice–principal if he felt there was a 'contradiction' between general training and training for future high school courses. Usually a thoughtful man, he rejected this interpretation out of hand without giving a cogent justification. I wondered, then, whether the term contradiction had a different, far more pejorative meaning for him, and whether he saw my comment as an evaluative statement about the lack of coherence in the school. Would it have allayed his concerns if I had noted that virtually all modern schools exhibit these kinds of contradictions (Carnoy and Levin, 1985)? Could he see that contradiction was a perhaps inevitable aspect of modern institutional life? And how would a student have responded if I had checked the same interpretation with him? Would he or she even have a good working sense of the term 'contradiction?'

I have had to accept that I am doing something rather different when I write in English for academic audiences and when I speak or write in Spanish to Mexicans. I remain vexed by the allegiances and constraints of the nation–state, bound to speak as a foreigner or as a border–crossing interpreter of other cultural worlds. In Mexico, I am telling Mexicans something for the most part they already know. I am reflecting back to them sides of themselves they may not so easily see, aspects of their social relations tangled up in the immediacies of everyday conduct. I hold up to them a strangely surfaced mirror. In the United States and elsewhere, I am presenting a foreign reality for domestic consumption. For better or worse, I am interpreting the 'other'. Even as I struggle against the exoticizing and distancing tropes of my discipline, I still pose the idiosyncrasies of Mexican student culture as a novel 'case' which can refine our understanding of educational dynamics around the globe. This is a different kind of mirror, a 'mirror for man' [sic] as the anthropologist Alfred Kroeber had once called it, a glimpse of the universal, and therefore of the self, in the particularities of the other. I still believe there is real value in this kind of work.

In the final analysis, how have the practices of reflexivity and social commitment been articulated in my research? I have tried to show that being reflexive, for me, has meant a more or less constant monitoring of the varying kinds and levels of social commitment made possible, or impossible, by the shifting contexts of research. In my case, such contexts have included the formulation of a research proposal and selection of a research site, the pursuit of research funding, the main period of conducting fieldwork itself, subsequent visits with research participants at the fieldwork site, my employment as a teacher at a small college, my publications and presentations in English, my publications and presentations in Spanish, and my employment as a researcher at a major university. Being aware of my commitments and limitations as a change agent in people's lives at the fieldwork site does not preclude awareness of the commitments I pursue in writing and disseminating the results of my research. Like those researchers I admire in the field of educational anthropology, I have tried to conduct a 'passionate ethnography' (Henry, 1963) which allows me to engage as social critic and interlocutor on various levels and in various contexts, including the seemingly distant realm of basic research and social reform. My main research project still falls squarely within the interpretive camp, but this does not obviate its claims to commitment and reflexivity. Nor does it prohibit me from envisioning a future project which might incorporate a stronger action component.[17] Ultimately, I would hope my experience points to an expanded conception of reflexivity in critical research, a heterodox meditation on the multiple frames for producing knowledge and enacting social commitment.

Notes

1 This is actually a rough translation from the original workshop title in Spanish, 'El Compromiso Social del Etnógrafo'. I am translating compromiso as 'commitment', but the term may also carry stronger connotations of 'obligation' or weaker connotations of 'engagement'. I thank Beatriz Calvo for the invitation to help conduct this dialogue. Selected papers from the Symposium (in Spanish and English), as well as a narrative summary of the workshop under discussion here, can be found in Calvo et al. (1997).

2 I am aware of the slippage here between a discussion of 'qualitative' research and 'ethnography'. This has been a subject of ongoing debate amongst the participants in

the Interamerican Symposium. Some advocate a more restricted use of the term ethnography for long–term, observation–based research. According to this view, projects of shorter duration, or which rely more heavily on interviews, written documents, and the like, merit the label of 'qualitative research'. Much of the work presented at the Symposium could only thereby be described as 'qualitative'. Others argue that all qualitative research is essentially ethnographic in that it is oriented to describing the social and cultural worlds of groups of people. While neither view has carried the day, the subtitle of the Symposium's latest edited volume (Calvo et al., 1997), 'experiences in qualitative research', would seem to suggest adherence to the more restricted definition of ethnography.

3   Elspeth Probyn (1993) makes a related point about the excessive 'discursivity' of recent anthropological experiments in ethnographic writing, such as those espoused by Clifford and Marcus (1986) and carried out by Dumont (1978) (pp. 58–81). The problem with such writing, according to Probyn, is that it defines reflexivity as a heightened self–consciousness about strategies for textual representation of the 'other'. Probyn calls for greater attention to the gendered 'ontological self' engaging in material fieldwork; I would extend this to advocate a closer analysis of the mutual entanglements of 'self' and 'other' in the negotiation of 'social commitments'.

4   Even in cases where social reform did not provide the initial impetus for anthropological research, many prominent anthropologists came to more radical commitments as a result of their research. Franz Boas, considered by many to be the institutional founder of US anthropology, spent much of his career advancing an enlightened relativism which might curb some of the more insidious effects of movements like racial eugenics, or the excesses of ethnocentric, imperialist foreign policy (see Stocking, 1968).

5   Actually, some of the earliest and best examples of such ethnography were accomplished by black anthropologists like Zora Neale Hurston (1935) and Hortense Powdermaker (1966). More recent examples include the study of Jewish senior citizens by Barbara Myerhoff (1978) and Doug Foley's (1995) account of Indian–White relations in his hometown of Tama, Iowa. There is also a burgeoning literature on the so–called 'halfie' anthropologist (see Narayan, 1994), the US citizen who conducts fieldwork in the country of her own family's origin. For examples, see Narayan (1989), Abu-Lughod (1986), and Kondo (1990). It is not coincidental that most of this work continues to be done by women. For an interesting discussion of such work outside of anthropology, see the recent essay by Sofia Villenas (1996), who recounts her dilemma as an Ecuadorian-born 'Chicana' positioned as both insider and outsider in her fieldwork amongst Mexican migrants and Anglo officials in a North Carolina town.

6   Ethical guidelines for research in anthropology were rather more stringently formulated in the early 1970s, after heated discussion of a few prominent cases of unethical conduct. See Weaver (1973).

7   One important form of applied research in educational anthropology is the new field of ethnographic 'evaluation' (Fetterman, 1984; Fetterman and Pitman, 1986). There are continuous debates within anthropological circles about the value of applied research within major corporations and government agencies. Increasingly, anthropologists have been hired by agencies such as the World Bank or AID to provide recommendations for projects and carry out evaluative studies, while others are employed by corporations to assist in research on marketing, product design, or employee work conditions. Some anthropologists find this work enables progressive change from 'within' dominant institutions, perhaps mitigating some of their more harmful initiatives. Others argue that constraints placed on working in such technocratic or imperialistic institutions require

anthropologists to toe the ideological line. There is a long history of critique of the applied anthropology of development, beginning with articles such as those of Manners (1956) and Bonfil Batalla (1966), both reprinted in Weaver (1973). More recently, the volumes by Hobart (1993) and Escobar (1995) have raised serious questions about the complicity of anthropology in a 'development' discourse which either ignores or demeans local knowledge and interests. For a measured critique and discussion of applied anthropology, see Gledhill (1994, pp. 214–16), and for a cogent defense of applied development anthropology, see the commentary by Little and Painter (1995).

8   See for instance the work of University of Chicago anthropologist Terence Turner with the Kayapó Indians of Brazil (Turner, 1991, 1993).

9   See the new volume by Blot, Schmertzing, and Niehaus (in press) for an important collection of essays about key founding figures in anthropology of education. See the recent work by Douglas Foley (1990, 1995) for a more contemporary example of an anthropologist who combines trenchant theoretical contributions to the literature on cultural process with passionate commitment to progressive social change and equity across class and ethnic lines.

10   See Anderson (1989), Angus (1986), Carspecken (1995), Quantz (1992), and Simon and Dippo (1986) for useful overviews and original statements of critical ethnography.

11   The problematic relation between reflexivity and commitment has been perhaps most thoroughly and trenchantly explored in the literature on feminist theory and methodology in the social sciences. See, for example, Gluck and Patai (1991), Stacey (1988), Fonow and Cook (1991).

12   A good example of a study that achieves this is Shirley Brice Heath's (1983) renowned research with community–based language practices in two Southern communities and their impact on children's schooling. More recent examples include Delgado–Gaitan's work on literacy and empowerment among Mexican immigrants (1990, 1993) and Doug Foley's (1995) work on the harmful discursive rendering of 'otherness' amongst Mesquaki Indians and their White neighbors. Foley contributes to the improvement of local ethnic relations even as he provides useful theoretical insights into similar situations of inter-ethnic strife.

13   Geertz's work is best approached through his two collections of essays (1973, 1983). See Rockwell (1986) for a statement about the importance of Geertzian 'thick description' in Mexican educational reform initiatives.

14   This prologue was eventually revised and published (Levinson, 1993a).

15   I often think of Rosita and her mother when critical researchers decry the 'exploitation' of interpretive research. As I've noted, I believe there are intrinsic rewards to participation, and these rewards are often overlooked. Moreover, part of the felt rewards come from some participants' satisfaction in being part of a larger study. Many of my research participants were remarkably generous in this regard. They expressed a sense of importance in contributing to something larger, and they expected little in return. I would note, however, that this sense of participation may in fact presuppose prior understandings of, and commitments to, the value of 'science' and social inquiry. Janise Hurtig (1997) calls our attention to the different 'research cultures' of ethnographers and informants, noting how expectations may converge or diverge.

16   For a fuller discussion of the epistemological and practical debates about my research with girls, see my manuscript, '(How) can a man do feminist ethnography of education?' (Levinson, n.d.).

17   One project I currently envision would involve a collaboration with Mexican migrant youth recently entering the public school system of the state of Indiana. Another project

would involve a historical–ethnographic study of evolving ethnic relations between middle–class Jews and recently settled Mexican migrants in my own hometown, near Los Angeles. Each of these projects would engage my subjectivity as a participant in ways quite different from my research in Mexico.

References

ABU-LUGHOD, L. (1986) *Veiled Sentiments: Honor and Poetry in a Bedouin Society*, Berkeley, CA: University of California Press.

ANDERSON, G. (1989) 'Critical ethnography in education: Origins, current status, and new directions', *Review of Educational Research*, **59**, pp. 249–70.

ANGUS, L. (1986) 'Developments in ethnographic research in education: From interpretive to critical ethnography', *Journal of Research and Development in Education*, **20**, pp. 59–67.

ASAD, T. (1973) *Anthropology and the Colonial Encounter*, London: Ithaca Press.

BEHAR, R. and GORDON, D. (Eds.) (1995) *Women Writing Culture*, Berkeley, CA: University of California Press.

BLOT, R., NIEHAUS, J. and SCHMERTZING, R. (Eds.) (in press) *Foundations of Anthropology and Education: Critical Perspectives*, New York: Bergin and Garvey.

BODLEY, J. (1976) *Anthropology and Contemporary Human Problems*, Menlo Park, CA: Cummings Publishing Co.

BONFIL BATALLA, G. (1966) 'Conservative thought in applied anthropology: A critique', *Human Organization*, **25**, 2, pp. 89–92.

BRIGGS, J. (1970) *Never in Anger*, Cambridge, MA: Harvard University Press.

BRODKEY, L. (1987) *Academic Writing as Social Practice*, Philadelphia, PA: Temple University Press.

CALVO, B., DELGADO, G. and RUEDA, M. (Eds.) (1997) *Nuevos Paradigmas, Compromisos Renovados: Experiencias en la Investigación Cualitativa de la Educación*, Ciudad Juarez, Chih, Mexico/Albuquerque, NM: UACJ/University of New Mexico Press.

CARNOY, M. and LEVIN, H. (1985) *Schooling and Work in the Democratic State*, Stanford, CA: Stanford University Press.

CARSPECKEN, P. (1995) *Critical Ethnography in Educational Research: A Theoretical and Practical Guide*, New York: Routledge.

CLIFFORD, J. (1983) 'On ethnographic authority', *Representations*, **1**, 2, pp. 118–46.

CLIFFORD, J. and MARCUS, G. (Eds.) (1986) *Writing Culture: The Poetics and Politics of Ethnography*, Berkeley, CA: University of California Press.

CRAPANZANO, V. (1980) *Tuhami: Portait of a Moroccan*, Chicago, IL: University of Chicago Press.

DELGADO–GAITAN, C. (1990) *Literacy for Empowerment: The Role of Parents in Children's Education*, London: Falmer Press.

DELGADO–GAITAN, C. (1993) 'Researching change and changing the researcher', *Harvard Educational Review*, **63**, pp. 389–411.

DENZIN, N. (1996) 'The epistemological crisis in the human disciplines: Letting the old do the work of the new', in JESSOR, R. et al. (Eds.) *Ethnography and Human Development: Context and Meaning in Social Inquiry*, Chicago, IL: University of Chicago Press, pp. 127–52.

DI LEONARDO, M. (1991) *Gender at the Crossroads of Knowledge: Feminist Anthropology in the Post–modern Era*, Berkeley, CA: University of California Press.

DUMONT, J. (1978) *The Headman and I*, Austin, TX: University of Texas Press.

EMERSON, R., FRETZ, R. and SHAW, L. (1996) *Writing Ethnographic Fieldnotes*, Chicago, IL: University of Chicago Press.

ESCOBAR, A. (1995) *Encountering Development: The Making and Unmaking of the Third World*, Princeton, NJ: Princeton University Press.

EVERHART, R. (1983) *Reading, Writing, and Resistance: Adolescence and Labor in a Junior High School*, London: Routledge and Kegan Paul.

FABIAN, J. (1983) *Time and the Other: How Anthropology Makes its Object*, New York: Columbia University Press.

FETTERMAN, D.M. (1984) 'Guilty knowledge, dirty hands, and other ethical dilemmas: The hazards of contract research', in FETTERMAN, D.M. (Ed.) *Ethnography in Educational Evaluation*, Beverly Hills, CA: Sage, pp. 211–36.

FETTERMAN, D.M. and PITMAN, M.A. (Eds.) (1986) *Educational Evaluation: Ethnography in Theory, Practice, and Politics*, Beverly Hills, CA: Sage.

FINE, M. (1991) *Framing Dropouts: Notes on the Politics of an Urban Public High School*, Albany, NY: SUNY Press.

FINE, M. (1994) 'Dis-stance and other stances: Negotiations of power inside feminist research', in GITLIN, A. (Ed.) *Power and Method: Political Activism and Educational Research*, New York, Routledge: pp. 13–35.

FOLEY, D. (1990) *Learning Capitalist Culture: Deep in the Heart of Texas*, Philadelphia, PA: University of Pennsylvania Press.

FOLEY, D. (1995) *The Heartland Chronicles*, Philadelphia, PA: University of Pennsylvania Press.

FONOW, M. and COOK, J. (Eds.) (1991) *Beyond Methodology: Feminist Scholarship as Lived Research*, Bloomington, IN: Indiana University Press.

FRANCIS, D. (1996) 'Moving from noninterventionist research to participatory action: Challenges for academe', *International Journal of Qualitative Studies in Education*, **9**, 1, pp. 75–86.

FREIRE, P. (1973) *Education for Critical Consciousness*, New York: Seabury Press.

GEARING, F.O. (1970) *The Face of the Fox*, Chicago: Aldine.

GEERTZ, C. (1973) *The Interpretation of Cultures: Selected Essays*, New York: Basic Books.

GEERTZ, C. (1983) *Local Knowledge: Further Essays in Interpretive Anthropology*, New York: Basic Books.

GLEDHILL, J. (1994) *Power and its Disguises: Anthropological Perspectives on Politics*, Boulder, CO: Pluto Press.

GLUCK, S. and PATAI, D. (Eds.) (1991) *Women's Words: The Feminist Practice of Oral History*, New York: Routledge.

GORELICK, S. (1989) 'The changer and the changed: Metholodogical reflections on studying Jewish feminists', in JAGGAR, A. and BORDO, S. (Eds.) *Gender/Body/Knowledge: Feminist Reconstructions of Being and Knowing*, New Brunswick, NJ: Rutgers University Press, pp. 336–58.

HARAWAY, D. (1991) 'Situated knowledges: The science question in feminism and the privilege of partial perspective', *Simians, Cyborgs, and Women: The Reinvention of Nature*, New York: Routledge, pp. 183–201.

HARDING, S. (1992) 'After the neutrality ideal: Science, politics, and "strong objectivity"', *Social Research*, **59**, pp. 567–87.

HEATH, S.B. (1983) *Ways With Words: Language, Life, and Work in Communities and Classrooms*, Cambridge: Cambridge University Press.

HENRY, J. (1963) *Culture Against Man*, New York: Random House.

HOBART, M. (Ed.) (1993) *An Anthropological Critique of Development: The Growth of Ignorance*, London: Routledge.

HOLMBERG, A.R. (1958) 'The research and development approach to the study of change', *Human Organization*, **17**, 1, pp. 12–16.

HURSTON, Z. (1990 [1935]) *Mules and Men*, New York: Harper Perennial.

HURTIG, J. (1997) 'Gender lessons' PhD dissertation, University of Michigan.

KELLY, D.M. (1993) *Last Chance High: How Girls and Boys Drop In and Out of Alternative Schools*, New Haven, CT: Yale University Press.

KONDO, D. (1990) *Crafting Selves: Power, Gender, and Discourses of Identity in a Japanese Workplace*, Chicago, IL: University of Chicago Press.

LATHER, P. (1986) 'Issues of validity in openly ideological research: Between a rock and a soft place', *Interchange*, **17**, 4, pp. 63–84.

LATHER, P. (1991) *Getting Smart: Feminist Research and Pedagogy With/In the Post-modern*, New York: Routledge.

LEVINSON, B. (n.d.) '(How) can a man do feminist ethnography of education?', unpublished manuscript.

LEVINSON, B. (1992) 'Ogbu's anthropology and the critical ethnography of education: A reciprocal interrogation', *International Journal of Qualitative Studies in Education*, **5**, 3, pp. 205–25.

LEVINSON, B. (1993a) 'Accommodating voices: Notes for a critical school ethnography', *Critical Pedagogy Networker*, **6**, 4, pp. 1–10.

LEVINSON, B. (1993b) Todos somos iguales: Cultural production and social difference at a Mexican secondary school, PhD dissertation, Department of Anthropology, University of North Carolina–Chapel Hill.

LEVINSON, B. (1996) 'Social difference and schooled identity at a Mexican *secundaria*', in LEVINSON, B. et al. (Eds.) *The Cultural Production of the Educated Person: Critical Ethnographies of Schooling and Local Practice*, Albany, NY: State University of New York Press, pp. 211–38.

LEVINSON, B. (1997) 'The balance of power: Gender relations and women's action at a Mexican secondary school', in CALVO, B. et al. (Eds.) *Nuevos Paradigmas, Compromisos Renovados: Experiencias en la Investigación Cualitativa de la Educación*, Ciudad Juarez, Chih, Mexico/Albuquerque, NM: UACJ/University of New Mexico Press.

LEVINSON, B. (in press) 'Contradictions of gender and the (dis)empowerment of women at a Mexican secondary school', in TARRES, M.L. (Ed.) *Estudios de género en América Latina*, Mexico City, El Colegio de Mexico/LASA.

LEVINSON, B. and HOLLAND, D. (1996) 'The cultural production of the educated person: An introduction', in LEVINSON, B. et al. (Eds.) *The Cultural Production of the Educated Person: Critical Ethnographies of Schooling and Local Practice*, Albany, NY: State University of New York Press, pp. 1–54.

LISTON, D. (1988) *Capitalist Schools: Explanation and Ethics in Radical Studies in Schooling*, London: Routledge and Kegan Paul.

LITTLE, P. and PAINTER, M. (1995) 'Discourse, politics, and the development process: Reflections on Escobar's "Anthropology and the Development Encounter"', *American Ethnologist*, **22**, 3, pp. 602–16.

MANNERS, R. (1956) 'Functionalism, realpolitik, and anthropology in underdeveloped Areas', *America Indigena*, **16**, 1, pp. 7–33.

MARCUS, G. and FISCHER, M. (1986) *Anthropology as Cultural Critique: An Experimental Moment in the Human Sciences*, Chicago, IL: University of Chicago Press.

McCURDY, D. (1994) 'Using Anthropology', in SPRADLEY, J. and McCURDY, D. (Eds.) *Conformity and Conflict*, 6th ed., New York: Longman.

MIES, M. (1983) 'Towards a methodology for feminist research', in BOWLES, G. and KLEIN, R. (Eds.) *Theories of Women's Studies*, Boston, MA: Routledge and Kegan Paul, pp. 117–39.

MILLER, J. (1990) *Creating Spaces and Finding Voices: Teachers Collaborating for Empowerment*, Albany, NY: SUNY Press.

MYERHOFF, B. (1978) *Number Our Days*, New York, Simon and Schuster.

NARAYAN, K. (1989) *Storytellers, Saints, and Scoundrels: Folk Narrative in Hindu Religious Teaching*, Philadelphia, PA: University of Pennsylvania Press.

NARAYAN, K. (1994) 'How native is a "native" anthropologist', *American Anthropologist*, **95**, pp. 671–86.

PATAI, D. (1994) (Response) 'When method becomes power', in GITLIN, A. (Ed.) *Power and Method: Political Activism and Educational Research*, New York: Routledge, pp. 61–73.

POWDERMAKER, H. (1966) *Stranger and Friend: The Way of the Anthropologist*, New York: Norton.

PROBYN, E. (1993) *Sexing the Self: Gendered Positions in Cultural Studies*, London: Routledge.

QUANTZ, R. (1992) 'On critical ethnography', in LECOMPTE, M. et al. (Eds.) *The Handbook of Qualitative Research in Education*, San Diego, CA: Academic Press, pp. 447–506.

RABINOW, P. (1991) 'For hire: Resolutely late modern', in FOX, R. (Ed.) *Recapturing Anthropology: Working in the Present*, Santa Fe, NM: School of American Research Press, pp. 59–72.

REINHARZ, S. (1992) *Feminist Methods in Social Research*, Oxford: Oxford University Press.

ROCKWELL, E. (1986) 'La relevancia de la etnografía para la transformación de la escuela', in *Tercer Seminario Nacional de Investigación en Educación*, Bógota, Colombia: Instituto Colombiano para el Fomento de la Educación Superior.

ROCKWELL, E. (Ed.) (1995) *La escuela cotidiana*, Mexico: Fondo de Cultura Económica.

ROCKWELL, E. (in press) 'Ethnography and the commitment to public schooling: A review of research at the DIE', in ANDERSON, G. et al. (Eds.) *Qualitative Educational Research in Latin America: The Struggle for a New Paradigm*, New York: Garland.

SANJEK, R. (Ed.) (1990) *Fieldnotes: The Makings of Anthropology*, Ithaca, NY: Cornell University Press.

SAVAGE, M. (1988) 'Ethnographic narrative as a neighborly act', *Anthropology and Education Quarterly*, **19**, 1, pp. 3–19.

SCHULTZ, K. (1996) Book review of Meredith Rogers Cherland's *Private Practices: Girls Reading Fiction and Constructing Identity* in *Anthropology and Education Quarterly*, **27**, 3, pp. 453–55.

SIMON, R. and DIPPO, D. (1986) 'On critical ethnographic work', *Anthropology and Education Quarterly*, **17**, 3, pp. 195–202.

STACEY, J. (1988) 'Can there be a feminist ethnography?', *Women's Studies International Forum*, **11**, 1, pp. 21–7.

STOCKING, G. (1968) *Race, Culture, and Evolution*, Chicago, IL: University of Chicago Press.

TEDLOCK, B. (1991) 'From participant observation to the observation of participation: The emergence of narrative ethnography', *Journal of Anthropological Research*, **47**, 1, pp. 69–94.

TURNER, T. (1991) 'Representing, resisting, rethinking: Historical transformations of Kayapo culture and anthropological consciousness', in STOCKING, G. (Ed.) *Colonial Situations: Essays in the Contextualization of Ethnographic Knowledge*, History of Anthropology, #7, Madison, WI: University of Wisconsin Press, pp. 285–313.

TURNER, T. (1993) 'The role of indigenous peoples in the environmental crisis: The case of the Brazilian Kayapo', *Perspectives in Biology and Medicine*, **36**, 3, pp. 526–45.

VAN GALEN, J. and EAKER, D. (1995) 'Beyond settling for scholarship: On defining the beginning and ending points of post–modern research', in PINK, W. et al. (Eds.) *Continuity and Contradiction: The Futures of the Sociology of Education*, Cresskill, NY: Hampton Press, pp. 113–31.

VILLENAS, S. (1996) 'The colonizer/colonized Chicana ethnographer: Identity, marginalization, and cooptation in the field', *Harvard Educational Review*, **66**, 4, pp. 711–31.

WEAVER, T. (1973) 'Toward an anthropological statement of relevance', in WEAVER, T. (Ed.) *To See Ourselves: Anthropology and Modern Social Issues*, Glenview, IL: Scott Foresman, pp. 1–4.

WILLIS, P. (1977) *Learning to Labor: How Working Class Kids Get Working Class Jobs*, New York: Columbia University Press.

7 On Writing Reflexive Realist Narratives

Douglas Foley

It took a while for the initial post–modern critiques of ethnographic writing (Marcus and Cushman, 1982; Clifford and Marcus, 1986) to catch on. First, a little spurt of books and articles (Geertz, 1988; Clifford, 1988; Rosaldo, 1989; Manganaro, 1990; Atkinson, 1990; Crapanzano, 1992, Clough, 1992) began seeping out the cracks in positivistic science. Soon the trickles turned into a torrent of philosophical statements and personal nostrums for writing 'experimental ethnographies'. Although I fancy myself a fledgling writer of such texts (Foley, 1990, 1995), I have almost given up trying to survey this rising commentary.

Over the years, I have experimented with socialist, dialectical, magical, and autobiographical realist practices in an effort to develop a more reflexive realist narrative style. This chapter first describes how I write ethnographies, then it contrasts my notions of 'hybrid voice' and 'reflexive realist narratives' to three recent feminist and feminist post–structuralist approaches (Behar, 1996; Britzman, 1995; Lather and Smithies, 1995). Hopefully, these reflections on my narrative practices will be of use to other ethnographers who are experimenting with narrative forms.

The Classical Scientific Realist Narrative

Unlike many ethnographers, I was never motivated to write in what Marcus and Cushman (1982) define as a 'scientific realist' narrative style. According to Marcus and Cushman, scientific realism, which dominated anthropological writing until the 1970s, uses several key writing conventions. First, the positionality and tone of the author is crucial. To evoke an authoritative voice, the author must speak in the third person and be physically, psychologically, and ideologically absent from the text. That lends the text an aura of omniscience. The all–knowing interpretive voice speaks from a distant, privileged vantage point in a detached, measured tone.

Second, the extensive use of conceptual language helps create a common denominator people of social archetypes and roles rather than complex, idiosyncratic individuals.

Third, detailed, typified descriptions of everyday life, for example, a day in the life of x people, or the life cycle of x people, help create common denominator events that convey a coherent, orderly cultural whole rather than a contradictory cultural scene.

Fourth, the native world view is faithfully represented through a closely edited and arranged set of typical statements that legitimate the author's perspective.

Ultimately, the ethnographer produces an abstract, generalizable portrait of a typical people doing typical things in a timeless space called the 'ethnographic present'. To be a literate academic anthropologist is to write in an abstract, formalistic intellectual language which freezes ordinary people and everyday life into a neat, coherent, timeless portrait.

Phenomenologist Alfred Schutz (1964) characterizes such language as a 'second order language of abstract typifications or constructs'. Ideally, a scientific language is relatively free of connotative and ambiguous expressions such as metaphor, irony, paradox, satire. Schutz (1967) makes clear, however, that second order language or sociological theorizing can never transcend its roots in ordinary language and common sense understandings of reality. Language philosophers like Wittgenstein (1953) gave up on the logical positivist fantasy of a purely denotative, objective language decades before the current post–modern critiques of writing and representational forms.

But notions of an authoritative formal, objective language, die hard. Many practitioners still believe that scientific narratives must be written in as abstract and formalistic a language as possible. Such narratives must be organized around a series of second order abstractions that characterize, compare, and classify the lived experience being observed. More importantly, such texts must not drift into the vortex of ordinary connotative, personal, expressive language and its endless forms of linguistic play. As Michel Foucault (1972) notes, there really is no author in academic writing. There are only authoritative discourses and their discursive regimes. Many of these authoritative discourses emerge from new academic disciplines that form a vast new social scientific surveillance apparatus.

Moreover, if we adopt Bourdieu's (1984) view of academia as the site of bourgeois taste cultures, academics are the new professional middle class of cultural workers (Ehrenreich, 1989). Even allegedly 'radical scholars' who break with their ideological role as scientific surveillance expert do not necessarily eschew the academic culture and its preferred discourse style. Many such scholars continue to ply the aesthetics, language games, and form of literacy that they mastered as graduate students and untenured assistant professors. Despite recent experimentation, most academic writers still convey their lived experiences in the vastly impoverished aesthetics and referential forms of a bourgeois academic discourse.

Having gone to graduate school in the 1960s, my dissertation (Foley, 1976) was definitely, as post–structuralists are fond of saying, 'an effect' of scientific realism's discursive regime. Social science at Stanford during that era had a decidedly fundamentalist, scientistic flavor. Nevertheless, the West coast of the 1960s was an interesting place politically and culturally. It fed my distrust of an academic elite and its myth of a neutral, detached social science. Being the son of a tenant farmer, academic literacy and writing in the scientific realist mode always felt like a bad bargain. My new academic language always left me feeling ill–prepared to write something that ordinary people could understand.

By 1977, I wrote my second ethnography entitled *From Peones to Politicos* (Foley, 1989). *Peones* was a study of the rise and fall of the La Raza Unida Party. That text is long on sixties' political ideology and short on narrative experimentation.

Nevertheless, the book has some narrative moments, primarily because of my initial training as a historian. Following Hayden White's (1973) typology of historical metanarratives, *Peones* captures the tragic, comic aspects of an epic racial/class struggle. It has a didactic, somewhat morally indignant tone. Its characters are social archetypes reminiscent of the simple, politically graphic characters in Bertold Brecht's epic theater (Brecht, 1964). These caricatures of complex people tend to get lost in overly detailed accounts of oppressive structures and heroic resistance. Chicano radicals — in the guise of grocers, migrant workers, and single parent mothers — overwhelm the white landed gentry and its corrupt political machines. *Peones* is more a socialist realist tract than an innovative popular ethnography, but it begins to break various academic and scientific writing conventions.

In a more recent ethnography, *Learning Capitalist Culture* (LCC) (1990), I portray how a South Texas high school stages the deployment of different kinds of linguistic capital. The study highlights how middle class Chicano students use deceptive and dehumanizing bourgeois speech styles to achieve school success, yet retain their ethnic distinctiveness and pride. Conversely, working class Chicanos deploy non–standard English and non–bourgeois manners and are labeled, punished, and pushed out of school. Their lack of communicative competence in deceptive speech preserves their working class language, thus increases their chances of failing. Theoretically, this work represents an extension of Marx's notion of alienated labor and Lukacs' (1972) reification thesis into the domain of everyday language or communicative labor.

Narratively, LCC breaks more thoroughly with the language of scientific ethnography than *Peones* did. To avoid jargon–filled descriptions of football, dating, and academic work, I placed my theoretical/interpretive perspective in an appendix. This narrative move violates a sacred convention of scientific realist narratives — the textual unity of a running theoretical commentary on the thick descriptions of everyday cultural practices. In addition, my interpretive perspective is presented in an autobiographical style. Personal class experiences are juxtaposed with academic readings. There is no pretense that I am deploying an abstract, universalistic scientific theory without personal roots.

In addition, vignettes of my interactions with kids and teachers are sprinkled throughout the text. They help convey that the narrative was mutually produced. There is no pretense that I am standing above or outside the experience and simply recording it. Narratively, I use what John Van Mannen (1988) calls an 'impressionist' first–person style. The story of how youth learn capitalist culture is told with a healthy dose of metaphor, irony, parody, and satire. Specific events and actual personal encounters are reported rather than composite typifications of events and characters. Such an extensive use of ordinary language narrative practices makes the story very accessible to non–academic readers.

Nevertheless, the tone and voice of LCC is still rather analytic and striving to make transcendent statements. The text is tightly structured around a unified theoretical perspective and its strong knowledge claims. The text is realist in the sense that Lukacs (1964) characterizes nineteenth century bourgeois novels. He argues that socialist intellectuals and nineteenth century bourgeois artists and novelists practice critical or dialectical realism when they uncover the hidden, dehumanizing reification of everyday life under capitalism. At the time, I did not describe my narrative practice as dialectical realism, but in retrospect, my primary goals were similar to these novelists. Like them, I wanted 'to reveal the driving forces of history which are invisible to actual consciousness'.

In this case, I wanted to portray the ordinary language games in classrooms, dating, and sports as a linguistic factory that stages ritualized speech events. During these events, humans treat each other as objects, thus reproduce the logic of capitalism. I, the transcendent ethnographic observer of capitalist ideology, was uncovering what most Americans take for granted as fun and fulfilling. I was providing a 'deep reading' of seemingly innocent everyday popular culture practices like football, dating, and horsing around in class.

Developing a More Hybrid Voice and Ordinary Language Narrative

After finishing LCC, I continued to question whether my realist portrayal of life in South Texas was a sharp enough break with scientific realism. After reading many post–modern and post–Marxist critiques of ethnographic writing, I decided to raise the emotional stakes in my next fieldwork. I reasoned that writing about and for old friends and relatives would force me to find a third, less academic, more reflexive, hybrid voice. Such a voice was supposed to bridge the vast cultural and linguistic gap between academics and ordinary people. So I returned to my hometown to write about white–Indian relations. *The Heartland Chronicles* (Foley, 1995) highlights the Mesquakis' struggle to survive culturally. It recounts their battle against the ideological hegemony of the media, well–intentioned academics, bumbling BIA policy, assimilationist schools, crusading missionaries, tourism, and local racists.

One ethnography that inspired me to develop a more hybrid voice is Barbara Myerhoff's *Number Our Days*, (1982). *Number Our Days* is a loving portrait of Holocaust survivors in a California nursing home. On some level, Myerhoff 'goes home' to study her people and cultural tradition. As Marc Kaminsky (1992) has noted, her narrative fuses the voice of the storyteller and the informants in an unusual way. Myerhoff deposits her authorial word inside informants' speech. Assuming the role of their cultural next–of–kin, she retains their Yiddish syntax and gives their fractured English an aura of wisdom and depth. This is done through a series of unusually powerful vignettes of conflicts at the nursing home. She then creates one elder who interprets these events with the wisdom of both a traditional Jew and a cultural anthropologist. This touching character becomes a kind of medium through which Myerhoff speaks authoritatively about cultural traditions. Although this literary device works well dramatically, it does not make the text more reflexive. Myerhoff's all–knowing third voice actually obscures the extent that she invents a fictionalized narrator.

In contrast, I tried to develop a hybrid or third voice that is rooted in my native dialect, thus blends 'Iowaese' into 'anthropologese'. The key to making this transformation was actually regaining my Iowa sense of humor. Having picked up the biting, sarcastic, detached voice of an urban academic, I had to rediscover the indirect, understated, self–deprecating voice that I learned growing up in rural Iowa. I had to relearn the art of sitting around and poking fun at events and people. I used this powerful, distinct oral speech style to leaven the abstract, generalizing, classifying, typologizing discourse of theoretical anthropology. In post–structuralist terms, I narrate and interpret events in a voice that breaks with the formal, detached voice of a disciplinary discourse. Put another way, I speak Marxese, Foucaultese, and Bourdieuese with a strong Iowa accent.

In retrospect, I wanted to pollute these academic scientific discourses with ordinary language. I wanted to speak/write in a way that met ordinary people half–way. In return, I expect the local folks to engage and learn from what is left of my anthropological voice. Countless methodological articles have been written about how researchers develop reciprocity with their informants. We all know how to do little favors for informants to get information. By speaking in a hybrid voice, I wanted to creates a new kind of 'linguistic reciprocity' that helps bridge the cultural and linguistic gap that disciplinary discursive regimes have created. I wanted to demonstrate my respect for and skill in the language of local people both during the fieldwork and in the final written ethnography.

The key narrative move that creates linguistic reciprocity is the foregrounding of people, characters, and events over theoretical commentary. Such a narrative makes displaying one's mastery of academic discourses, hence one's cultural capital, secondary. Unfortunately, colleagues who do not read carefully — and there are many — may caricature and devalue such hybrid texts as untheoretical, popularizing accounts. My own students are quick to label this narrative style 'informal', 'loose', and 'professionally risky'. Professional preferences for a formal, theory–driven, impersonal academic discursive style die hard. This call for backgrounding theoretical discussions is not, however, an argument for ethnographic texts devoid of theory. The *Chronicles* is actually full of social scientific constructs, but my explanatory ideas rarely interrupt the narrative flow. They are either integrated into the stories being chronicled or are in the background and explicated succinctly.

Backgrounding theory and foregrounding personal experiences also helps convey the complex, constructed nature of the authorial self. Whatever essentialist, unified authorial self remains, the text conveys that I am both implicated in and detached from local white culture. *Chronicles* tries to disrupt various scientific and post–modern self–representations of the heroic author as the all–knowing scientist, philosopher, or poet. Instead, I speak from a subject position that makes situated, partial knowledge claims rather than grand universalistic knowledge claims. Conveying such a subject position helps disrupt the omniscient observer of scientific realist narratives. Another major way that I decenter my authorial voice is through a series of native tales and theories.

Diversifying the Voice Through Native Tales and Theories

Typically, the scientific narrator in ethnographic texts is like the rational, interpretive talking heads one finds in documentary films. After describing various everyday events, the narrator intrudes and announces authoritatively what it all means. During these interpretive moments, the narrator dispassionately deploys abstract theories and a literature review. Rather than rely on a single expert interpretive voice, an ethnographic text can also let local people explain their own reality. To this end, *Chronicles* elevates a variety of stories told by Mesquakis to the status of formal or 'official' interpretations of their lived reality. For example, I use several 'native theories' of cultural change to represent how Mesquakis adapt to white cultural intrusions.

After considerable fieldwork, I realized that tribal historian Jonas CutCow's explanation of how Mesquaki culture changes is very similar to Eugene Roosen's (1989) theory of ethnogenesis and self–determination. CutCow argues that the traditionalists and the progressives are locked into a constructive dialogue that moves the tribe forward. After presenting his theory, I recount how anthropologists and journalists have consistently misread this intertribal dialogue as destructive factionalism and assimilation. Ultimately Jonas' idea becomes my second order construct that explains how Mesquakis make their own history. This narrative technique undermines the usual assumption that only professional researchers produce superior second order languages. By elevating Jonas' voice to an authoritative, generalizing discourse, I am undermining this distancing practice of academics. In effect, I am saying that CutCow's theory is as good, if not better, than Roosen's theory.

Like Meyerhoff, I am using the wisdom of a Mesquaki organic intellectual to interpret Mesquaki cultural life. But unlike Meyerhoff, I am not creating a character who speaks for me in Mesquaki and anthropologese. CutCow speaks as a cultural insider for himself with anthropological–like ideas. This encounter signals readers that my interpretations often flow from intense intellectual and emotional engagements with people like Jonas. Similar encounters occurred with the poet Ted Facepaint about narratives, with the politician Claude Windsong about ethics, and with traditionalists Lone Trueblood and Ernest Truetongue about tribal tradition. In all these encounters, we all speak in our own voice, and the encounters produce important stories and interpretations. Narrating in this manner helps portray how mutually constructed and situational my knowledge claims actually are.

In addition, I present several Mesquaki stories that many whites felt were fantastic superstitions. For example, the *Chronicles* includes a story about a BIA agent who sought to terminate the tribal school and died in a plane crash shortly after the termination. Traditionalists on the settlement believe that God terminated the agent who was trying to kill Mesquaki culture. Another example is the story of the wind that God sent to blow down the powwow tent placed near the casino. In this case, God was sending the Mesqukais a warning that they were off their chosen path and veering towards white culture and materialism. I present these tales somewhat like Gabriel Garcia Marquez uses 'magical realist' stories in his fiction. These Mesquaki stories are presented as events that may mean what the Mesquakis say they mean. By presenting the stories without qualifying interpretive commentary, I hope to cast some shadows of doubt on my interpretive powers. They also provide a window into this unique culture.

Douglas Foley

Blurring the Genre with Autobiography and Travel Writing

Another way I try to make *Chronicles* more reflexive, thus disruptive of naive real-ism, is through 'blurring' the ethnographic genre (Geertz, 1983). I borrow narrative practices from cognate genres such as autoethnography, autobiography, and travel writing. Some time back, David Hayano (1979) labeled the writings of 'native ethnographers' who study their own culture 'autoethnographies'. In some sense, I qualify as an autoethnographer. Researching my hometown gave me a measure of credibility and acceptance among selected whites and Mesquakis. To a degree, I was a cultural insider with prior knowledge of the people being studied. I had some ability to be accepted or pass as a native member. Utilizing one's insider connec-tions embraces the epistemological importance of intimacy over detachment. Gener-ally, Hanyano finds the written style of such autoethnographies to be more intimate, descriptive, holistic and less theoretical.

Chronicles also makes explicit use of autobiographical memories in a man-ner advocated by feminist ethnographer Lila Abu–Lughod (1990, 1991). She argues for replacing the language of generalization with a language of 'tactical human-ism.' For her, the little–known body of anthropological writing by non–professional anthropological wives (Fernea, 1969; Shostak, 1981) exemplify what she calls an 'ethnography of the particular'. Like autoethnographies, autobiographical ethno-graphies shift the basis of the researcher's authority to subjective and intersubjective experiences. Such a narrative move helps convey that the author speaks from a partial, bounded position rather than an impartial god–like position. These richly textured, highly personal, more autobiographical books fulfill what feminist philo-sophers like Donna Haraway (1988) are advocating. They replace the objective knowledge claims of the omniscient, transcendent observer with the situated, partial knowledge claims of a historical observer.

For example, the *Chronicles* begins with me recounting my youthful feelings about and experiences with Indians and racism. I recount my romanticizations of Indians, my timidity to speak out against white school bullies, and my general indifference to and ignorance of local racism. I claim to be a metaphor for most local whites. Many townspeople bear no intense malice towards the Mesquaki, but we have little interest in and knowledge of their way of life. The *Chronicles* then recounts what I missed about the mysterious Mesquakis. I pour over old newspaper and find many derogatory white attitudes and actions. White anti–Indian sentiments culminate in a hysterical, comic temperance campaign. As the fieldwork progresses, I experience first–hand more of Mesquaki culture and historical memory. I recount what I see and hear about everyday reservation life, traditional ceremonies, and politics. In the end, Mesquaki culture is portrayed as a very dynamic mix of Indian and white cultural traditions.

In retrospect, the *Chronicles* narrative reads a little like a travelogue of my discoveries. Post–modernist James Clifford (1988), having recounted how profes-sional anthropology broke with travel writing, finds more kinship between these two genres than most scientific anthropologists admit. Most early anthropologists worked hard to distance themselves from travel writing to establish ethnography as a professional science. More recently, anthropologists, who share Mary Louise Pratt's (1992) critical view of colonial travel writing, work hard to distance their work from the ideological excesses of that genre.

I would, however, claim some kinship with the best of modern, non–professional travel writing, which is often produced by ex–Peace Corps volunteers. In Maurice Thomsen's *Living Poor*, (1972) one finds an American dedicated to working in and learning about a strange place. Such travelers are less imperial and chauvinistic than many military, business, government, and academic travelers are. Some of these new amateur travel writers simply want to engage the cultural other in deeply personal ways. The best of these intimate accounts are reminiscent of another group of talented amateurs, the anthropological wives. If nothing else, *Chronicles* is written in the spirit of exploration and personal engagement that these non–professionals often exude.

A final way that *Chronicles* disrupts and breaks with scientific and dialectical realism is by contexualizing my representations within a field of past representations. George Marcus (1994) argues that reflexivity is generally conveyed in three basic ways through: (i) personal confessionals; (ii) multiple, conflicting representations of cultural others; and (iii) epistemological ruminations.

As already indicated, the text has a steady undercurrent of confessional autobiographical moments. In addition, the text is dedicated to presenting multiple, conflicting representations of cultural others. Instead of structuring the narrative around a unifying master theory, I structure it around the stories that whites and Indians tell about each other. The cultural divide between the races is portrayed as a series of 'discursive skirmishes'. Mesquakis and whites disagree over local politics, education, speech styles, sports, alcohol consumption, the powwow celebration, the casino, and mysterious deaths on the train tracks. Each of these topics spawn a flood of white talk that is countered by a torrent of Indian talk. This everyday war of words — expressed through homilies, jokes, laments, divine occurrences, and newspaper accounts — is strung together into one long story. The narrative makes public the private feelings of each group.

In post–modern jargon, *The Heartland Chronicles* portrays how racial groups 'other' or invent and misrepresent each other. It also details how outside academics and journalists and a new crop of Mesquaki writers feed images into the local authoring process. My voice is presented as one more in a long line of voices. More importantly, I also try to 'deconstruct' my account with a community review process. Forty of the key characters read and critiqued a draft of the *Chronicles*, and the highlights of their commentary are published in the epilogue. Several reviewers claim I misrepresent and romanticize events and characters. They also say that my story is just a story, not an objective, scientific account.

What the *Chronicles* lacks in terms of reflexive practices are long technical discussions about epistemology and representation. I do address these weighty matters, however, through a series of parodies and humorous stories. Perhaps the most powerful is the parody of anthropologists in the act of searching for and salvaging 'authentic Mesquaki culture'. Using the old fieldnotes of several student anthropologists, I retell the story of how they try to buy their way into a clan ceremony. After much confusion and teeth–gnashing, they come to the ceremonial house with chicken in hand, slip in — despite gentle protests — and end up ignored and unfed. Their elaborate rationalizations of these events are both intense and comic. Later in the text, I draw some parallels with my own nervous, foolish behavior at ceremonies, which is also recounted humorously. Finally, I use a parable about scientists as vampires, and a comic encounter with a Mesquaki 'post–modern poet', to throw into question my interpretive powers.

I avoid, however, much explicit discussion about epistemological and ethical questions. I eschew such discussions because expressing philosophical scepticism seems to be a new rhetoric that is replacing the old scientific rhetoric of sample, validity, and reliability. Worrying over epistemology and representational issues has become another rhetorical convention to establish, not undermine, the author's authority. Worse still, this new rhetoric still reproduces the academic high culture. The ethnographer as sceptical philosopher–poet is some improvement over the ethnographer as objective scientist, but the agents of the academy are still doing most of the talking and writing.

'Reflexive Realism' as a Response to Post–modern Critiques

What all the aforementioned narrative practices add up to is my response to the post–modern critique of realism. But unlike many post–modernists, I cannot abandon realist narrative practices so quickly — not because I cling to modernist notions of identity, language, and reality — but because I cling to the goal of communicating with ordinary people. The place to start may be with what Gramsci (1971) calls the contradictory common sense understanding of people. In this case, we must start with ordinary peoples' familiarity with realist story–telling conventions. We cannot expect people to respond to unfamiliar avant-garde ethnographies any more than they respond to cubism or other high modernist expressive forms. The challenge is to create new forms of realism that engage ordinary people, but also disrupt any tendencies they have to read the books of experts uncritically.

In retrospect, the kind of realist narrative that I am trying to create has some kinship with the realism of Bertold Brecht's epic theater (1964). I try to avoid his use of archetypical characters to propagandize the audience, but I break the realist frame the way he does. Brecht uses narrators who announce to the audience that his plays are 'just a play'. At various points, my narrative signals the audience that they are reading 'just an ethnographic account', i.e., just a chronicle of my experience, not a carbon copy of reality. Nevertheless, some locals, and many non–locals, will still read my account as an 'official' objective history. I try to counter this tendency with a epilogue that presents local views of the *Chronicles*. In this epilogue, several locals point out that I am biased and was probably duped by my informants. These readers do not read the text the way a naive realist would. I apparently sent them enough disruptive signals to make clear how constructed and personal the text is.

Ultimately, all of us who are claiming to produce more reflexive texts need more audience response data on how non–technical readers make sense of our texts

(Moores, 1993). As indicated, I have some idea how locals read and understood my text, but none of us really know that much about how our texts work. Post–modernists are quick to lament the powerful 'discursive effects' of realism, but they provide little evidence that the realist texts they flog are irredeemably hegemonic. One would hope that ordinary people will be able to deconstruct and critique the newer reflexive realists texts more easily. As I continue to collect reader responses to the *Chronicles*, it may turn out that not everyone is a philosopher, as Gramsci claims. On the other hand, not everyone will be a dupe. No doubt, many will express the healthy scepticism that my local reviewers did.

I would like to conclude this paper with brief reviews of two post–structuralist ethnographies (Lather and Smithies, 1995; Britzman, 1991) and one feminist auto–biographical ethnography (Behar, 1993, 1996). Reading the works of these fine ethnographers has helped me clarify what I was apparently doing in the *Chronicles*. Let me begin with Pattie Lather's innovative new manuscript entitled *Troubling Angels* (Lather and Smithies, 1995).

Patti Lather's *Troubling Angels: Women Living with HIV*

In a recent article, Lather (1996) champions a 'hypertext pistache' narrative style that seeks to thoroughly disrupt realist textual assumptions and practices. She graphically and visually splits the text into a clearly demarcated set of stories organized around topics generated in focus group discussions with HIV positive women. At the bottom of the text, Lather and her coauthor make running commentaries that tack back and forth between a personal, autobiographical voice and a formal, academic voice.

She and Smithies make no attempt, however, to write a unified, seamless text mediated through the authors' omniscient pen and voice. According to Lather, such narratives lapse too easily into naive realism. To disrupt and break the ideological grip of realism, yet produce a popular, accessible 'KMart text', Lather creates a messy, disjointed jumble of unorchestrated voices. It is not clear how edited and selected the dialogues with these women are, but they do seem less constructed than the usual ethnography.

Lather feels that her split text, which features parallel ways of speaking in different registers, helps undermine her authorial authority and voice. But something much more personal, the horror and grandeur of these HIV–positive women, sends the inveterate theorizer of *Getting Smart* (Lather, 1991) packing. Early on in the fieldwork, it strikes Lather that the inexplicable events and people she is witnessing must be the return of mythical angels. This metaphor apparently helps Lather quell old academic habits to produce neat, dichotomous explanations. Ultimately, the main interpretive commentary is expressed obliquely through angel stories and through boxed off 'factoids', i.e., the latest and best information we presently have on AIDs. Thus we have the rational, sceptical ex–Catholic, ex–Marxist, ex–scientist speaking in metaphors and factoids rather than in a formal, second order academic discourse.

In many ways, *Troubling Angels* does allow everyone — the researchers and the women who are HIV–positive — to have their own say. Many of their stories are particularly touching, and judging from the preliminary reader response, the women like the text very much. It gives them a voice in a relatively unmediated way. Since Lather thinks of herself as breaking radically with realist assumptions and practices, she exhibits little interest, however, in explaining the residual realism of her text. Her narrative practice seem very similar to the surrealist representational practices of French ethnologists in the 1920s and 1930s (Clifford, 1988). Like Lather, the French surrealists placed a heavy emphasis on juxtapositions or montages that jarred the reader/observer's common sense reality.

The price of letting everybody speak the way they feel like speaking is, however, a disjointed, chaotic text. The reader has to work to make sense out of the various stories, the factoids, the reflections on angels, and the epistemological laments. No authorial engine and organizing voice coordinates and blends these voices. There is no easily marked beginning, middle, and end. No linear chronology, argument, or plot structures the narrative. Consequently, I ended up browsing the text, reading bits and pieces, reading it like I watch MTV. I tuned in when something struck my fancy and tuned out when something bored me. It clearly disrupted my desire for a clear, transparent realist ethnography about these women, but the text is a little too surrealistic for my tastes. I did not necessarily work harder to make the meaning that the authors defer to the reader, and I suspect that other readers will react the same way. My reader response is obviously a function of my preference for linear, modernist texts with clear story lines and strong characters. Nevertheless, still I found the text interesting and engaging in a strange way.

What I find more problematic about Lather's new text, however, is her spirited polemic against clear, accessible language (Lather and Smithies, 1995). She evokes the work of post–structuralist Freudian Jacque Lacan that the unconscious is like a language, a language that is often unspeakable and resistant to easy translation. Lacan takes this notion of the unspeakable so far as to argue that 'not being understood is some kind of ethical imperative'. She then supports Lacan's call for a deep, complex language of interpretation with a quote from critical theorist Henry Giroux. He seems to be parroting Adorno and Marcuse when he says, 'sometimes we need a density that fits the thoughts being expressed. In such places, clear and concise plain prose would be a sort of cheat tied to the anti–intellectualism rife in US society . . .'. Taken at face value, this kind of justification of a deep, complex language over clear, assessable language privileges the high culture language of intellectuals.

It turns out, however, that Lather is not simply parroting a modernist defense of the Western high culture and its intelligensia. She is defending the rights of marginalized academics, such as women and people of color, to be intellectuals and theorists, too. She narrates a tale of oppressive academic politics and cites Toril Moi's view that women must not be content to leave high theory to men. She also recounts Wahemma Lubiano's observation that marginalized intellectuals must elbow themselves into the theory game. Unfortunately, this line of argument still seems to preserve the ordinary culture/high culture language dichotomy in some unintended, uncomfortable ways.

Moreover, her polemic against unnamed clear and accessible speech advocates — who apparently deride 'high theory as a masturbatory activity aimed at the privileged few' — highlights the worst possible defense of clear, accessible academic writing. This sort of bombast may settle some old scores, but it ends up distracting Lather from a more careful examination of realist thought and narrative experimentation. She seems to reduce all forms of realist philosophy and realist representational practices to what Putnam (1987) calls 'naive realism'. Such a notion of realism excludes more nuanced philosophical discussions of realism (Putnam, 1990; Bhaskar, 1989) and early modernist representational experiments in literature, theater, and art (Bradbury and McFarlane, 1972). These experiments have inspired a number of experimental ethnographies that Lather probably finds promising (Clifford, 1988; Marcus and Fischer, 1986; Behar and Gordon, 1995).

Deborah Britzman's *Practice Makes Practice: A Critical Study of Learning to Teach*

Britzman's *Practice Makes Practice* represents a rather different post–structuralist textual solution than Lather's *Troubling Angels*. In a recent article, she claims that 'post–structuralist concerns haunt my ethnographic research, writing, and reading' about student teachers. Following Foucault and Raymond Williams, she seeks to do an 'archaeology' of the 'discursive regime' and 'structure of feelings' that affect the way student teachers think and feel about teaching. She reframes Lukacs' Hegelian–Marxian jargon with Foucault's post–structuralist's jargon, and advocates going beyond descriptions of surface reality to a 'deeper reading' of her subjects' lived reality. In this instance, Britzman is studying the ideology, or as she puts it, the 'mythology of professionalism' that young teachers struggle against as they learn to teach. This leads her to study 'how student teachers become an invention of the educational apparatus, how they become constituted as a problem population'.

Narratively, Britzman portrays, this complex, contradictory learning process with rich, detailed cases of two student teachers. These cases are set within an organizational nexus of cooperating teachers, principals, peers, and university teacher education specialists and the wider educational discourses of crises of the Reagan years. She highlights how teachers cope with antagonistic discourses and three fundamental mythologies that teachers are — autonomous, expert, and self–made.

Britzman (1995) describes her break with 'conventional, essentializing realist narratives with unitary subjects and linear chronologies' as a difficult personal struggle. Ultimately, she uses Walter Benjamin's notion of a photographic metaphorically to describe her new post–structural narrative style as enlarging the snapshot, hence revealing 'new structural formations of the subject'. She reasons that the student teaching experience is a 'discursive site of struggle', thus a 'disorderly, discontinuous, and chaotic narrative' will best capture the unruly process of constructing a professional identity. Moreover, since subjects are always constrained by the discourses and histories that pre–figure them, their stories, thus the stories of their ethnographer, are always partial.

121

In effect, Britzman's solution to the problem of realist narratives and representations relies more on a new critical discourse/theory rather than on highly innovative narrative practices. She seems to be arguing that if one starts with a more sophisticated notion of reality, i.e., a discursively constructed reality, then it follows that one's narrative will be more complex, hence more representative or truthful. Her approach is much closer to what Clifford and Marcus (1986) call the anthropology cultural critique than to the old scientific realist tradition. In this tradition, the scientist who objectively records reality is replaced with the engaged, passionate social critic who unmasks hidden, naturalized reality.

Narratively, Britzman's *Practice makes Practice* is a more conventional academic ethnography that Lather's more surrealistic *Troubling Angels*. She speaks in a detached, authoritative Foucaldian discourse/voice throughout her text. Britzman weaves the theoretical and the descriptive into one seamless, linear, theory–driven argument that demonstrates the utility of her post–structuralist world view. She tacks back and forth between relatively descriptive material on the student teachers and their peers and rather dense interpretive commentary. And like many good critical ethnographers, Britzman is not particularly autobiographical or openly subjective. But she does make an effort to be reflexive in other ways and to foreground how she produces her account.

Ruth Behar's *The Vulnerable Observer and Translated Woman*

Another narrative strand of feminist ethnographic writing emphasizes using an autobiographical voice (Okely and Callaway, 1992; Behar and Gordon, 1995). This new style of autobiographical writing breaks, however, with the old Western, modernist notion of autobiography as the linear progression of a lone individual outside history and culture. In sharp contrast, Behar constructs the autobiography of both the anthropologist and the cultural other. Her accounts explore personal and scientific authority, as well as ego boundaries. This new style of autobiographical ethnography reintroduces a powerful authorial voice, but is based on a less unified, essentialist modern notion of personal identity. The end result is a highly reflexive portrayal of the author as a constructed, conflicted, multiple–self.

No one ethnographer personifies these new trends, but the work of Ruth Behar (1993, 1996) provides an excellent starting point. Behar summarizes her approach in *The Vulnerable Observer* (1996) by saying 'anthropology that does not break your heart is not worth doing'. She understands ethnography as a long, irreversible voyage through a tunnel with no apparent exit. Hence, anyone presumptuous enough to witness and retell the stories of others must surrender 'to the intractableness of reality' and find a way of witnessing that is neither cold nor afraid to reveal what she calls 'the hidden dialectic between connection and otherness that is at the center of all forms of historical and cultural representation'. Behar claims that exploring the self–other tunnel has no easy exits and requires a great deal of emotional openness and honesty. Most scientific studies repress such emotion through distancing methodologies, theoretical discourses, and posturing as the invulnerable objective decoder of reality.

In sharp contrast, Behar advocates 'inscribing of the self' into descriptive accounts of others through heartfelt autobiographic memories. She constantly foregrounds how her observations are filtered through sorrow, shame, fear, loathing, guilt, vanity, and self–deception. Behar, the stepchild of the Cuban diaspora and a budding anthropological star/diva, is always tacking restlessly between her field experience and the personal memories that these experiences evoke. A powerful example of this narrative technique is her ethnography *Translated Woman* and her stunning essay about death in a Spanish village (Behar, 1996). She begins the essay on death as a green, distracted young ethnographer who leaves her dying grandfather to study how traditional villagers view death. After several years, a nagging conscience forces her to see the monstrous irony of betraying her dying grandfather to 'collect data' on dying. Exploring her reaction to his death allows her to grasp how the villagers feel about death. By being more subjective and vulnerable, thus surrendering to the intractability of life/death, Behar actually finds a more honest, 'objective' vantage point from which to apprehend what the villagers are telling her.

Since traditional academics abhor open subjectivity, some may dismiss her method as a whining, solipsistic ethnographic soap opera. A more generous reading (Marcus, 1994) credits feminists like Behar for using autobiography as a form of reflexivity that undermines the cultural and linguistic privilege of the scientific author and text. According to Marcus, the feminist penchant to be autobiographical and confessional is a more subjective type of reflexivity than Bourdieu's theory of practice. In sharp contrast, Marcus characterizes Bourdieu's theoretical project as a more rational, less subjective form of reflexivity. Such a conceptual distinction misses what feminist like Behar are actually doing.

Behar puts it this way, 'The exposure of the self who is also a spectator has to take us somewhere we couldn't otherwise get to. It has to be essential to the argument, not a decorative flourish, not exposure for it own sake.' Her analogizing between personal and public field experiences collapses a series of false dichotomies that have long plagued Western thinkers (Haraway, 1988). This strikes me as doing much more than mediating objectivity through subjectivity. Behar is trying to undermine the modernist, masculinist privileging and separating of the rational over the emotional. If the feminists are correct, good 'rational' generalizing and theorizing springs from engaging life as a whole thinking-feeling being. In contrast, Bourdieu's theory of practice will not produce an emotionally engaged interpreter willing to go into Behar's long tunnel and wrestle with the self–other connection. What such an ethnographic practice encourages are emotionally controlled, deep readings of 'ideological hegemony', 'discursive regimes', or the 'habitus' of actors. What Behar is advocating sounds similar to Gadamer's (1988) notion of the 'double hermeneutic' that occurs as an interpreter tacks back and forth between experience and being. The difference might be that Behar places more emphasis on emotions and vulnerability.

Ultimately, Behar is trying to create a new hybrid genre of ethnographic writing that builds upon what 'native anthropologists,' psychological trauma victims, ethnic minority essayists and feminists are writing. She contends that this new hybrid genre works when readers take the voyage through anthropology's tunnel and see themselves in the observer who is serving as their guide. She cites a number of reader responses that praise her for making the connections between her life and the lives of those being studied. Such a narrative move allows the readers openly identify with the author, thus makes the text accessible and popular. Another reason why readers may embrace her texts passionately is because they are what John Fiske (1989) calls 'producerly texts'. Foregrounding her vulnerability and struggle to know conveys a less infallible interpretive voice, thus invites readers to produce their own meanings. In contrast, the 'writerly texts' of conventional academics foreground the author's official interpretation in an unwavering authoritative voice free of guilt, angst, and self–doubt. Such texts are less likely to promote as much 'producerly' meaning–making.

Post–modernists like Crapanzano (1992) might protest that Behar's representation of the vulnerable self is no more 'authentic' and 'whole' than any other authorial representation. He generally argues that all autobiographical narratives are 'autobiographical illusions'. Behar seems quite aware, however, that her constructed self is an artifice. The kind of autobiography she practices anticipates such criticisms. She consciously uses the 'artifice of her self' to make telling points about whatever scene she is describing. Narratively, her book entitled *The Vulnerable Observer: Anthropology that Breaks Your Heart* (1996) illustrates how she often deploys self–parodies to enhance her ethnographic interpretation. In the aforementioned book, Behar tells the tale of being a commentator on an American Ethnological Society panel. Her assignment was to comment on a set of papers that were especially critical of her friend and mentor Renato Rosaldo. After recounting a bit of her fear and loathing to be cast in that role, she ends up defending Rosaldo's exploration of his grief over his wife's death in an academic article. The two young anthropological critics take Rosaldo to task for exploiting the memory of his wife to help explain grief and rage among a group of headhunters. In response, Behar recasts Rosaldo as the vulnerable, reflexive observer seeking to understand himself in order to understand the cultural other.

As Behar portrays these merciless critics, she recounts how she found herself playing the same role in an academic meeting with feminist colleagues. She uses this painful, ironic memory to parody her present performance against two relentless critics. These two tales about Behar–the–academic–critic are part of her general account of the conference and her performance as a rising academic star. She plays her role as diva–critic reluctantly. She plays it to the hilt. In the end, she produces a tragic–comic account of the whole enterprise narrated in a distancing, self–parodic voice.

By recounting her emotional struggle with being a diva–critic, Behar helps the reader understand these two young critics and their cultural milieu. Her engaged, complex self becomes the window through which we view the entire anthropological tribe and its degradation and socialization rituals. The story of her performance becomes an ethnography of the anthropological academy. She captures the pathos and spectacle of fresh young academics picking the bones of eminent elders, thus leaving others to restore order and civility. A curious little academic squabble becomes a moving event because Behar makes the reader pay attention to its emotional undercurrents.

When I compare what I did in *Chronicles* to what Behar is doing, I find many parallels. My account also has autobiographical moments of tacking back and forth between my personal memories and my present encounters. Like Behar, I use these stories to make generalizing statements about the cultural scene I am describing. Not infrequently, I use past memories and stories to draw analogies the way Behar does, but she seems to place personal stories more center stage than I do. I rely more on a pervasive hybrid voice to make *Chronicles* reflexive than on analogizing from intimate, vulnerable feelings. Consequently, I come in and out of my stories about the cultural other in a somewhat less dramatic, confessional way. The voice I narrate in is generally more understated and comic than dramatic and tragic. In addition, I rely more on the reflexive practice of framing one's representation with previous representations to convey how constructed and personal my interpretation is.

But as reflexive as the *Chronicles* is, I do not interrogate the 'tunnel' or the self–other as consistently and intensively as Behar does. At times, I narrate as the engaged, vulnerable observer. At other times, I am still the emotionally detached, politically engaged observer of dialectical realist tales. Since I take Behar's call for a more vulnerable ethnography very seriously, I am left wondering why we end up with a different mix of reflexive practices. Our differences narratively may spring from intrinsic differences in our writing skills and personal sensitivities. Or our differences narratively may flow from differences in class and gender. I am a working–class male brought up by grandparents who survived the depression. My family, and most rural midwesterners, are not particularly open and expressive about personal feelings. My notions of privacy, reserve, stoicism, and machismo probably keep me from being too open and vulnerable.

In addition, some strong philosophical convictions keep me searching for a sensible, defensible middle ground in ethnographic practice. As important as the new post–modern critiques are, I have grown weary of what Marshall Sahlins refers to as a 'climate of epistemological hypochondria'. Philosophically, I wanted *The Heartland Chronicles* to be a restrained, understated, unsentimental expression of the present debates and experiments in ethnographic writing. I wanted to balance an older style of narrating with the newer more personal, introspective style of narrating. In retrospect, I apparently did just that.

For me, doing ethnography has never been a particularly angst–ridden pursuit. Perhaps I have always had diminished expectations for ethnography. I am not sure that I take it, or my role as an 'anthropological witness', as seriously as Behar does. The discipline of anthropology certainly has some useful things to say, but ethnography now seems more like thoughtful travel writing than some grand scientific, philosophical, or poetic statement. I do not feel the weight of my discipline riding on my writings. Perhaps this is because I am an 'educational anthropologist'. I write from the margins of the discipline rather than from its center. I also do not feel the weight of my race or gender riding on my writing. I write mainly as an individual, although I sometimes imagine myself an 'organic working class intellectual' speaking passionately for 'my class'. And like Behar, I want to touch, or as she says so eloquently, 'break people's hearts', but I would settle for breaking their sober faces with a smile.

Summary

I have tried to present some good reasons for why we all need to write in ways that break with the old scientific realist narrative style. To this end, I have advocated writing in a 'hybrid voice' and 'reflexive realist' narrative style that engages ordinary readers' common sense understanding of representational practices. I have argued for a realist narrative form that is more familiar to ordinary readers than a highly experimental, avant-garde narrative form. My main reasons for this approach are political. Using more familiar realist narrative forms should help bridge the vast and growing cultural gulf between academics and ordinary people. I want social science writers to distance themselves from their emerging role as normalizing, ideological sciences. I want academic ethnographers to write highly accessible, popular ethnographies in ordinary language that challenge the normalized consciousness of ordinary readers.

On the other hand, I want to avoid writing 'radical' realist accounts that are in the all–knowing voice of a 'deep reading' of reality. Instead, any critical realist account that I write must also disrupt its own truth claims, thus put ordinary language readers on guard about all truth claims. Such ethnographies would continue to make knowledge claims, but they would be smaller, more situated, personal knowledge claims. Again, this type of ethnographic narrative may have a better chance of breaking with both the discursive regime of the bourgeois academy and with allegedly radical, counter–hegemonic academic discourses.

Some post–modern and post–structuralist ethnographers may not find my notions of a 'hybrid voice' and a 'reflexive realist narrative' a radical enough break with modernist assumptions about the self, authorship, and realism. They may say that *Chronicles* is far too author–centered, autobiographical, and seamless a narrative to disrupt realist assumptions. I have tried to show that some of out best post–structuralist thinkers have overlooked interesting experiments in realist representation and thought. Ruth Behar's autobiographical ethnographic writing seems particularly promising because she breaks with both modernist notions of autobiography (Okely and Callaway, 1992) and with post–structuralist notions (Foucault, 1972) of authors as nothing more than discourses.

Writing in a highly reflexive autobiographical voice and ordinary language breaks more completely with formal academic discourse style than most post–structuralists do. Such a narrative style actually deconstructs the authority of the author more thoroughly. In this style of ethnographic writing, the author becomes a situated, subjective, historical observer making modest knowledge claims rather than a transcendent, objective observer making grand knowledge claims. I would urge the new generation of post–everything ethnographers to revisit the experimental moments of modernism and realist thought. Behar, myself, and many others are demonstrating that we have just begun to mine that tradition for new ways of writing ethnographies. It feels like we are living in an exciting era of crumbling discursive regimes, so I urge this new generation of ethnographers to continue experimenting. Surely the next generation of ethnographers will surely surpass what this generation has done.

References

ABU–LUGHOD, L. (1990) 'Can there be a feminist ethnography?', *Women and Performance: A Journal of Feminist Theory*, **5**, pp. 7–27.

ABU–LUGHOD, L. (1991) 'Writing against culture', in Fox, R. (Ed.) *Recapturing Anthropology: Working in the Present*, Santa Fe, NM: School of American Research Press.

ATKINSON, P. (1990) *The Ethnographic Imagination: Textual Construction of Reality*, New York: Routledge.

BEHAR, R. (1993) *Translated Woman: Crossing the Border with Esperanza*, Boston, MA: Beacon Press.

BEHAR, R. (1996) *The Vulnerable Observer: Anthropology that Breaks Your Heart*, Boston, MA: Beacon Press.

BEHAR, R. and GORDON, D. (Eds.) (1995) *Women Writing Culture*, Berkeley, CA: University of California Press.

BHASKAR, R. (1989) *Reclaiming Reality: A Critical Introduction to Contemporary Philosophy*, London: Verso.

BOURDIEU, P. (1984) *Distinctions: A Social Critique of the Judgement of Taste*, Cambridge, MA: Harvard University Press.

BRADBURY, M. and MCFARLANE, J. (1972) *Modernism, 1890–1930*, New York: Doubleday Press.

BRECHT, B. (1964) (John Willet, translator) *Brecht on Theater: The Development of an Aesthetic*, New York: Hill and Wang.

BRITZMAN, D. (1991) *Practice Makes Practice: A Critical Study of Learning to Teach*, New York: State University of New York Press.

BRITZMAN, D. (1995) 'The question of belief: Writing post–structuralist ethnography', *Qualititatitve Studies in Education*, **89**, 3, pp. 233–41.

CLIFFORD, J. (1988) *The Predicament of Culture: Twentieth–Century Ethnography, Literature and Art*, Cambridge, MA: Harvard University Press.

CLIFFORD, J. and MARCUS, G. (Eds.) (1986) *Writing Culture: The Poetics and Politics of Ethnography*, Berkeley, CA: University of California Press.

CLOUGH, P. (1992) *The Ends of Ethnography: From Realism to Social Criticism*, Newbury Park, CA: Sage.

CRAPANZANO, V. (1992) *Hermes' Dilemma & Hamlet's Desire: On the Epistemology of Interpretation*, Cambridge, MA: Harvard University Press.

EHRENREICH, B. (1989) *Fear of Falling: The Inner Life of the Middle Class*, New York: Harper Perennial.

FERNEA, E. (1969) *Guests of the Sheik: An Ethnography of an Iraqi Village*. Garden City, NY: Anchor Books.

FISKE, J. (1989) *Understanding Popular Culture*, Boston, MA: Unwin Hyman.

FOLEY, D. (1976) *Philippine Rural Education: An Anthropological Perspective*, De Kalb, IL: University of Northern Illinois Press.

FOLEY, D. (1989) *From Peones to Politicos: Class and Ethnicity in a South Texas Town, 1900–1989* (2nd ed), Austin, TX: University of Texas Press.

FOLEY, D. (1990) *Learning Capitalist Culture: Deep in the Heart of Texas*, Philadelphia, PA: University of Pennsylvania Press.

FOLEY, D. (1995) *The Heartland Chronicles*, Philadelphia, PA: University of Pennsylvania Press.

FOUCAULT, M. (1972) *Truth and Power: Selected Interviews & Other Writings, 1972–1977*, New York: Pantheon Books.

GADAMER, H. (1988) *Truth and Method*, New York: Crossroads.

GEERTZ, C. (1988) *Works and Lives: The Anthropologist as Author*, Stanford, CA: Stanford University Press.

GEERTZ, C. (1983) *Local Knowledge: Further Essays in Interpretive Anthropology*, New York: Basic Books.

GRAMSCI, A. (1971) *Prison Notebooks*, New York: International Publishers.

HARAWAY, D. (1988) 'Situated knowledges: The science question in feminism as a site of discourse on the privilege of partial perspective', *Feminist Studies*, **14**, pp. 575–99.

HAYANO, D. (1979) 'Auto–ethnography: Paradigms, problems, and prospects', *Human Organization*, **38**, 1, pp. 99–104.

KAMINSKY, M. (1992) 'Myerhoff's "Third voice": Ideology and genre in ethnographic narrative', *Social Text*, **33**, pp. 124–44.

LATHER, P. (1991) *Getting Smart: Feminist Research and Pedagogy with/in the Postmodern*, New York: Routledge.

LATHER, P. (1996) 'Troubling clarity: The politics of accessible language', *Harvard Educational Review*, **66**, 3, pp. 7525–45.

LATHER, P. and SMITHIES, C. (1995) *Troubling Angels: Women Living with HIV/AIDs*, Atheena's Pen DTP, Columbus, OH: Greyden Press.

LUKACS, G. (1964) *Realism in our Time: Literature and the Class Struggle*, New York: Harper Torchbooks.

LUKACS, G. (1972) *History and Class Consciousness*, Cambridge, MA: MIT Press.

MANGANARO, M. (Ed.) (1990) *Modernist Anthropology: From Fieldwork to Text*, Princeton, NJ: Princeton University Press.

MARCUS, G. (1994) 'What comes (just) after "post"? The case of ethnography', in DENZIN, N. and LINCOLN, E. (Eds.) *Handbook of Qualitative Research*. Newbury, CA: Sage, pp. 563–73.

MARCUS, G. and FISCHER, M.M.J. (1986) *Anthropology of Cultural Critique: An Experimental Moment in the Human Sciences*, Chicago, IL: University of Chicago Press.

MARCUS, G. and CUSHMAN, D. (1982) 'Ethnographies as texts', *Annual Review of Anthropology*, **11**, pp. 25–69.

MOORES, S. (1993) *Interpreting Audiences: The Ethnography of Media Consumption*, Thousand Oaks, CA: Sage.

MYERHOFF, B. (1982) *Number Our Days*, New York: Simon and Schuster.

OKELY, J. and CALLAWAY, H. (Eds.) (1992) *Anthropology and Autobiography*, London: Routledge.

PRATT, M.L. (1992) *Imperial Eyes: Travel Writing and Transculturation*, New York: Routledge.

PUTNAM, H. (1987) *The Many Faces of Realism*, LaSalle, IL: Open Court.

PUTNAM, H. (1990) *Realism with a Human Face*, Cambridge, MA: Harvard University Press.

ROOSENS, E. (1989) *Creating Ethnicity. The Process of Ethnogenesis*, Thousand Oaks, CA: Sage.

ROSALDO, R. (1989) *Culture and Truth: The Remaking of Social Analysis*, Boston, MA: Beacon Press.

SCHUTZ, A. (1964) *Collected Papers I: The Problem of Social Reality*, The Hague: Martinus Nijhoff.

SHOSTAK, M. (1981) *Nisa: The Life and Words of a !Kung Woman*, Cambridge, MA: Harvard University Press.

THOMSEN, M. (1969) *Living Poor: A Peace Corps Chronicle*, Seattle, WA: University of Washington Press.

VAN MANNEN, J. (1988) *Tales of the Field: On Writing Ethnography*. Chicago, IL: University of Chicago Press.

WHITE, H. (1973) *Metahistory: The Historical Imagination in Nineteenth–Century Europe*. Baltimore, MA: Johns Hopkins University Press.

WITTGENSTEIN, L. (1953) *Philosophical Investigations* (Translated by G.E.M. Anscombe) New York: Macmillan.

8 Journey from Exotic Horror to Bitter Wisdom: International Development and Research Efforts in Bosnia and Herzegovina

Noreen B Garman

For almost two years I have been involved in an educational program in Bosnia and Herzegovina. In retrospect, it's been a tough journey! I took on the codirectorship of two initiatives funded by international agencies with a naive belief that our colleagues at the University of Pittsburgh could make a contribution to the educational needs in BiH. By many indications I think we have done so. Along the way, however, we have lost our innocence; we have been consumed by the demands of the work and energized by our successes; and we have experienced the pain of duplicity and deceit. These realizations provided points of departure for the writings that have become part of the Bosnian program.

Writing this chapter has given me the opportunity to reconstruct a text about our Bosnian experiences, and in so doing, I was reminded of Laurel Richardson's (1994) affectionate irreverence toward research.

> Although we usually think about writing as a mode of 'telling' about the social world, writing is not just a mopping–up activity at the end of a research project. Writing is also a way of 'knowing' — a method of discovery and analysis. By writing in different ways, we discover new aspects of our topic and our relationship to it. Form and content are inseparable. (p. 516)

I discovered anew that writing is a *method of inquiry*, a way of finding out about myself and my topic. As I reviewed the various artifacts of the Bosnian project, I realized that I had created a series of narratives which reflected a sense that (as Heidegger (1971) expressed it) 'there is more in our experience of the world than can possibly meet the unreflecting eye' and, in my first encounters in Bosnia, I wrote 'to unconceal' (pp. 52–3).

During my first two trips I sent several email vignettes to family and a few friends and, as I discovered, these 'Postcards from Bosnia' were widely circulated on the email networks by the few people that received them. The postcards became the subject of an article for the School of Education Bulletin, and again reached a large audience. I thought it was ironic that these simple narratives had perhaps reached a broader audience than any of my other publications and decided it was, perhaps, the vitality inherent in narrative inquiry that caught people's interest. As we continued our work in Bosnia, however, I began to realize that the writing had served a crucial part of my existence there. It provided the opportunity for the creation of 'reflexive space' as I lived out the other aspects of the project. The postcards, as text, or rather as 'becoming-text' provided the dialectic of self. As Ricoeur (1991) suggests, 'To understand oneself is to understand oneself as one confronts the text and to receive from it the conditions for a self other than that which first undertakes the reading' (p. 17). As I confronted the horrors of war, the struggle to find satisfaction in doing important work, and the pain of duplicity, I wondered whether the writing was, after all, a form of therapy. Still I agreed with Natalie Goldberg (1986) that 'Writing is not therapy, though it may have a thera-peutic effect . . . Writing is deeper than therapy. You write *through* your pain, and even your suffering must be written out and let go of' (p. 114). As the world moved and shook beneath my feet, I was challenged daily to find new ways of coping and making sense of it all. Similarly, Stone (1996) reminds us,

> Needing to ground ourselves in the realities at hand, while also searching for a perspective that allows us to find purpose in the events, feelings, and ideas that surround us, we desperately need tools that can help us keep it all together, giving a sense of wholeness to what would otherwise be a fractured reality.
>
> The narrative structure of story impresses understandable patterns of meaning on experience, no matter how discontinuous an event is with our core beliefs and current view of things. This shows up most vividly in the midst of crisis. (p. 49)

Thus the email 'postcards' provided the reflexive medium for the 'dialectic of self' that served to sustain other aspects of the project. They were points of depar-ture for the events and writings that provided insights into the Bosnian inquiry. As a result I began to realize that the concept, *research stance*, is a useful way to articulate a particular perspective which directs the meaning given to experience. There seemed to be at least three research stances inherent in our writings. I call these stances: *exotic horror*, *alien dwelling*, and *bitter wisdom*. There is also a sense in which the stances take on an evolutionary purpose as the project continued. That is, it seemed necessary to write within one stance before I could move into the next. In this brief chapter it isn't possible to detail the complexities that we encountered, but rather it is intended to portray the reflexive qualities of the postcards through the three research stances. In the following sections the postcards will serve to explicate the notion of *exotic horror* as well as to advance the story of the project.

Exotic Horror

In this section I present many of the postcards from Bosnia that I wrote during my first two trips to Bosnia as well as an introduction and coda from the published article. I began to realize that writing these email vignettes was a way for me to try to come to terms with the devastating experience of being in the middle of a war torn country. I was facing such conflicting feelings. In some sense it was akin to encountering the 'exotic' that ethnographers describe (Peacock, 1988). In a strange way I realized how I might be inclined to romanticize the situations I found myself a part of, and yet, the overwhelming experience was ineffable. The stance reflected in the following piece is one I have identified as *exotic horror*.

On 2 December 1995 I sent an email postcard to my family and a few university friends. I had been in Bosnia for two weeks. It was before the Dayton Agreement was signed and I was a bit nervous about traveling in a war zone. I promised my family that I would let them know how the trip was going. I was in Bosnia on a mission for the Institute for International Studies (IISE) in the School of Education. The Institute, as an implementing partner of UNICEF, has been working to foster collaborative efforts between national and cantonal educators in Bosnia and Herzegovina and the University of Pittsburgh Education Faculty and graduate students. The program is officially known as the University of Pittsburgh/Bosnia Program for Renewal of Teacher Education in Bosnia and Herzegovina. The Pitt program officially began in early 1995 when IISE sent Lauren Caldwell as the Program Coordinator to Bosnia to establish our offices and our presence there. The war was going on and Lauren held the program together during the latter part of the fighting. By the time I traveled to Bosnia it was clear that the war was coming to an end. The intent was to establish program priorities for the next phase of our involvement. During this trip I found myself torn between our programmatic duties and the awesome images of a war torn country that called my attention. I wrote the first email postcard after I left Bosnia and stopped at the UNICEF office in Croatia for the return to Pittsburgh.

Dear Friends and Family

Greetings from Zagreb, Croatia. I just returned on a UN transport/cargo plane from Sarajevo. With UNICEF credentials and vehicle we could travel more freely between war zones in Bosnia. (Crossing Serb lines was scary.) Last Sunday we drove to Mostar through unbelievable devastation in the city as well as the countrysides, then on to Sarajevo with a UN convoy. Our meetings in Sarajevo were productive. The UNICEF folks here are a unique and dedicated group of locals and internationals. (They are our partner in the Pitt program.) I stayed with a family in an apartment in Sarajevo . . . no running water, heat or electricity most of the time. We arrived at dusk and it was pitch dark as we tried to get settled with a few candles, no heat and water. Walking at night in the city (with a few streetlights only and fog settling around) is eerie, definitely Kafkaesque. During the day the smoky shells of buildings and rubble are awesome, and yet the beauty of the city lurks in the devastation. The people that I've talked to in Sarajevo are so courageous . . . and so proud that they did not abandon their city, and that they've prevailed! I'm haunted by how personal this war is . . . neighbor against neighbor. As we were driven around Sarajevo, I found the terrain remarkably similar to Pittsburgh. The hills begin just on the other side of the river. Like Mt. Washington, the beautiful city is spread out below. It made me wonder how young men who lived in the city could go up on the mountain and begin to relentlessly destroy their homes with shells, and as snipers, to shoot and kill their neighbors. How profoundly tragic this war! I am struck with the way it forces us to face our dark sides, the consequences of our hatred. If it can happen here in this rich, beautiful industrial country, it can happen in Pittsburgh. Where do we find the wellspring of love to move us away from the dark? And then I think of you as the source of my own love. It gives me sustenance as well as hope. Thank you for the warmth. Hope all of you are well . . . I look forward to seeing you soon.

Love, Noreen.

Postcards from Bosnia

On 10 February 1996, I returned to Bosnia to continue our efforts. At that time I wrote more postcards. I share these with you, hoping that they will tell a story of my profound and troubling experiences.

When I returned, there was a tenuous feeling of hope in the air. The Dayton Peace Agreement had been signed. The Paris meeting was near. This latest cease fire seemed to be holding. I got to Split, Croatia, where our Pitt/UNICEF driver met me. Split is a beautiful city on the Adriatic Sea. It has no war damage. The weather was mild and the coastal scenery, breathtaking. I wasn't prepared for the impending experience.

GREETINGS FROM ZENICA: (pronounced zen ee' za).

I flew from Zagreb to Split (both in Croatia) at 6 this morning and Sanel Hodzic, our field assistant and driver, met me for what was to be a truly 'white knuckle' trip through the Bosnian mountains. I was trying to be brave and also enjoy the beauty of the vast scenery and the pine trees, heavily laden with snow. It was the two feet of snow on the narrow road that kept distracting me. I kept gripping the seat belt as if it would save me when we slid down the steep mountain or off into a minefield. (I was afraid to ask where they were.) This time we drove through towns like Dongi Vakuf, known as Serb towns that were tragically devastated. The people were out on the streets in the cold weather, visiting one another. There are miles of houses, the shells and holes where windows and doors once were. . . . their 'faces' haunt the countryside like gloomy spectres. What waste! And what dual feelings. On one hand, the desire to appreciate the natural beauty of the countryside and its people, on the other, trying to muster courage to survive the hardships of this war torn environment. Welcome to Bosnia! I must close before this email goes down. I send warm regards to all. Just to let you know I am safe and in good hands here.

Much love. . . . Noreen

POSTCARD FROM ZENICA:

Lauren Caldwell and the Pitt/UNICEF staff (two young Bosnians) have their main office here on the eighth floor of a modern building. (The elevator is out a lot of the time.) Lodging is difficult to find in Bosnia. I am staying at Dom Penzionera. (The Old People's Home.) It is quite pleasant, actually. The officials have divided the home in two; one section is a hotel, the other houses 'old people'. (Please don't ask which part I'm in.) Rooms are sparse, clean, sunny. This is how the home gets funds to support the elderly. Good idea, eh? The sounds of the city (about the size of Cincinnati, I think) . . . interesting. Five times a day there is chanting–like song, known as 'ezan', coming from the Muslim mosques over the city . . . in concert with the church bells ringing from one Serb orthodox and five catholic churches. Imagine the melody! We are working late into the evening planning our many site visits around Bosnia.

Much love . . . Noreen G.

A BOSNIAN VALENTINE:

It's Valentine's Day and for some reason I was remembering the box I helped decorate with red hearts in the fourth grade . . . all those school valentine exchanges. In 1989 when I taught in the Philippines, the college kids had quite an ambitious enterprise, selling their services to deliver sentimental messages and roses around campus. Valentine traditions are big there. Here two young people told me that they don't buy valentines 'because it's an American holiday'. I got to thinking that valentines are really tokens of affection . . . extended moments of caring, like a smile, kind words, an embrace (sometimes an empty ritual if it's without love). I suppose it really is what keeps us humans together, these extended moments . . . the glue of social units. It may be that these moments somehow broke down in this country, came unglued. People I've met here are struggling to find new ways to care for one another now. Really a great Valentine gift. HAPPY VALENTINES DAY FROM BOSNIA!

Much love, Noreen

POSTCARD FROM SARAJEVO:

Today we drove to Sarajevo with Sanel (our driver). Sanel's mother was worried. We had to drive through Ilidza, a suburb of Sarajevo, also known as Serb territory. There have been isolated incidents of snipers and hijackings. Sanel is Muslim — said he wasn't worried. The destruction in Sarajevo is incredible. Every building has considerable damage, if not total destruction. I didn't see a single building that was untouched by either shells, bullets or fire. The sights are so grim. I don't seem to have cognitive images in my repertoire of experiences to help me make sense out of the landscape (even tho I've been here before). But then maybe that's the message my brain keeps sending. Yet everyone says how much better it is now! At least they don't have to haul water into the high rise buildings and up several flights of stairs . . . and there is water and heat every other day. Today wasn't the day. It was very cold this morning in the UNICEF office. I don't know how this staff continues to work in the bitter cold. We stayed with a friends overnight. What beautiful and courageous people live in their apartment. More later. . . .

Love, Noreen G.

(P.S.) The email is extremely difficult to type here. It keeps kicking out. Hope you get this.

27 February 1996:

People here in Bosnia have been telling me how much they need books and materials in their language. The educational books are all but gone . . . Libraries have been bombed. What a tragedy!! The National Library in Sarajevo has been totally destroyed. We visited the shell of that once beautiful building which housed rare artifacts of history dating back to the twelfth century. Although some of the materials were evacuated to basements, it's not clear how they've been preserved.

Remnants of cultural heritage wiped out. I never thought much about how so many books disappeared. I just assumed it was the war. Yesterday I had a conversation with Svetlana Pavelic–Durovic, the assistant UNICEF officer here. She happened to mention that last year she got a call from her father asking her if it was OK to burn her University notebooks. She said, 'I told him, of course, I can always buy new ones.' I realized that people have been burning their books to keep warm!!! Svetlana described how her mother would carefully tear each page separately and in that way cook the lunch with the heat. They endured three winters without modern heat. There are wood burning stoves in most areas and people burned everything they could to keep warm and cook. In a country that puts such a high value on education, this is yet another tragic irony of the war. I'm glad we're translating our materials into Bosnian. It's a meager effort, but greatly appreciated . . .

Much love, Noreen.

Coda

My memories of Bosnia linger still. I returned in August to continue our work. Several people have asked me if I think peace is possible in the Balkans. It probably depends on what we mean by 'peace'. I'm not convinced that peace is probable in the US. I think we have to do a lot more to counter the hatred that is being peddled by some fringe groups and our politicians. Mostly, I guess, we have to search our own hearts and minds where I think peace really begins. I'm not convinced that the US is a peaceful place right now. As for Bosnia . . . there is one theme that seems to permeate the discourses there . . . people are tired of fighting, they're tired of the war, they're cold and hungry and much poorer than before and there isn't anything to gain by continuing the war. It is quite sobering to think that it takes such killing and devastation for people to convince themselves about how futile hate wars really are. Most important, we, as educators are compelled to ask what our responsibilities are in helping to understand what peace might mean. We can't morally ignore the challenge of Bosnia.

Alien Dwelling

When I returned to Sarajevo in August, 1996 I realized that I was 'seeing' the surroundings differently. In my earlier trips I found it hard to understand how people could walk among the devastation and carry on the dailiness of their lives. They were now strolling down Sniper Alley, a street where only 10 months before they were risking their lives to get water from a common supply. Now I was walking among the buildings without much notice. I began to accommodate to the lack of water and electricity. The strangeness, the exotic horror, was beginning to subside. I realized that my earlier writing had allowed me to begin to come to terms with war torn Bosnia, at least so that I might find a way to 'dwell' there and, in so doing, hear our Bosnian colleagues more deeply.

In traveling around the Bosnian countryside, it was clear that the consequences of war could not be ignored, nor should they be forgotten. I was continually torn between the need to take in, and deliberate about, the devastating images as symbols of injustice and evil, and yet to find ways to be committed and productive in the work Bosnian educators had brought us there to do. At some point I was no longer feeling as if I were outside of my previous experiences. I settled into the difficult tasks at hand. I began to know the Bosnian educators as colleagues rather than counterparts. The educational environment, as well as the physical landscape, became familiar. Our research and development associated with the project took on a different perspective, one that I am calling *alien dwelling*.

I am reminded here that Clifford Geertz was criticized by a colleague for 'paying lip service to the "problem of other"', referring to the fears and anxieties stirred up by the confrontation with an alien set of beliefs'. But, as Berreby (1995) describes 'Geertz's interpretations revealed a confidence in objectivity and in his own ability to grasp the essence of other people — a confidence he could not have if he really put the other culture on an equal footing with his own'. It gives this feeling of 'Aha, now I know them'. It is for this reason that 'alien' in another culture is crucial to the research stance we assume here.

My colleague, Steve Koziol, and I officially took over the codirectorship of the Program for Educational Renewal in Bosnia and Herzegovina in June 1996. There were two initiatives associated with the program. One was a continuing project funded by UNICEF known as 'Teacher Development Through Active Learning'. The second, a new project funded by the World Bank, was intended to create a national dialogue to reform teacher education. The project title, 'Participatory Planning for Renewal of Teacher Education in Bosnia and Herzegovina', became known as *Obnova* (Bosnian for 'renewal') and the UNICEF project was called *active learning*.

Active Learning

The active learning initiative included Faculty, master teachers, and professional staff from the School of Education at Pitt in collaboration with educators in BiH. It was begun in 1994 and focused on establishing an active learning center to support pre–service training programs, in–service professional development programs and a network of Bosnians who would continue the active learning dissemination. At first Pitt Faculty and staff offered workshops in Zenica, Tuzla, Mostar, and Sarajevo. We also developed materials known as active learning modules which included *An Introduction to Active Learning, Informal Drama, Journal Writing, Elementary Mathematics and Science*, and *Instructional Supervision and Mentoring*. These materials provided the basis for the workshops We went to great lengths to have them translated into the Bosnian language.

Both projects were being funded for a brief period of time. As it turned out we had less that a year to accomplish our mission. Bosnian language translation became a major challenge at the University. The first translator left the project and we had to quickly replace her. Ideally we wanted to have more of the translation done in Bosnia, however there were enormous difficulties in sending large amounts of text. There was no mail system in place and we had to carry all materials each time one of us traveled there. Each month either Steve or I went to Bosnia with other staff to conduct a workshop and meet with demonstration teachers.

In our reports to the funders we emphasized the collaborative nature of our efforts. At first, however, 'collaboration' with our Bosnian colleagues meant that we would meet with the administrators from the Pedagogical Academy in Zenica to share our plans and materials with them. They provided the space, organized the workshop participants from various cantons and generally hosted the meetings. It was clear, however that these three men were dedicated educators who believed that active learning would provide a better way for children to be engaged in learning. They found a way to establish an Active Learning Center in a school across from the Academy. They began publishing a journal which included a great deal of our translations, and generally continued to offer workshops that fostered active learning as the basis for the training. We could see that our collaborative efforts were beginning to pay off.

Our move into more collaborative efforts took shape when we began to work with demonstration teachers from Zenica and Sarajevo. They wrote lesson plans and made videotapes of their lessons which were intended to be used in the two active learning centers and to set the stage for their leadership in the coming workshops. More important, the teachers developed a network which they intend to continue as a result of their work. The meeting in Tuzla is typical of our encounters throughout the Federation:

POSTCARD FROM TUZLA:

Mostly I've been meeting with various educators and education 'officials', and working on reports. Today we met with the Tuzla Minister of Education, Faculty at the University of Tuzla Pedagogical Academy, school directors (principals) and teachers. Quite a trip through the bureaucracy. The Pitt team has been doing a program here in 'active learning' to help educators move away from their didactic teaching in primary schools, also working with policy planners to help rebuild the educational system. (We keep questioning how presumptuous we might be, yet people here are enthusiastic.) Teachers here have been working without pay for four years, keeping the schools open . . . the bottom line, they recognize that kids are no longer the same as they were before the war . . . they've lost their innocence, their faith in the social systems. Still, those who are in charge are continuing to recreate the old. Interesting meeting with the teachers and directors. Those teachers that have attended the 'active learning training' are enthusiastic. They report that when they go back to their schools they get mixed reactions. Many teachers are excited while others teachers seem to resent them, and in some schools, the directors are insisting that every teacher prepare an active learning lesson. Some teachers complain that they are already overburdened, others are compliant, and still others are remarkably creative. Directors say that their biggest challenge is 'motivating the teachers'. It's deja vu all over again. I heard the same situations last month in Pittsburgh. There is, indeed, a kinship among teachers the world over!! . . . It's very cold here today. The heat has been suspended for the remainder of the winter. All seems normal in Bosnia . . .

Much love, Noreen.

Obnova

Collaboration between our Bosnian colleagues and Pitt Faculty were a central theme in this project, titled 'Participatory Planning for Renewal of Teacher Education in BiH'. The intent of the project was to support a Federation–wide dialogue which could lead to reforms in teacher education. Initially funded by the World Bank, it began on 1 July 1996. The expected results of *Obnova* were to produce a substantive plan including legislation and policy and to establish the endorsement of the Federal Ministry of Education. The efforts began in Sarajevo where the Pittsburgh Team met with our field office team in order to organize the project. At that time Steve and I conducted focus groups with Bosnian educators from Sarajevo, Tuzla, and Zenica in order to generate substantive needs and issues for future planning materials. At this time educational leaders were identified from all ten cantons as the participants. They included six Muslims (Bosniaks) and four Croats.

The Bosnian leaders traveled to Pittsburgh in October for three weeks where the study and planning began in earnest. To facilitate the planning process, Pitt faculty conducted seminars on various topics related to teacher education. We agreed that we would not lecture during these sessions, but rather, we wrote information papers which were translated into Bosnian. Having read the papers prior to the sessions, the Bosnians would meet with the authors of the papers, ask questions and discuss the implications of the information as it related to their context. By the end of the second week they organized themselves into smaller groups and began the planning. It was during their three weeks in Pittsburgh that the Bosnian educational leaders developed the commitment to each other and to the challenging tasks at hand. The experience was a new one for citizens of the former socialist Yugoslavia, where participatory planning and decentralization were new ideas.

Designing new programs for pre–service and in–service education has been identified as a critical educational priority in eastern European countries making the transition from what were highly centralized systems to ones in which there is decentralized decision–making and authority. In Bosnia and Herzegovina the task has been additionally complicated by the great needs for physical facility and infrastructure reconstruction following the war. Participants in the *Obnova* project were learning to engage in democratic–like collaboration, a relatively unfamiliar concept in the Eastern European transition efforts.

After their Pittsburgh experience the group began meeting for one weekend each month to continue the planning efforts and to hammer out recommendations for policy and practice to support the needed reforms. Steve and I managed to alternate our travel plans to BiH so that one or the other of us attended the work sessions, which were hosted in different cantons monthly. A defining moment came in February when a series of events made it clear to our colleagues that this was not a Pittsburgh–directed project. Although we had acted as if they were in charge of the planning, there were still confusions about our role in the project. The planning continued with a deeper commitment to the process.

One of the goals of the project was to widen the dialogue to include a larger representation of the educational community. In order to accomplish this, an educational conference was planned for June. The working document that was being created would be the centerpiece of the meeting. The Bosnian team worked very hard to finalize the report and plan for the June conference.

In 1997 April the World Bank funding ran out. The funding agreement had been rather problematic. When we first proposed the project, the Bank officer led us to believe that there would be funding for the entire project. A month into it, however, we were told that the Bank would only fund half of the effort, and would, supposedly, 'help us find the rest'. From early on we spent considerable energy looking for funds to complete the planning and finance the conference. In May we were able to continue the project through funding from the Open Society/Soros Foundation (without help from the Bank). A Federation–wide working conference was held at the University of Sarajevo (sponsored by the Ministry of Education and the University of Pittsburgh). The Bosnian Team published their working document which included recommendations for reform. Sections of the document served as the agenda for several working groups and members of the Bosnian Team organized and chaired each session. Tapes from the conference became useful data for subsequent recommendations. Most important, however, was the wide representation. There were Muslim, and Croatian educators from all of the cantons, as well as a few Serb educators from Sarajevo.

The *Obnova* project is considered by many Bosnian officials as an historic event. At a time when little collaboration is happening in other sectors of the country, *Obnova* has become a symbol of the larger goal of a multicultural state in BiH. The work has not been easy. For two months, during a highly charged political climate, the Croat contingent of the Team did not attend the monthly meetings. As the June conference grew near, however, the whole group came together with a high degree of commitment to each other and to their task at hand. One official in the Ministry of Education remarked that it was a 'small miracle' that Bosniaks and Croats have collaborated in the efforts and that there were also Bosnian–Serbs that contributed to the Sarajevo conference.

Our working relationships with our Bosnian colleagues in *Obnova*, as well as the active learning project, were productive and profound. We began to discover how to work within an atmosphere of mutual respect and reciprocity. We were all learning together. The perspective which I identified earlier seemed to serve us well. Our foreign passports, lack of Bosnian language, manager of project funding, cultural differences, etc. were clear images of the alien status we carried. Yet we found ways to 'be' with our colleagues, to dwell with them in mutual respect and caring. There were always expressions of meaning through special handshakes and hugging. We learned that there are many different ways to communicate through gestures and hugs. We learned to listen, even as the translations may have distorted the literal meanings of the words. There were always other ways to interpret meanings.

We were proud of the materials we had written for both projects. Our Bosnian colleagues reported that they found them useful, and in some cases, invaluable, especially when they located their own voices in the materials. They were especially grateful that we had them translated into the Bosnian language. Likewise, the Bosnian documents reflected our mutual discourse as well as their cultural perspective and intellectual rigor. We appreciated the Bosnian to English translations. In US educational research communities this effort is often referred to as 'development' (as differentiated from 'research'). I would argue that what we were doing here was a particular kind of research/development. It is impossible to locate the distinctions. The traditional assumptions related to research and development are blurred in this Bosnian project.

Bitter Wisdom

For Steve and I the project has yielded a good deal of bitter wisdom as well as deep fulfillment. Although we earned the gratitude and affection from our Bosnian colleagues, our relationship with two of the funding agencies was less than satisfactory. Much of the situation was acerbated by our own staff member. We learned, too late, that the Pitt field office manager was continually undermining our efforts from her position in Bosnia. We've come away from the project with psychic bruises from the duplicity we experienced. Even more painful was the sense of betrayal I felt when I remembered my earlier impressions of Lauren. I wrote Bosnian Tribute to her and later realized my need to romanticize her accomplishments in the program.

BOSNIAN TRIBUTE:
Since I've been here I've come to realize what a truly remarkable person Lauren Caldwell is. She's the Pitt Field Coordinator and one of our doctoral students. She came here in February 1995 with two suitcases and a document giving her legitimacy to fashion a program as a UNICEF partner. The war was still raging when she began conversations with Bosnian educators at all levels, including the Federal Ministry in Sarajevo. She heard their requests for some new teaching methods that would help sustain teachers who were keeping the kids in school. She designed workshops for 'active learning'. She was evacuated along with other UNICEF partners from Sarajevo, but continued the work in Tuzla. Just as the workshops were to become a reality, there was a massacre in a Tuzla square, killing 74 young people. Two hundred more were badly injured. UNICEF officials insisted she leave Tuzla. She took up residence in Zagreb (Croatia) where it was supposed to be relatively safe. The UNICEF main office had also moved there from Sarajevo during the siege. They urged her to go back to the US until 'things got better', but Lauren knew that if she left the Program would die. She said, 'I promised the Bosnian educators we'd do this. They've been disappointed so much. I just couldn't leave.' She held out in Zagreb for six weeks and returned to continue the work. She was evacuated one more time from Zenica, but went back again. She's lived under grim conditions including months of shelling. (One hit close to where she was living.) She's managed to organize two Pitt offices and staff. We now have our own vehicle. Last year's report documented the scope of her work. . . .
She's reached out to 220 educators from at least 100 primary schools, as well as 118 mentors who have been themselves working with teachers. She's done this with a minimum of help from Pitt during the war. Pitt faculty and students are now able to help expand the Program. Lauren's efforts have renewed my faith in the

notion that one person can truly make a difference. There's not enough in our language to give appropriate tribute to Lauren. The Bosnian word for thanks is 'hvala' and the Bosnian word for Bravo is 'Bravo!' . . . to you, Lauren . . .

Much love, Noreen.

Subversion

Our field manager, graduate student Lauren Caldwell, (not her real name) was hired by the former Faculty Program director. She was given carte blanche in 1994 when she arrived in Bosnia to establish our field office and contact our counterparts. In one of my 'postcards' I wrote the tribute to her because I believed, at that time, that she was a courageous educator who worked for the good of the Program. It represents my interpretation of her disposition at that time. It is a romanticized version, yet I am still willing to acknowledge her early accomplishments. During the first year of the UNICEF project, she directed most of the Pitt activities from the field with very little attention from the previous Pitt Faculty Director. She complained at great length that she had little access to Pitt Faculty who would be willing to take part in the Program, yet she seemed to enjoy the freedom she had to make all the decisions regarding the activities in Bosnia, including budget concerns. She was, in most ways, a maverick in the field who could direct the course of events. When Steve and I took over the direction of the Program, we began to create a team approach. Several Faculty were brought into the activities at Pitt. We wrote the second phase of the UNICEF initiative with specific directions regarding the educational experiences. This was a difficult transition for Lauren. She never quite adjusted to the change.

One thing I learned about staff in the international agencies in Bosnia (and perhaps most other nations in crisis) is that the 'humanitarian' workers form a tight community with an active social life that rivals their professional concerns. It's understandable given the need for support in difficult environments. And, although Lauren continually chided us for not 'understanding' our counterparts, it became clear that she had not spent much time listening to their perspectives. Her focus seemed primarily on the social contacts with the internationals rather than professional concerns of the Bosnians. It seemed that she was living, but not *dwelling* in Bosnia and Herzegovina.

We began to realize that our plans were being subverted, imperceptibly at first, but as time went on, it became clear. Lauren was undermining our credibility with the officers of both funding agencies, since they were part of the small social group of internationals who had their own concerns about the restructuring going on in their agencies. Fortunately, our field assistant, a young Bosnian, became a helpful ally to us. Lauren had turned over much of the office management to him. He was also an excellent liaison and interpreter with our Bosnian colleagues and we were able to continue our relationships with them through his efforts. He had a strong dedication to the success of the Program. Before the June conference Lauren took a job with an international agency in Bosnia. Her networking proved to be successful for her, but quite devastating to the Program.

Bitter Irony

Perhaps the most unfortunate episode happened through our association with the World Bank and the person who was the World Bank officer for the *Obnova* project. He was located in Eastern Europe and made infrequent trips to Sarajevo. We had little contact with him directly during most of the project. As the date grew near for the Bosnians to complete their report, I had an impromptu meeting with John (pseudonym) and Lauren in our Sarajevo office. At that time John stated his concern that the Bosnian document might not meet the Bank's expectations. It would, perhaps, be an inferior report. It became clear that Lauren was intending to write the final document. She claimed that she had all of the notes from the monthly planning meetings. (At this time we still didn't have funding to complete the project and we were considering the possibility of finishing the document and ending the initiative.) In the meeting I insisted that we had worked very hard to get all of the voices of the Bosnian educators included in the process and it was imperative that they produce the final report themselves. John continued to talk about his concern for the quality of the document and, in particular, that it should be 'useful to the Bank'. He mentioned that their office had gotten a report from another group in Eastern Europe that was unsatisfactory so they had to hire 'an expensive consultant to come in and write the final report for them'. He did not think they had the resources to do this for the Bosnians, but rather he insisted that the Bosnian team send the draft to him and others who could review the report and provide necessary editing before they finalized the report. I suggested that he convey his request directly to the Bosnian team leaders.

A week later we got the confirmation that the Soros Foundation would fund the remainder of the project. We could now proceed with the plans for the conference and a final report based on the results of the conference. The draft that the Bosnians were writing would serve as a working document for conference discourse. When John requested that the Bosnian team send out their draft for review before they print the conference document, the Bosnians refused to do so. They decided together that this document represented their efforts and insisted that any review and suggestions would be most welcome at the conference. They would remain the authors of their work. I got an angry call from John. He was annoyed that the Bosnians had taken such a hard position. I said that I thought it was quite appropriate. The Bosnian document reflected the Federation–wide dialogue and, as such, had achieved one of the major goals of our *Obnova* proposal sanctioned by the Bank. Furthermore, the Bosnian position was a clear indication that they had become owners of the planning process. John disregarded my view. He was certain that the document would not be 'up to Bank standards and would reflect badly on the project'. He said to me, 'Can't you people in Pittsburgh control those people and their decision?' I said that I assumed that our mission was not to 'control' our colleagues, but rather to stand by them as they took over the process. John ended the conversation, saying, 'Well, we'll see what it looks like'. When John received a copy of the working document he wrote a heated email, saying that the document 'was a great disappointment and the project was a failure'.

He later sent word that he was not able to attend the conference because he was on holiday.

The two day conference in June was quite successful. Two hundred educators were invited and 165 attended. They were sent the working document prior to the conference and many Bosnian educators reported their enthusiasm for the contents. The working groups used the findings and recommendations as a point of departure for further recommendations. The Bosnian team is currently putting together a final report. They have agreed to share the draft with the Bank and with the Pittsburgh colleagues, however they have made it clear that the audience for the final document, like the first draft, is meant for a Bosnian audience, including members of the Ministry of Education.

The irony here is disturbing. Although the Bank appeared to support a process to engender a sense of national empowerment, in reality, the efforts of the Bosnians were diminished for taking ownership of their process. It didn't seem to matter that the collaborative efforts accomplished the 'minor miracle' mentioned by a member of the Ministry of Education. The most important indicator of success became the way in which the Bosnian document would reflect the Bank expectations.

As I consider the implications of the World Bank story here, I also acknowledge our naiveté as we began the project. My experienced colleagues will respond by saying, 'Why would you have expected anything different?' After all, there is a body of critical literature, known as *Fifty Years is Enough* (Danaher, 1994) which reached a groundswell when the World Bank celebrated its fiftieth anniversary (for example, Jones, 1992). Rich (1994) adds to this literature with his treatise called *The Cuckoo in the Nest: Fifty Years of Political Meddling by the World Bank*. And, although this is an account of the duplicity of agencies like the World Bank and the way in which they play out their agenda, this is also a sad story of Lauren and John, who, while they are perpetrators, get caught up in the wider web of duplicity of the international agencies.

It seems that our experience was not uncommon. It did, however, serve to add to our wisdom about international humanitarian projects and the individuals who are successful in these endeavors, as well as the various criteria for success. We have continued to revisit the situations of our journey and to question our own actions. We realize that we need to interrogate the experiences in order to portray the lessons learned. In addition, there is a critical lens that we must use to give theoretic meaning to our story. Our bitter wisdom may help us gain a deeper perspective for this challenge. Maxwell (1992) poses the challenge to researchers for an inquiry that would 'have as its basic aim to improve, not just knowledge, but also personal and global *wisdom* — wisdom being understood to be the capacity to realize what is of value in life. To develop this new kind of inquiry, we will need to change almost every branch and aspect of the academic enterprise' (p. 205).

Postcards and Stances: Reflexively Narrating Research Writing

In this chapter I have attempted to introduce three research stances that reflect different perspectives on our Bosnian experience. Through my writing I began to realize that a research stance gives direction to the author's interpretive voice and position in the text. The significance of the text is, to an extent, established through the author's stance. One's stance can also serve as a lens into deeper meanings of one's text. I examined my early writing through the lens of *exotic horror*, realizing that it was important to move beyond the preoccupation with the devastating conditions in Bosnia so that I might become more productive. I described briefly the situations which helped us create educational materials through our sense of *alien dwelling*, when the strange became familiar and we discovered our ability to be 'at home' with our colleagues and their work. Finally, I narrated the events and ironies which led to our *bitter wisdom* and, as such, a stance which can give rise to critical, theoretic research. I continue to revisit our Bosnian experience, recognizing the profound metaphor it has become.

BOSNIA AND POSTMODERNISM:

24 February 1996: I've talked and written a lot over these past few years about post–modernism . . . among other things, questioning the utility of modern structures. As an academic, of course, I am referring to mental structures, forms of representation socially contrived and assumed as 'reality' or rather the way the world 'really' is in some correspondence to the physical world. It may be that Bosnia presents a compelling metaphor of post–modernism!! Physical structures that once made sense are now symbols of frustration . . . no longer providing comforts of the modern world. The sink faucets are here, but there's no running water much of the time. The toilets are here, but they don't flush everywhere. Gas heaters stand cold and quiet. Elevators run sometimes. There're more kind of chocolate bars than vegetables in the markets. The television ads from Germany sell exercise equipment. IFOR military convoys carrying weapons trail behind horse drawn carts carrying wood. These modern physical structures will eventually be fixed and all will serve the good life again. Unfortunately the social structures aren't so clearly repairable. Remnants of psychic fixtures are still around, but so badly broken, and their repair, or rather our salvation, depends on our ability to face the question, 'What does "the good life" mean in regard to our lives together?' That's what we're facing as educators here. Truly a post–modern dilemma! . . .

Much love, Noreen.

References

BERREBY, D. (1995) 'Unabsolute truths: Clifford Geertz', *The New York Times Magazine*.

DANAHER, K. (Ed.) (1994) *Fifty Years is Enough: The Case Against the World Bank and the International Monetary Fund*, Boston, MA: South End Press.

GOLDBERG, N. (1986) *Writing Down the Bones*, Boston, MA: Shambhala.

HEIDEGGER, M. (1971) *Poetry, Language and Thought*, New York: Harper & Row.

JONES, P. (1992) *World Bank Financing of Education: Lending, Learning and Development*, London: Routledge.

MAXWELL, N. (1992) 'What kind of inquiry can best help us create a good world?', *Science, Technology, & Human Values*, **17**, 2, pp. 205–27.

PEACOCK, J.L. (1998) *The Anthropological Lens: Harsh Light, Soft Focus*, Cambridge: Cambridge University Press.

RICH, B. (1994) 'The cuckoo in the nest: Fifty years of political meddling by the world bank', *The Ecologist*, **24**, 1, pp. 8–13.

RICHARDSON, L. (1994) 'Writing: A method of inquiry', in DENZIN, N. and YVONNA, L. (Eds.) *Handbook of Qualitative Research*, Thousand Oaks, CA: Sage Publications.

RICOEUR, P. (1991) *From Text to Action: Essays in Hermeneutics, II*, Evanston, IL: Northwestern University Press.

STONE, R. (1996) *The Healing Art of Storytelling: A Sacred Journey of Personal Discovery*, New York: Hyperion.

In/forming *Inside Nursing*:
Ethical Dilemmas in Critical Research

Annette Street

Introduction

I recently visited a small country town in Victoria, Australia which is widely known
for its retention of the charm and character of the 1880s gold rush period. The main
street is lined with mellow sandstone buildings with wide shapely verandahs, and
the businesses tastefully recreate this bygone era in the presentation of their wares or
trades to the public. Yet a wander down the back lane behind this street took me into
a very different world. It was evident that many businesses had a well–preserved
facade which hid endless variety — modern factory units, extensive workshops,
tumbling down or patched sheds coated in dust and grime, and small family homes
of any vintage; diversity and incongruities abounded. Clearly the view provided
from the horse drawn carriage which took tourists along the main streets was very
different from the realities of the lives of the people who lived and worked there.
The disjunction between the carefully created homogeneity of the artifice that was
the streetscape and the haphazard individuality and uneasy alliances provided by the
contrasts glimpsed in the lane was disrupting and fascinating. It clearly portrayed
my own contrary feelings as I reflect on the whitewashing practices in which many
of us engage to re/present the ethical dilemmas we encounter in critical research.
Although as a reflective project I did disclose and discuss many of the problems
I encountered at the time, it was not until I revisited the journals kept during the
research process that I found a more revealing picture.

In this chapter I intend to peer into the backyard of my doctoral research
which was reported as *Inside Nursing* (1992) and in my journal notes of the time,
through the gaze of my more recent experience and my changing theoretical position as a feminist whose critical work is currently largely informed by cultural studies
and post–modern perspectives.

Situating the Research

Inside Nursing was a product of its time and the political location of the research.
The research was conducted in 1987 in Melbourne, Australia. It was structured as
a critical ethnography of clinical nursing practice at a time when the only other
example of this form of research practice I could locate was the work of Willis

(1977), and when very few people were interested in the culture of nursing practice. Not only was critical research alien to the medically dominated nursing community I was to work with, but it was generally considered very radical and totally ignored by mainstream academia. Critical research of the time in Australia was largely informed by the work of the Frankfurt School, by Habermas and Freire. It was a quintessential modernist exercise in which we agreed with Fay's (1987) contention that humans were agents capable of reflecting upon their worlds collaboratively and taking action to change it. With radical fervour we echoed the weighty words of *enlightenment, empowerment* and *emancipation*. It was exciting to read and speak but daunting to make central to your research process, something that troubled me daily during the research. I encountered Foucault's books (1972, 1977, 1980) late in the research process. His ideas were not well known in my academic circle at that time but his work on the power/knowledge relationship became important as an analytical focus of the study. Soon after I had completed my thesis the shops were flooded with post–modern texts which soundly challenged the enlightenment project that my coresearchers and I had been struggling to reflect in our research activities, and generally anointed Foucault the latest theoretical guru.

My understanding of feminist critical research ethics was fed by the early papers of Lather which were later published in 1991 and the work of Oakley (1981) and Finch (1984) in addressing the subjective nature of the feminist interview encounter and the attending ethical responsibility. I find that many of the dilemmas raised by these authors and their colleagues are still just as relevant for my students today.

Since the publication of *Inside Nursing* I have more often been asked to speak about ethical dilemmas than any other area. As I had chosen to do my critical ethnographic work within a hospital (perhaps the last bastion of positivist and paternalistic ethics committees) the ethical tensions inherent in my chosen approach and in the values of that particular scientific, institutional context, were thrown into sharp relief. During those times, armed with enthusiasm and the theoretical discussions of the university community we had some slick answers to the ethical questions. There was a temptation to argue self–righteously that participatory critical research designs did not deal in deception or treat its participants (subjects) as objects of the research, rather they were collaborators who were active in the meaning making, decision making and implementation processes. There was a tendency to minimize the problem of confidentiality as the assumption was that we were exploring issues not personal lives and the collegial research structures enabled us to collaboratively manage the data. Participants were presumed to be volunteers able to decide when, how and what to divulge. The recruitment process was structured to cover informed consent.

As I locate myself now 10 years further on from the particular research project reported in *Inside Nursing*, I can discern changes in my attitudes to ethics in critical projects and in the ethical conduct of my research practice. With Eisner (1991) I share a desire to be ethical with an acknowledgment that at times the ethical facade is shielded by the research rhetoric and undermined by the complexity of actual research decision making in real life research situations.

Inside Nursing: A Critical Ethnography of Clinical Nursing Practice

I began this study with an interest in the everyday lives of nurses. It was a highly neglected area. As Oakley (1986) was to discover about her own practice as a feminist medical sociologist, nurses were invisible in the explorations of health care. Doctors and patients loomed large as subjects of sociological interest but nurses were barely mentioned. Despite the predominantly female population of nursing and its position as a discipline marginalized and hierarchically subordinated to the male–dominated medical profession, feminists were also not interested in nurses or nursing. Nurses themselves mostly described their work in practical or scientific ways, intent on legitimating their professional base. I was a feminist interested in the roles and work of nurses, in how they made sense of their daily lives, in the power relationships which shaped their knowledge and action, in the value of reflection as a process for change. I chose to collaborate with interested nurses to reveal something of the way nurses thought, acted and reflected on their practice. This attempt to be a collaborator as an outsider to the setting was a new experience and stretched my faith in *emancipatory* research designs from the start. As recorded in my journal:

> I went into the setting armed with my previous experience of inviting emancipatory research (partnerships) from the inside as a colleague and participant . . . the confidence I had developed through this soon disappeared when I realized the difficulties of doing emancipatory research with nurses on the wards who were not friends, nor colleagues who shared my angst, nor compelled to cooperate and do research 'my' way by a higher authority who had something invested in the research product. Question: Is emancipatory research able to be initiated by an outsider? Would nurses have initiated this kind of emancipatory research themselves? On both counts the answer is 'probably not'!!! — a classic dilemma to start with.

I began with a great respect for nurses which was enhanced through the opportunity to see the good, bad and ugly in nursing. The project was an ethnography because it explored the everyday world of five clinical nurses over a period of nine months through the processes of participant observation, in–depth interviews, group discussion and document analysis. It was a *critical* ethnography because the 'key informants' took the role of coresearchers in the process; they gave me running commentaries on their thoughts and actions as I observed; they read, discussed and debated the data I collected; they contributed their own reflections; they began to theorise with me. It was a *feminist* ethnography because it situated nursing as a female dominated profession whose knowledge and practice was marginalized and silenced by the dominance of the male domains of science and medicine. I argued that nurses carried the double load of being both nurses and mainly women with a large part–time work force, home and family responsibilities, and a largely oral, personal and subjective culture. It was both *critical* and *feminist* because it shared a concern with the exercise of power/knowledge in the lives of women/nurses, a commitment to collaborative action, a desire to find more authentic ways of under-standing and practising nursing, and a desire to communicate the findings in ways that were relevant to the wider audience of nurses.

Exploring The Exercise of Power in Research Relationships

Obtaining Ethics Approval

I was not a novice critical researcher when I embarked on this particular project; I had been well prepared and mentored by Stephen Kemmis and John Smyth. At that time, the School of Education at Deakin University, Geelong provided a very stimulating intellectual climate for a would–be academic. I had been privy to count-less debates about the roles of all people who participated in critical research; endless theoretical discussions on whether they were to be called researchers, coresearchers, participants or even 'teachers–as–intellectuals'. I had worked with both Stephen and John on other projects to develop procedures for ethical conduct of critical projects. My own set of procedures and consent forms were based on this previous work and were highly praised by the Doctoral Committee for their congruency with the the-oretical tenets of critical research as we understood it at that time. My proposal discussed negotiation at some length: negotiation of access, of the boundaries of what is included and excluded, of accounts, of release of information, of publication. I addressed the issues of privileged access to data; the representation of differing views; the confidentiality of information and reporting; I outlined my accountabil-ity to the various parties involved. I explored my role as researcher and the role of the key informants as coresearchers. Why then did the hospital Medical Ethics Committee regard my procedures as inadequate? Why did they say they couldn't understand why I was discussing negotiation, that I obviously had no idea about confidentiality, that I had no clear 'subjects' in my study, that I had no appropriate analytical (quantitative) methods, that my study was obviously biased, capable of misrepresentation, intent on disclosing personal medical information, and finally unethical?

Of key interest to the Ethics Committee was what data I would collect and what I would do with it. This concern was echoed by the nursing administration and by the nurses who were planning to become coresearchers with me, albeit for entirely different reasons. After much hard work and countless explanations I was finally allowed to begin my research under the watchful eye of the Research Projects Director who had changed from gatekeeper to sponsor.

I understood that this assault on the integrity of my project by doctors and medical scientists was because they did not have an understanding of what a critical project was and how it could be done ethically. As I have continued to conduct my research in demanding health care environments dominated by scientism I have faced continual challenges to the veracity of my work and I have found that indeed, despite our rhetoric, there are times when the ethical facades of our critical streets cover a range of less desirable backyards. In recognition of the ethical squalor of these backyards I have become much more thoughtful about providing appropriate answers to ethics committees.

How Informed is Informed Consent?

In the production of scientific knowledge with 'human subjects' the ethical concern lies with the manner by which people are recruited into the project and treated during their involvement. The concern is that the research does not harm these people whilst it enables the researcher to collect the information or body product or conduct the test which is part of the trial. The issues of *power* in the contact with the human subject in these forms of research is not discussed. Ethics committees are interested in whether the researcher has the knowledge to protect the interests of the person and to do the research. The relationships are brief and the interests of the person are generally irrelevant to the research.

Conversely, the exercise of power is a central interest of critical research and, as such, the structure and ongoing negotiation of the research relationships are continually in the spotlight. The adage *do no harm* is hardly enough of a safeguard for relationships within a critical project, rather the emphasis must be on how we collaborate, develop collegiality and how we treat each other respectfully as fellow human beings. This kind of rhetoric reads well but is hard to achieve; it requires constant thoughtfulness.

When we invite other people to collaborate with us in our critical research, in other paradigms this is called our recruitment strategy, we are ethically bound to acquaint them with all the potential issues that their involvement might entail. This assumes in us a capacity of foresight which requires a reliable crystal ball. As a critical project takes a collaborative and collegial approach with a specified intent of either social redress, improvement in practice or change in policy, then the outcome is never predictable. The outcome will be redefined as the emergent issues are addressed. If we are unsure of where our research activities will take us how can we provide *informed* consent to those we travel the research journey with?

Even as I faithfully followed my ethical procedures I was aware that these nurses were consenting to become part of something from outside any of their own frames of reference. They accepted my explanations in good faith. They all remembered negative experiences as data collectors in medical research so expressed excitement at the prospect of being coresearchers and exploring their nursing practice. To all appearances there was no coercion and these nurses were all volunteers, yet I later discovered that two of the nurses were directed to participate by superiors and one nurse was the 'representative' of another group with a different agenda.

During the life of the ethnography there were a number of changes at the hospital which meant that information I/we were collecting was politically compromising for a couple of the nurses. In order to protect their jobs and their union activities we agreed that I would not use some of the excellent material we had collected, analysed, and theorized. I felt that the good faith they had entrusted in me needed to be reciprocated but as a researcher it was an agonising decision and I felt guilty leaving out that part of the picture.

My reflection on that situation enabled me to develop a strategy to prepare people for their participation in critical projects. I have run workshops exploring the research strategies and also work with groups to explore the ethical issues for themselves and the potential impact on their jobs or their workplace. These workshops have supported prospective participants to think about how they will deal with the technologies of power inherent in the situation and the research process. They are required to propose their own strategies to deal with ethical issues of coercion, confidentiality, negotiation, obligations, responsibilities, and potential for upset or harm. After the workshop there is a cooling off period of three–seven days duration to enable people to think further on the implications before signing consent. I still suspect that, despite these measures, people join in with my critical projects because a superior has intimated it would be a good idea, because they think it will enable them to control the research results, or because they think it will bring about a quick solution to a long time problem.

The Ethics of Access: Re/presenting the Self as Researcher

As part of the probation process I was required to show my early documentation to selected senior medical and nursing staff. As I was intending to not only show my work to the coresearchers but then to actively engage them in coauthoring position papers with me for wider distribution, this requirement did not create the consternation in me that I think the Committee expected. As an ethnographer I was interested in how codes of dress were used as demarkators of status and prestige such that the wearer was able to exercise power in certain forms or have power exercised over them. In a hospital where everyone's clothing is overlaid with structured and unstructured meanings, exploring dress codes provided me with a place to start. I continually discussed the information on dress codes with the coresearchers as I collected it. They rapidly caught the spirit of the inquiry and highlighted all kinds of subtleties which I may not have noticed. I wrote a position paper showing how I was representing their views and they loved it and wanted to show it to everyone in their areas. We gave a copy to the required senior staff and anyone else who was interested. Everyone was interested and thought the paper fascinating, but the seeming threat that I had posed as a researcher was dissipated. I was harmless after all. I wasn't even interested in important things like the new breakthroughs in heart/lung transplants; for some crazy reason I was interested in codes of dress, roles, routines and rituals; questions about who did what to whom, how power was exercised, how nurses understood their practice world and acted to change it.

The presentation of self in my persona as a researcher was not only directed towards the medical and senior nursing establishment. In *Inside Nursing* I discussed the clothing strategies I adopted to 'blend in' and yet hold my distinct place in the hospital as a researcher interested in nurses. A further issue related to the strategies I needed to adopt in order to discard my usual professional role as a very experienced crisis counsellor. This was not too difficult in structured situations as I could pre–plan how I would speak and act as a researcher and how I would ignore cues to adopt a counselling role. However in the high drama of a busy intensive care unit where many relatives and even staff needed debriefing and sometimes therapeutic interventions, it was very difficult for me not to respond. I had to learn to ignore distress cues from relatives when alone with them and their loved one, and to call for a nurse. I had to watch nurses handle counselling in a less skilled way than I would have done–this was their professional environment and not mine. I had to safeguard my research ethics whilst also safeguarding both sets of professional ethics.

Confidentiality

In all textbooks on ethics the issue of confidentiality is central to the discussion. How can we protect personal privacy and guarantee confidentiality? The issue of confidentiality relates to the collection of information, storage of records and the dissemination of the research findings. In this study the Ethics Committee were particularly interested in what information I would collect about sensitive patient data. As I was conducting participant observation in the hospital for nine months this was a legitimate concern. What was I going to write and would that impinge on people's privacy? Patient information was important to nursing decision making and would be included in the field notes but as we discussed this issue we recognized that it was possible to use a number of descriptors that kept the integrity of the patient situated contextually in the account without disclosing identifying information. For example, there were many males having coronary artery grafts during the research period which was usually enough identification for the purposes of an explanation and was not traceable. When patients had particular, specific, highly individual conditions or experiences which were necessary to be elaborated to make sense of the data, then other identifiers were changed such as marital status, number of offspring or even on occasions gender. As the nurses read through the various drafts of the thesis it was possible to make sure that identifying data about doctors, nurses, patients and others were altered. A critical project has the potential for the coresearchers to actively shape and vet the information to assist the researcher decide if confidentiality has been breached or if material is compromising to themselves or others in a way that is harmful.

Some staff were initially concerned that my obvious presence would 'corrupt' and 'bias' the data. I was able to counter that argument with the example that when guests stay in our home we can only put on a 'good face' for a short time and then fall back into our normal patterns. As I was to be present in the setting for a long time I would see the situation 'warts and all'. The one thing that really concerned me about protecting privacy was the impact of my presence on the privacy of the person, but this was not discussed by the staff of this large university teaching hospital. It was common practice for students of various health disciplines to observe or participate in activities with patients and, technically, patients agreed to this when they entered the hospital. I was very sensitive to the intrusive nature of my research situation when I was privy to discussions with families about their loved one on issues such as turning off life support machinery. My background in family counselling probably contributed to my personal awareness at being incorporated into such discussions and also helped me act to minimize my intrusion. I did ask oral consent of most people to stay and be present in the situation. I was never refused but I knew that it was hard for very anxious people to make an informed decision about my participation when I was already standing there with notebook in hand. The situation called for constant consideration of the effects of the intrusive nature of participant observation and a reminder of the need to use as much discretion as possible. It also made me very careful with the handling and storage of my fieldnotes when in public places.

Disrupting the Power of the Data Collector

Eisner (1991) questions the ethical responsibility of the researcher when they are present during an unethical encounter, such as when a racially bigoted teacher subtly encourages children to be bigots. As an educational ethnographer, Burgess (1989) describes how he was present when racist remarks were made about a teacher in the farewell speeches and that he felt as a researcher he was able to distance himself from the comments. He explains that the head kept looking at him:

> I could only imagine that he, unlike some teachers, realized that all these remarks were destined for my fieldnote book and ultimately for publication (p. 64).

As a critical researcher my process gave me no such luxury. When I was relatively new to the field and writing down every word and action, I observed a coresearcher engage in highly inappropriate behaviour which could be classed as sexual harassment. It was then that I was faced with the effects of an open notebook policy where everything I had recorded was presented for collaborative discussion. I was sorely tempted to not to disclose my notes on the episode as I felt it was none of my business. I was afraid that it could disrupt the rapport with the person and, as I and my research was still 'on probation', it could result in the termination of the research. But, ethically I had committed myself to collaboration, to work together with these women to construct shared meanings and not to have 'hidden' notes. After a sleepless night I presented the nurse with the account in the notes and asked her to talk about it. I then explained how it had appeared to me which was surprising and confronting for her and difficult for me. The next day we theorized the structured patriarchy of health care institutions and the way power and sexuality is exercised in them. We discussed the impact on nurses who feel powerless and adopted those methods which had marginalized them.

I was to have to deal with a similar ethical dilemma with each of the researchers in relation to habitual practices which appeared to me as an outsider to be discriminatory, exploitative, manipulative or immoral. In each instance we discussed them and explored the reasons why the practices developed and their grounding in the technologies of power which permeated the structure of these nurse's lives. I shared with them my own journal accounts of my own actions as a researcher and my similar responses to feeling marginalized. It was never easy but these incidents contributed to a climate of developing mutual trust where 'failings' could be acknowledged and theorized because my notebooks were also full of rich accounts of superb nursing practice.

The ethical contention that coresearchers will edit their own data to make themselves appear 'better' has never been sustained in my experience. The reflective sharing process enabled us all to examine and stand back far enough from the data enough to theorize it, deal with its practical implications and collaboratively decide how to deal with it in the text.

The Right to Withdraw

In all informed consent forms the 'right to withdraw' is central to the understanding that the person participating is a volunteer, and as such a free agent able to withdraw themselves or their data at any time. This may not create too many problems in studies with a large sample size but in a critical ethnography when you have only a few coresearchers (key informants) then the loss of one person and their data can adversely affect the research. Nurses are often very professionally mobile and this was the case at the time of the study. Nurses were moving from unit to unit, from hospital to hospital, from place to place. In this study I had recruited six nurses from two settings who agreed to participate on the understanding that they would be present at the hospital. But this was not to be. Almost immediately one nurse began six weeks of night duty and then decided to move to a country hospital to be near her sick mother. So I wrote her out of the study. Another nurse left the study halfway through to move overseas with her husband who was a doctor doing specialty postgraduate work. We discussed her involvement and as the data I collected with her showed a different picture to that of the others we decided that I would negotiate its meanings with her and use that in the early part of the findings. Then another nurse decided to go into a specialist course. As the course still involved her in clinical practice and she was very committed to what was by then 'our research', she became a regular visitor to my house to share her experiences on tape. By this stage of the research I was reaching data saturation in the clinical setting and was working at a more analytical level so this strategy helped us get a more reflective approach to the data. In this way I minimized the loss of coresearchers and was able to include their data in the process.

Democratic Intent: From Annette's Research to 'Our' Research?

Critical research projects avow a democratic intent which is intended to critique and disrupt existing power relationships. An exploration of language and discourses is crucial to critical projects, often displaying the changing ownership of the project as the talk moves from *Annette's* project or *the (name)* project to *our* project. An ethical issue in critical research relates to the question of 'ownership' of the project. For example, the language in the following journal account and excerpts from the project data demonstrates the subtle distinctions as this process occurs:

> 'I have just thought of something I wanted to tell you about for *your* project' . . . so far I have found that the nurses generally are more interested in pursuing questions related to themselves as individual nurses than they are in examining nursing, its knowledge and its power structures. They are not uncooperative . . . they are all very patient and interested in talking to me and answering *my* questions (journal).
>
> I have been thinking further about why not many nurses are feminist . . . *the* project has got me thinking about this and I asked (another senior nurse) what she thought and *we* all started to talk about it at lunchtime . . . (fieldnotes)

If you come to this unit meeting with me *we'll* see some interesting things about medical dominance to write about for *our* project . . . (fieldnotes)

Yet, this apparent progression of ownership misrepresents the situation. There was no sense that the nurses shared equal ownership of the entire research. The words 'our project' meant the collaborative activity of data collection, analysis and theorizing. Accounts from my journal at that time reveal my feelings when the critical intent was not supported through negotiation of the final theorizing and thesis writing.

> . . . I have just recognized the impact that this oral culture is having on the hierarchical relationships in the research process. I worked hard to successfully develop a non–hierarchical reciprocal relationship with the nurses in the study. This was working well as it was obvious to them that I thought about nursing in ways that they hadn't considered but at the same time, they had knowledge and expertise that I didn't. However these nurses who were steeped in a talking culture were very reluctant to write anything and as I had no power over them I could not make them (oh for the ease of working with students who have to jump through hoops or fail!!). Therefore I wrote and then handed them my notes also handing them the power to challenge or amplify or correct. They did respond to specific misunderstandings of their actions on my part and corrected technical information. One nurse wrote some very brief critiques of herself in the margin. Yet it became apparent to me that the previous flattened hierarchy which meant that nurses had no qualms about changing, challenging or orally correcting me and participating actively in making sense of the data was changed as soon as we began working with the recorded data. The nurses acted as if I was the 'expert' and had the right to choose what should be recorded and that their role was only to respond to my initiatives.

I had so much more to gain from the process — a Ph D — and so was required to be the majority shareholder of the final reporting and to raise the theorizing to another level of analysis. We discussed this situation on occasions and, although the nurses didn't want to write a thesis of 100,000 words, I felt concerned at the power that is inherent in the one who chooses what words are reported and how ideas and situations are re/presented. As Eisner (1991) reminds us:

> We do not like to think of ourselves as using others as a means to our own professional ends, but if we embark upon a research study that we conceptualize, direct, and write, we virtually assure that we will use others for our purposes. (p. 226)

Negotiation of Outcomes

As explained previously, the term negotiation occurred frequently in my ethical document. I understood that negotiation would need to take place over time but I did not really understand the way that my research design reflected my research interests and that the outcomes I was attempting to negotiate were most consistent with an academic approach. For example, I intended to negotiate with the coresearchers to coauthor some position papers for publication and inclusion in the thesis. I had read of Tripp's (1983) work on coauthoring and discussed it with academic colleagues who were very encouraging. We addressed the issue of withdrawal of data which had affected Tripp's efforts but we assumed that the interests of the academy in publishing were central research outcomes. I envisioned myself collegially collaborating with and empowering the nurses to get papers published with me, something I was unable to achieve. Consider the reality of the situation I discovered:

> By writing down what I saw as useful or relevant knowledge and data meant that I disempowered them by moving on to terrain (the written word) in which they did not feel comfortable . . . The nurses were happy to discuss the data orally but became passive when it was written down. To change this I used my tape recorder to record the dialogue with two nurses. This was particularly time consuming for me and on reflection I found myself having to be selective about what was included in the text for the next discussion. This again gave me the power as editor. To deal with this the second time through I did not edit the conversation but this act did not reassure the nurses as they were embarrassed by the amount of 'waffle' and personal detail in the transcript. They found it difficult to edit themselves. Two nurses responded to this situation by making notes as the thoughts occurred to them — something I had been constantly encouraging them to do. Neither of them wrote more than a few words to prompt them and then proceeded to tell me what they had been thinking. Both were reluctant to show me the notes and when I saw them they consisted of a few isolated words and phrases covering half a page. They had no meaning for me (journal).

This experience led me to reflect on research writing as a technology of power which relocates the position of the coresearcher and their oral discursive practice to the position of respondent rather than interpreter of the meanings.

> It seems to me that when I change the domain from the oral to the written word I also change the balance of power. This raises the question whether a researcher who functions through a process of writing to describe and analyse a culture that is based on oral transmission of knowledge can develop *emancipatory* research.
> It is evident that there are ethical issues involved in inviting people to become coresearchers in projects which are based in academic discourses which, in this

instance, marginalized the oral discourses of their practice as nurses and, more generally, the orally structured discursive practices of many aspects of women's cultures. Too often the power of the editor is glossed over and the question of who speaks for whom, in what circumstances and under what conditions, becomes a central issue (journal).

Discussing this issue in *Inside Nursing* I attributed my failure firstly, to the oral tradition of nurses where they wished to talk not write; and secondly, to the fact that they valued action whereas a pre–occupation with writing was an interest of the academy. This analysis was one with which they concurred, but I have more recently coauthored papers with nurse coresearchers and realise that this explanation was based on a modernist concern with consensus.

Benefits to the Participants

In every ethics proposal researchers are expected to detail the benefits of the re-search process to the participants. This strategy enables the evaluating committee to decide if the research work is so worthwhile the committee can support the use of human subjects. As previously discussed, I had enticed these nurses with the intangibles of collaboration and the tangible reward of academic publication! When publication was obviously not what they valued I needed to think clearly about my responsibility to them in tangible terms. Over time as I came to know these nurses very well they began to discuss their personal and professional lives, their aspirations and problems. I became an academic resource and increasingly they used me as someone to debrief with. I understood that their desired outcomes related to learning from me in the research and by using me as an academic adviser on courses and on how to prepare assignments. I also discovered that they wanted me to help them cope with the burn out and critical decision making which was central to their lives. At the time it seemed a fair exchange to negotiate as a successful outcome for us all.

Looking Back . . . Moving Forward

Through the process of deconstructing my journal depicting the modernist critical research world of *Inside Nursing*, I charted my shifting subjectivity, the techno-logies of power which I constantly questioned and the ethical messiness of research work.

I remain a researcher. I constantly engage with these contentious ethical questions in the health field. I have found that it is much harder to be theoretically and ethically consistent in the realities of field work. Although my theorizing is in/formed by post–modern thinkers I still have to deal with a research field traversed by public and private discourses shaped by health economics, evidence–based medicine, quality improvement, productivity measures, population statistics, and the received 'truth'.

My research work adopts a critical feminist ethical research process to coconstruct texts in the field. I then analyse them through a feminist post–modern lens.

My research work is still critical enough to be interested in gathering groups of people who have enough in common on a particular issue to be prepared to work together to improve a situation. But I no longer expect the kind of consensual agreement I had expected in the past where power was exercised illegitimately under the guise of the 'common good'. A post–modern project enables the divergent voices and expectations to disrupt the symmetry of the consensus process where power can be exercised subtly when we adopt an artificial semblance of agreement. Now I tend to work with looser alliances of stakeholders and tolerate ambiguity and dissension. When I negotiate I try to enable each member of the group to explore what a satisfying outcome of the research activity is for them personally. Those who choose to write for publication I coauthor with, but those who regard an improvement in a situation or the development of policy is what they want, then we affirm this. The power–sharing democratic focus is not on equality in contribution and outcomes but on the level of satisfaction of personal, professional, group, community or social goals. Research remains a constantly challenging and humbling engagement with ethical dilemmas.

References

BURGESS, R.G. (1989) 'Grey areas: Ethical dilemmas in educational ethnography', in BURGESS, R.G. (Ed.) *The Ethics of Educational Research*, New York: Falmer Press, pp. 60–76.

EISNER, E.W. (1991) *The Enlightened Eye*. New York: Macmillan Publishing Company.

FAY, B. (1987) *Critical Social Science*. Ithaca, NY: Cornell University Press.

FINCH, J. (1984) 'Its great to have someone to talk to: The ethics and the politics of interviewing women', in BELL, C.R. (Ed.) *Social Researching: Politics, Problems and Practice*, London: Routledge and Kegan Paul, pp. 70–87.

FOUCAULT, M. (1972) *The Archeology of Knowledge*, London: Tavistock Publications.

FOUCAULT, M. (1977) *Discipline and Punish: The Birth of the Prison*, New York: Pantheon.

FOUCAULT, M. (1980) 'Two Lectures' in GORDON, G. (Ed.) *Power and Knowledge: Selected interviews and other writings 1972–1977'* New York: Pantheon.

LATHER, P. (1991) *Getting Smart*, New York: Routledge.

OAKLEY, A. (1986) *Telling the Truth about Jerusalem*, London: Routledge and Kegan Paul.

SMITH, L.M. (1990) 'Ethics in Qualitative Field Research: An Insider Perspective', in EISNER, E.W. and PESHKIN, A. (Eds.) *Qualitative Inquiry in Education*, New York: Teachers College Press, pp. 258–76.

STREET, A. (1992) *Inside Nursing*, New York: SUNY Press.

TRIPP, D.H. (1983) 'Coauthorship and negotiation: The interview as act of creation', *Interchange*, **14**, 3 pp. 32–45.

WILLIS, P. (1977) *Learning to Labor*, London: Saxon House.

10 On What Might Have Been: Some Reflections on Critical Multiculturalism

Stephen May

In January 1997 I received a letter in Bristol, England — where I currently live and work — which both surprised and saddened me. In the letter, the Japanese correspondent outlined how she had left her lecturing position in Japan, where she had taught English, to undertake further postgraduate study in the USA on multicultural education. What so surprised me was her reason for doing so: she had made this move, she said, as a direct result of reading my critical ethnography of Richmond Road School in Auckland, New Zealand (May, 1994; see also, May, 1995). Perhaps I should not have been so surprised. After all, the educational innovation apparent at Richmond Road had already received international attention (see Cazden, 1989). Moreover, I had specifically argued in the conclusion to my own ethnography that the school's approach to multiculturalism — what I had termed 'critical multiculturalism' — was applicable internationally. In particular, I had argued that the example of this small inner–city New Zealand primary (elementary) school had much to offer to the wider debates on the theory, policy and practice of multiculturalism. I still believe this to be the case but it nevertheless came as somewhat of a shock to be taken at my word. We may all acknowledge the internationalism of academia, but it is not until an event like this occurs that you really start to believe it.

However, the letter also saddened me because the writer specifically wanted to visit Richmond Road to observe at first hand the school's approach to multiculturalism. Regretfully, I had to inform her that, to my knowledge, what I had outlined in my critical ethnography was now no longer being practised. I had heard that a different principal had since been appointed to Richmond Road and had returned the school to a more 'traditional' and monocultural approach; an approach that its two previous principals, Jim Laughton and Lionel Pedersen, had spent 20 years attempting to subvert. While I still believe that Richmond Road — from the time of Laughton's arrival in the early 1970s to the early 1990s when I examined the school — provides an exemplary model of just what can be achieved in multicultural education, the project now appears at an end. Having to inform my correspondent to this effect brought into sharp relief my own feelings about Richmond Road and the enthusiasm and commitment with which I had undertaken my account of all that had been achieved at the school. The school had fired my imagination — in the same way, it seems, as my correspondent — and the sense of disappointment and loss at its subsequent fate remains palpable. It is with this background in mind that I want to return to my own involvement in the research and to explore the various theoretical, epistemological and methodological issues with which I grappled at the time. They say that hindsight is a wonderful thing but some of the ambiguities and tensions that I encountered during the course of my research *are* much clearer now than they were then, although in the light of what has happened, no less troubling.

Origins and Principal Concerns

My first research contact with Richmond Road School in February 1990 was, like most things, an accident. In terms of my own 'biographical positioning' (Coe, 1991; Sparkes, 1994) in relation to the research, I was a graduate student at the time, having recently left secondary teaching to return to academic study at Massey University in Palmerston North, New Zealand. It was in the process of establishing a project on school language policies that Richmond Road School's name (and reputation) was mentioned. As I happened to be flying to Auckland (some 600 miles away) the following week, I rang the school on the off chance that they might see me. Lionel Pedersen, the Principal at the time, agreed that I could visit the school for the day. Little did I know at that point what this seemingly casual arrangement was to lead to.

The day that I was there proved a revelation. As an erstwhile high school teacher I had little experience of primary schools and even less experience of the link between educational theory and practice. Like most New Zealand trained high school teachers, my only previous experience of the latter had been a cursory one–year graduate course at a teachers' training institution in the mid–1980s. I say cursory because my teaching subject (and my undergraduate degree) was in English and we spent most of that all too brief year addressing English curriculum content and delivery. Precious little time was spent on the educational theories of teaching and learning and even less on the wider structural factors that impinge on these. (As an aside, this now helps to explain why I found my first years of teaching so difficult!) I was thus wholly unprepared for the depth of educational engagement that I experienced on that first visit to Richmond Road. Having only just begun to experience and address these issues for myself, and having left teaching to do so, it came as a shock to find teachers in situ who had been grappling with educational theory and practice, and their interconnections, for some considerable time. Coupled with the rather imperious view that we secondary teachers had of our primary colleagues, this came as a double shock. As I was soon to find out, there was far more yet to learn about education than I had ever expected.

On that first day, I spent the morning talking informally with Lionel Pedersen, the Principal, and Shona Pepe, the Associate Principal, about the ethos and operation of the school and the afternoon observing it at first hand. While my initial brief had been to explore issues pertaining to 'whole language', I soon became intrigued by the much broader educational approach adopted by Richmond Road. As Pedersen observed in that initial discussion, there is no point in developing whole language programmes and then implementing them in age related classrooms where all children are expected to be at the same developmental level. What is needed is a more integrated and consistent approach to (language) learning and teaching. Moreover, developing such an approach may mean challenging and changing the traditional structures of schooling and, crucially, the power relations that underlie them.

This was to be my introduction to the theoretical tenets underlying the emancipatory ethos and practice of the school. Richmond Road was in many ways a typical inner–city school, with the majority of its school population drawn from ethnic minority groups. Many of these pupils were also second language learners of English who were, on entry to school, below the national norms of academic achievement for their age. What was not typical was the school's educational approach. Over a period of some 20 years — much of which had been under the direction of its previous Principal, Jim Laughton — the school had developed a theorized, educationally coherent and emancipatory approach to multiculturalism which challenged and subverted the *structural* constraints that disadvantaged ethnic minority children within education. This combination of critical theory and practice centred on the promotion of cultural and linguistic diversity *alongside* a pedagogy of social access for all students. At the same time, however, Richmond Road was involved in challenging and reconstituting the traditional forms of cultural knowledge production and reproduction which dominate in most schools. As I argued in my subsequent ethnography, drawing on Bourdieu (1990a, 1990b; see also, Bourdieu and Passeron, 1990), the habitus of ethnic minority children, so often devalued within the realms of the school, was specifically recognized as cultural and linguistic capital at Richmond Road. Consequently, the 'cultural arbitrary' of the dominant group was not confounded with necessary school knowledge, as is so often the case. Rather, multiple forms of cultural and linguistic knowledge were promoted, and given credence by the school's critical multicultural approach.

Unlike the majority of multicultural programmes, these developments were also intrinsic rather than additional and had resulted in the significant reform of traditional school structures. Along with school organization, the 'message systems' (Bernstein 1971, 1990) of pedagogy, curriculum, and evaluation were all reconstituted to the benefit of ethnic minority children at Richmond Road. Maintenance bilingualism was fostered in dual–medium bilingual units while vertical family groups — comprising the entire age range of pupils within the school — replaced traditional age–related classrooms. Collaborative and participatory relationships were modelled at all levels of the school: between staff and pupils, among staff, and between the school and its local community. In family groups, peer tutoring, the direct involvement of parents, and the role of teacher as facilitator rather than leader, promoted the key notion of 'provisional authority' (Peters, 1973) — whoever has knowledge teaches. Staff development — instigated by Laughton on his arrival at the school in 1972 and continued after his death in 1988 — was central to staff involvement in, and ownership of, the systemic educational change undertaken at the school. Child–centred and process approaches to learning were paramount and were supported by an extensive teacher–made resource programme and by the close formative evaluation and monitoring of children which was a central feature of the school. And so on.

Of course, I did not produce this synopsis, and its theoretical parameters, on that first day. What followed over the course of 1990 was an increasing engagement with the school and its wider project, although the actual amount of time spent at the school during that year was limited to two or three subsequent short–term visits. It was not until the beginning of 1991 that I spent my first sustained period of time at the school — six weeks. Two comparable periods were to follow later in that year and again in 1992, by which time I had returned to teaching — now in teacher education. The constraint of living some 600 miles from Auckland necessarily limited the time that I could actually spend in the school. This is reflected, to some extent, in the published account of Richmond Road in which I placed greater emphasis on interviews (with teachers, ex–teachers, education officials, pupils and ex–pupils) than on my role as a participant observer. There were methodological reasons for this which related to my increasing interest in Jim Laughton's historical role in, and influence on, the school's approach; an issue which I wish to explore further in the next section. Nonetheless, in retrospect, there is less participant observation included within the actual account than I would have liked; the observation was there but I did not let it 'speak' as much as I should. This is an issue to which I will also return in due course.

The Man in the Principal's Office

One of the greatest ironies arising from my research on Richmond Road was the confident prediction I made that the school would continue along the radical educational approach it had developed over some 20 years. Indeed, I specifically invoked the contrast with the Kensington School of Smith and Keith (1971) ethnographic fame — arguing that the subsequent slide into normalcy of this once radical school (see Smith et al., 1987) would not be replicated at Richmond Road. So much for that. However, what I also recognized at the time, and what has become clearer since, is that the Principal's influence is critical to any subsequent process of continuity or change. At Kensington, subsequent principals had not continued the radical agenda of its founding Principal, Shelby. At Richmond Road, I had thought that the educational agenda established by Jim Laughton would outlast him. It did, but only for a time.

When I began my research at Richmond Road, it was only 14 months after Laughton's death and his 'presence' was still clearly felt within the school. Teachers still talked about him as if he was there and the older pupils remembered him clearly and fondly. His immediate successor, Lionel Pedersen, had long been associated with the school (and with Laughton), as indeed had many of the teachers and all were committed to continuing what he had established there. The inclusive and collaborative systems of staff training and development also meant that any new teachers were quickly inducted into the established ethos and practice of the school. Clearly, the transition period after his death in 1988 had been a difficult one but the school appeared to be emerging from this — adapting and evolving certainly, but still pursuing the broad educational remit that Laughton had established. Or so I thought. The subsequent change of direction, and the concomitant dismantling of much of what had been associated with the school's radical agenda, has caused me to reflect further on Laughton's central influence on the school and how much of this pervaded my own ethnography. The warning signs were there at the time but I did not fully heed them.

My initial intention in researching Richmond Road had been to provide a contemporary critical ethnographic account of the school and its approach to multiculturalism. However, it became almost immediately apparent that this would prove of little value unless it was situated within the context of the school's history under Laughton. Perhaps it was also a matter of timing since, as I have already indicated, I came to the school at a time when Laughton's historical influence was still strongly felt. Accordingly, my increasing interest in tracing the historical antecedents of the school's educational approach led me to a detailed examination of the school's documentation (of which there was a copious amount) and, in addition to those staff who were currently at Richmond Road, to the interviewing of ex–staff members and others long associated with the school. The latter were chosen on the basis of their personal knowledge of Laughton and/or their direct involvement in the changes he brought about. The result, perhaps inevitably, was that Laughton came to dominate the subsequent account. As one of my respondents observed: 'you cannot talk about Richmond Road without talking about . . . Laughton' (May, 1994, p. 66) and that certainly proved to be the case. I will explore the methodological implications of this development more fully below. Here, I want to concentrate on some of the educational tensions to which this emphasis gave rise.

The difficulty of educational change outlasting the visionary leader who implemented it is an issue to which I have already alluded. However, there is a related tension that I wish to explore further here concerning the key role of the principal as instigator and visionary and the *democratic* participation of the wider school community. I had argued that the school, under Laughton, had been able to combine the both. However, in so doing, I now believe that I underplayed the *directive* influence that Laughton clearly exerted. However facilitative, consensual and inclusive his approach, however well–established the support systems that he set in place, it was still in the end *his* school that I was describing, even retrospectively. This tension was evident at various points in respondents' accounts of his leadership style as well as in my own analysis. For example, while the school was moving towards a flatter management hierarchy when I was there, it was clear that under Laughton the traditional authority attributed to the Principal was employed by him, sometimes forcefully. Specifically, a number of incidents were highlighted by previous staff members where Laughton clearly had (and used) the whip hand. At one point in my discussion with a former Deputy Principal, he observed that Laughton retained the final say about overall curriculum development: 'He held that to himself because if he handed it over you've got varying points of view and you ended up with a curriculum that didn't match . . .' (ibid, p. 100). Another instance recounted by an ex–staff member concerned a time when Laughton overruled her and other staff members about the introduction of structured timetabling (see ibid, p. 125). Even Laughton's ambivalence concerning full–immersion bilingual units related, at least to some extent, to his unwillingness to allow developments within the school with which he could not be fully involved (see ibid, p. 118). As for my own analysis, there is a certain contradiction in my comment about staff development that 'Laughton *made* teachers learn theory as the basis of their practice' (ibid, p. 80). He clearly did, and Rousseau's well known aphorism that people can (or should) be forced to be free aside, this does run counter to the notion of democratic participation. Relatedly, my observation that teachers were involved in a continual process of action research at Richmond Road (ibid, p. 197) needs to be tempered by the fact that, unlike much action research, the initial impetus for this involvement had not necessarily come from the teachers themselves. I will return to this point in my discussion on methodology below.

Theory into Practice (Applying Bourdieu)

Another related tension within the research was the congruence of my own critical conception of Richmond Road's endeavours with that of Laughton's own view and the views of those who followed him. This raises the wider issue of the role of critical theory in the framing of my account of Richmond Road and its relationship to the theory and practice that I encountered there. As I have already indicated, I drew principally on Bourdieu and his notions of habitus, cultural capital and the cultural arbitrary as the theoretical frame of my account. Or more precisely perhaps, I argued that Bourdieu's key concepts could be employed as social *method* rather than as social *theory* — that is, as a way of thinking and a manner of asking questions, which is actually Bourdieu's preference (see Harker et al., 1990). By this, I could explore and explicate the processes of cultural reproduction that are found in schools generally *and* the possibilities of resistance that could be demonstrated by Richmond Road's alternative approach. Indeed, I contended that the work of Bourdieu was ideally suited to such a task. This was because it was clear that much of his intellectual project was not structuralist as it has come to be (mis)represented but was actually directed towards dismantling and/or circumventing the absurd dichotomy between agency and structure (ibid, pp. 23–7; see also, Harker and May, 1993). To this end, key concepts such as habitus aim to reintroduce 'individual agents and their individual actions without falling back into the amorphous anecdotes of factual history . . . Notions like that of habitus (or systems of dispositions) . . . are linked to [an] effort to escape from structuralist objectivism without relapsing into subjectivism' (Bourdieu, 1990a, pp. 46, 61).

My use of Bourdieu again relates to my time at Massey University. As a result of the work of Richard Harker and others, the first significant English–language edited collection on Bourdieu's corpus had been published in 1990 (Harker et al., 1990), just as I arrived in the Education Department of which Harker was a member. Not surprisingly perhaps, the intellectual culture of the Department led me to explore Bourdieu's work in greater detail. This burgeoning interest became increasingly allied with my long–standing preoccupation with, and involvement in issues of multiculturalism at both a personal and professional level. My own educational history played a significant part in this latter regard. Coming from a white lower middle–class family much concerned with academic achievement, I had been plucked from a local and predominantly working–class primary school to attend an elite, traditional and entirely monocultural private secondary school. My parents' best intentions notwithstanding, it was not an experience that I particularly enjoyed. However inchoately, I was disturbed even then by the idea that academic excellence was defined by its traditionalism and that a school's status was determined by the social, economic and cultural capital of its clientele. This discomfort was further heightened by the stark differences that I encountered between the social and cultural milieu of the school and my own home background, let alone the multiethnic New Zealand that I experienced elsewhere.

I am not suggesting that this sense of unease led me to pursue a social and educational trajectory that was markedly different from my peers. I proceeded to do the usual things for someone of my class and educational background. However, my growing disquiet at the blatant unfairness of the educational system was further concentrated by my first teaching appointment in a multiethnic urban secondary school — a 'sink' school, in effect. It was as a result of this at times difficult initiation into teaching that I first became convinced of the need for an alternative approach — one that combined a recognition of cultural and linguistic diversity with a pedagogy of social access for those students who were usually denied the merits of both. How to accomplish this though was another matter entirely. My own teaching experience offered few clues in this regard. Indeed, my abiding memory of that time was the overwhelming sense of frustration and impotence that I felt at the consistent failure visited on the minority students there and how little I, or others, could apparently do to change this. It was only on coming upon Richmond Road some five years later that I could see how the alternative might possibly be achieved. In this respect, my own experience of teaching (and teacher training) was also behind an allied aim of the research — to break down the infamous divide between educational theory and practice. I had experienced this disjuncture at first hand while teaching in schools and subsequently, from the other side of the fence, in educational research. Moreover, for all the benefits that I could see in critical research, it seemed to me to be one of the worst offenders in its failure to operationalize itself effectively in school practice. I thus saw in Richmond Road the opportunity to highlight that rare phenomenon in education — critical theory *in action* — as a possible way forward.

But there were problems with this; notably, in the lack of fit at times between my own critical understanding and positioning as these applied to practice, and those of the school. For example, while I was involved with Richmond Road, staff did clearly engage with the theoretical tenets of Bourdieu and with the discussions surrounding critical multiculturalism as part of their ongoing staff development programme. The introduction of these debates within this established forum was part of the reciprocity of the research process itself — a 'trading point' (Goodson, 1991) between myself as the external researcher and the school staff. My reciprocal obligation to the school required me not simply to observe, or even to participate, but to be actively engaged in the school's endeavours — offering my own expertise and input where appropriate. However, it would be fair to say that the principal theoretical influences remained those established under Laughton — particularly, the work of Stenhouse (1975) and Peters (1973). After all, an external researcher whose time in the school is invariably limited cannot hope to shape the educational agenda in the same way as an ongoing participant. The question then arises — to what extent did the theoretical frame that I applied to Richmond Road actually reflect the school's own practice? The answer must be to a limited extent only.

This apparent disjuncture might also help to explain why the work of Bourdieu does not feature as prominently in the ethnographic account of the school as perhaps its should have. Applying Bourdieu in this way would have strengthened the account and integrated the theory/practice dimension more effectively; an approach that is demonstrated in the work of more recent commentators (see, for example, James, 1995; Reay, 1995). However, that I did not do so may relate to the implicit tension I felt at the time between representing the school as it perceived itself and how I perceived it — or, perhaps, how I *wanted* to perceive it. Again, the predominant emphasis in the account on the various historical antecedents that informed the school's practice may have contributed to my dilemma here. One way that this might have been overcome would have been to have provided a closer examination of the *current* theoretical engagement with theory among staff and how this compared with what had gone before. While I did explore the ongoing evolution of the school's theory and practice, it did not feature as much as it should.

Critical Ethnography or Action Research?

A final dimension of the research that I want to explore in this chapter concerns the methodological choices that I was faced with during the research process. One key choice was to combine the use of both qualitative and quantitative research methods in my analysis of the educational outcomes of Richmond Road's students. This was not something that I had originally intended — principally, because of my scepticism towards the use of quantitative analysis in previous research on ethnic minority children (see Troyna, 1993, for a useful critique here). Aside from its positivist associations, quantitative analysis was (and remains), in my view, an extremely blunt instrument for measuring and/or comparing the educational achievement of different ethnic groups within education. In effect, quantitative analysis simply codifies existing inequalities and does little, if anything, to explain why they exist (or what to do about them). However, faced with the inevitable question of some form of 'external' validation concerning the purported academic achievement of Richmond Road's students, I chose what seemed to me to be a useful compromise. Rather than adopting a straightforward criterion–referenced or norm–referenced evaluation, which would have militated against both the school's and my own critical inclinations (see May, 1994, pp. 139–43), I opted for a form of evaluation which also included *personally referenced evaluation* (Eisner, 1991) — that is, an internal comparison of students' past and present performances.

In this respect, I took one variable — English language literacy — as the means of analysis. This was not entirely unproblematic since it could be argued that using literacy *in English* as a key performance indicator understated the many alternative forms of cultural and linguistic capital which the school was so concerned to acknowledge and foster among its students. Nonetheless, it did provide a useful reference point in illustrating *one* key aspect of the educational *progress* that students at Richmond Road made over their time there. It also did so in a manner which took account of the relative disadvantage of such students to begin with, without this factor skewing the subsequent analysis. Even more importantly perhaps, confirming the educational achievements of the school was crucial in demonstrating that resistance to hegemonic patterns within education does not inevitably lead to the further ghettoisation or failure of traditionally marginalized students (cf. Willis', 1973 'lads'). As I concluded in the account, delivering necessary school knowledge need not be limited to the cultural arbitrary of the dominant group in a pluralistic and critically conceived educational approach (May, 1994, pp. 190–94).

More problematic, however, were factors relating to the broader critical ethnographic approach of the study, both in terms of my application of it and in relation to the methodology of critical ethnography itself. With regard to the former, for example, the relatively sparse engagement with the views of students in the final account of Richmond Road militated against its critical intentions. Again, my interest in the evolution of the school over time ended up weighing in favour of staff and other educationalists involved with the school. In retrospect, this perpetuated a traditional hierarchizing of respondents which a critical research project such as mine should have been concerned to prevent.

More broadly, my research highlighted some of the limitations of critical ethnography as a research methodology. One such limitation — as I discussed at the time — had been its relative inability to link critical theory with critical practice. As Anderson (1989) has observed along these lines, educational critical theory has often been criticized for 'its tendency toward social critique *without developing a theory of action* that educational practitioners can draw upon to develop a "counter–hegemonic" practice in which dominant structures of classroom and organizational meaning are challenged' (p. 257; my emphasis). Most critical ethnographies had simply critiqued the malign influence of unequal power relations in education and consequently had given little practical advice, or much hope for change to practitioners. This tendency was reflected by the fact that so few had taken critical practitioners as objects of study — a feature that I was determined to change.

However, I was also frustrated to some extent in this task by another weakness of critical ethnography. Jordan and Yeomans (1995) highlight this methodological drawback clearly when they argue that, for all its democratizing intentions, critical ethnography still invariably involves a relationship between an *academic* researcher and *non–academic* research participants. As a result, the academic/non–academic distinction continues to perpetuate an implicit power imbalance between the two — an imbalance that my own research did little to challenge or subvert. In this respect, critical ethnography continues to reflect the inherent exploitation of ethnography *per se*. As Stacey (1988) summarizes it: 'In the last instance an ethnography is a written document structured primarily by a researcher's purposes, offering a researcher's interpretation, registered in a researcher's voice' (p. 23; see also Gorelick,

1991). Add to this my own privileged educational background — and my position as a white, middle class, male researcher — and it is not hard to see why my story of the school may have ended up being somewhat different from their own. Barone (1992) argues that honest and critical storytelling is all that is required of critical researchers but I am left with the feeling that, important though this is, it is still not enough.

But there is an alternative. Jordan and Yeomans (1995) assert, for example, that the aims of critical ethnography should be redirected away from the privileged role of the academic researcher to facilitating the active engagement of the participants themselves. And this returns me to the questions that I raised earlier concerning the role of action research within Richmond Road. The tenets of action research accord with the critical reflexivity and ethnographic praxis of critical ethnography but extend these to include practitioners in the active formulation of, and engagement with critical practice (see, for example, Carr and Kemmis, 1986; 1993; Elliott, 1991; Smyth, 1991). That this kind of *self-initiated* and *ongoing* critical engagement has not survived among practitioners at Richmond Road explains, at least to some degree, the limitations of both my own account of the school *and* the critical educational practice of the school itself. The combination of critical theory and practice which both I and the school espoused may thus have been better served in the long term by the incorporation of a stronger action research basis.

Conclusion

In this chapter, I have attempted to provide a *situated* account — in both the personal and political sense of the term — of the critical ethnography that I conducted of Richmond Road School. In so doing, I have tried to be as open and as critical as I can about some of the key dilemmas that I faced during the actual research process itself. Many of these dilemmas and the ways I responded to them have, in retrospect, contributed to some of the shortcomings of the research in its published form. Making different choices would have inevitably led to the crafting of another tale and, perhaps, a better one. I would certainly have done things differently now. But this, in a way, is the central point. In one sense, I have to be judged on the story that I chose to tell. However, in another sense, acknowledging its limitations is an essential aspect of ongoing reflexive critical research and practice. The 'front–endedness' (Anderson, 1989) of critical social science, and the considerable forces arraigned against it, require a constant vigilance and critique of our own individual and corporate endeavours. As I had to tell my Japanese correspondent, the emancipatory possibilities that inhere in such a task are enormous but they are also fragile and easily lost; something which, as events have unfolded in the course of this research, I have found to my cost.

References

ANDERSON, G. (1989) 'Critical ethnography in education: Origins, current status, and new directions', *Review of Educational Research*, **59**, pp. 249–70.

BARONE, T. (1992) 'Beyond theory and method: A case of critical storytelling', *Theory into Practice*, **31**, pp. 142–6.

BERNSTEIN, B. (1971) 'On the classification and framing of educational knowledge', YOUNG M. (Ed.) *Knowledge and Control: New Directions for the Sociology of Education*, London: Collier-Macmillan, pp. 47–69.

BERNSTEIN, B. (1990) *The Structuring of Pedagogic Discourse: Class, Codes, and Control* (vol. 4), London: Routledge and Kegan Paul.

BOURDIEU, P. (1990a) *In Other Words: Essays Towards a Reflexive Sociology*, Cambridge: Polity Press.

BOURDIEU, P. (1990b) *The Logic of Practice*, Cambridge: Polity Press.

BOURDIEU, P. and PASSERON, J. (1990) *Reproduction in Education, Society and Culture* (2nd Ed.), London: Sage Publications.

CARR, W. and KEMMIS, S. (1986) *Becoming Critical: Education, Knowledge and Action Research*, Lewes: Falmer Press.

CARR, W. and KEMMIS, S. (1993) 'Action research in education', in HAMMERSLEY, M. (Ed.) *Controversies in Classroom Research* (2nd Ed.), Milton Keynes: Open University Press.

CAZDEN, C. (1989) 'Richmond Road: A multilingual/multicultural primary school in Auckland, New Zealand', *Language and Education*, **3**, pp. 143–66.

COE, D. (1991) 'Levels of knowing in ethnographic inquiry', *International Journal of Qualitative Studies in Education*, **4**, pp. 313–31.

EISNER, E. (1991) *The Enlightened Eye: Qualitative Inquiry and the Enhancement of Educational Practice*, New York: Macmillan.

ELLIOTT, J. (1991) *Action Research for Educational Change*, Milton Keynes: Open University Press.

GOODSON, I. (1991) 'Teachers' lives and educational research', in GOODSON, I. and WALKER, R. (Eds.) *Biography, Identity and Schooling: Episodes in Educational Research*, Lewes: Falmer Press, pp. 137–49.

GORELICK, S. (1991) 'Contradictions of feminist methodology', *Gender and Society*, **5**, pp. 459–77.

HARKER, R., MAHAR, C. and WILKES, C. (Eds.) (1990) *An Introduction to the Work of Pierre Bourdieu*, London: Macmillan.

HARKER, R. and MAY, S. (1993) 'Code and habitus: Comparing the accounts of Bernstein and Bourdieu', *British Journal of Sociology of Education*, **14**, pp. 169–78.

JAMES, D. (1995) 'Mature studentship in higher education: Beyond a "species" approach', *British Journal of Sociology of Education*, **16**, pp. 451–66.

JORDAN, S. and YEOMANS, S. (1995) 'Critical ethnography: Problems in contemporary theory and practice', *British Journal of Sociology of Education*, **16**, pp. 389–408.

MAY, S. (1994) *Making Multicultural Education Work*, Clevedon/Toronto: Multilingual Matters/OISE Press.

MAY, S. (1995) 'Deconstructing traditional discourses of schooling: An example of school reform', *Language and Education*, **9**, pp. 1–29.

PETERS, R. (Ed.) (1973) *The Philosophy of Education*, London: Oxford University Press.

REAY, D. (1995) '"They employ cleaners to do that": Habitus in the primary classroom', *British Journal of Sociology of Education*, **16**, pp. 353–71.

SMITH, L. and KEITH, P. (1971) *Anatomy of Educational Innovation*, New York: Wiley.

SMITH, L., PRUNTY, J., DWYER, D. and KLEINE, P. (1987) *The Fate of an Innovative School: The History and Present Status of the Kensington School*, New York: Falmer Press.

SMYTH, J. (1991) *Teachers as Collaborative Learners: Challenging Dominant Forms of Supervision*, Milton Keynes: Open University Press.

SPARKES, A. (1994) 'Life histories and the issue of voice: Reflections on an emerging relationship', *International Journal of Qualitative Studies in Education*, **7**, pp. 165–83.

STACEY, J. (1988) 'Can there be a feminist ethnography?' *Women's Studies International Forum*, **11**, pp. 21–7.

STENHOUSE, L. (1975) *An Introduction to Curriculum Research and Development*, London: Heinemann.

TROYNA, B. (1993) *Racism and Education*, Buckingham: Open University Press.

WILLIS, P. (1977) *Learning to Labour*, Farnborough: Saxon House.

11   Raising Consciousness about Reflection, Validity, and Meaning

Phil Francis Carspecken and Laurie MacGillivray

The Validity/Reflection Problematic

Hello readers! Laurie and Phil here. We are about to talk to you in a non–traditional manner. Or, rather, we have just started talking to you in a way unusual for an academic article. We are talking about three complex and interrelated things: reflection, validity, and meaning. We talk directly to you and we talk to each other, in distinctive sections of this chapter. Right now we are talking to you. Later on you can watch us talk to each other. This format helps us *show* things that are otherwise hard to talk *about*. We hope you will be open to reading a chapter that breaks academic norms.[1]

We, Laurie and Phil, talk about various internal connections between reflection, validity and meaning. And we do this from the perspective of qualitative researchers. We think that understanding the internal connections between validity, reflection, and meaning can help qualitative researchers get clearer about:

- the relationship between researcher and researched (researcher stances or roles);
- the nature of reconstructive analysis (validity reconstructions as substantive findings);
- the issue of researcher bias;
- other issues like the difference between systems analysis and reconstructive analysis which, however, we lack space to probe here.

Consciousness Raising

We think that you, readers, sort of know already what we are going to say! But we think you don't know this explicitly. No, we are not being condescending, we also don't know explicitly, here at the beginning, what we are going to say next, but we do have a vague yet fundamental understanding of it. You and we differ only through the roles we are playing. This time, we talk and you both watch and listen. All of us will understand this same text to the extent that we *recognize* meanings in it. We don't pretend to start with a problem, clearly articulated and defined, and end with a solution. We think instead that we start with a problematic, already understood but not clearly. A problematic that clarifies as we talk about it. We are more engaged in consciousness raising than in problem–solving. And this effort involves you, though our format robs you of a first person role. We must lock you into roles of the second and third person positions only. Your participation as a first person is something only anticipated by us. Your participation in our consciousness raising is virtual, but it is a structuring principle, nevertheless, which helps to constitute what we say.

Beginnings, Metaphors

We have already begun talking to you. Now we will suggest metaphors for what has already been said and for what we will soon say.

Beginnings involve difficult choices, especially when we are talking about a problematic we find ourselves already within; and when the point of the talk is to raise our consciousness, from within. The validity/reflection/meaning problematic is thus like a pool of water into which we have already jumped. We have started to swim but in just one of many possible directions. We will change direction as we swim but will not try to swim across the whole pool, nor plunge through all its depths, in one short chapter. A beginning for this chapter is a direction of swim within a pool.

Except that the problematic isn't exactly like a pool, it is more like a fractal, such that patterns are repeated indefinitely as one shifts locations, perspectives, and scales. The problematic has a fractal shape in that the parts resemble the whole. It is scale–symmetric. For example, an examination of researcher to subject interactions from within the validity problematic will trace out patterns repeated when examining subject–subject interactions and how to validly analyse them. And these patterns will be found again when examining the validity claims made in this chapter to you, our audience. And so it goes. A beginning for this chapter is a direction of swim within a fractal pool.

Except that the problematic is not exactly something within which to swim, but something that swimming (also) produces, or reproduces. The movement of the swimmer, in terms of how the arms and legs *can* be employed, is what the fractal *represents*. The progress of our writing, as it produces figure after figure, is what the figures are (also) describing. Product symbolizes process. Reflection occurs as self–reference. Our statements about validity in research can not avoid demonstrating the way that validity claims inform our writing activities. Our statements about reflection can not avoid employing reflections. We mean what we write but also mean what is necessarily beyond what we write. What is beyond *could* be written about, but only by creating another beyond. The fractal image *almost* captures this state of affairs: it's failure to fully capture it could itself be represented with fractal properties.

Retracing: Laurie and Phil reflect on the beginning
I hope the readers notice that our idea of the problematic is suggested through three images that progressively take up and reject features of each other: (i) pool; (ii) fractal; (iii) equation of shape with activity. Meaning is intimately tied to

figurative language, so our beginning displays a pattern that is repeated else-where within the meaning, reflection, and validity problematic. I think readers should notice that this beginning is also a progressive example of sous rature or 'under erasure': ~~pool~~ with the line through it, ~~fractal~~ with the line drawn through it, shape ~~is~~ movement with the line through 'is'. Like telling the readers: 'First, understand that what we have in mind is like a pool. Then understand that only the implied acts of jumping in and swimming suggest the pool, and that the metaphoric shape must be modified to the shape of a fractal. Next, understand that it is the motion rather than the figure we are interested in and the way that the figure can stand for (represent) the motion. Finally, understand as a sort of corollary that the movement from one metaphoric figure to the next is a pattern within the very fractal image we employ.'

Sous rature, 'writing under erasure', is first illustrated weakly via a concrete metaphor (pool) but then stepped up twice to arrive at the stronger example of put-ting identity itself under erasure: 'movement ~~is~~ shape'. At bottom we have, 'the act of representing ~~is~~ represented by our representation: to claim that the problematic is like a fractal is to trace one pattern in this very fractal'.

And thus the reflection. The concept of reflection. A sous rature is a type of reflection. We hint to the reader that what we are <u>doing</u> is also what we are trying to <u>describe</u> but that one can not exhaust the structures of any doing in a description.

In qualitative research, reconstructing the cultural themes referenced in the action of our subjects is iterating that same action on different levels and scales. It is doing what our subjects do, but not exactly. Our articulations are symbols point-ing back to states of being and acting. We must reflect to produce the articulations, and readers of our research reports must reflect to understand our texts.

I hope the readers intuit that, put all together, in this beginning we have hinted our own knowledge of what we are doing: that is, that we have anticipated at least some of the objections, affirmations, and digressions our beginning might produce in reader's minds, and that all such objections, affirmations, and digres-sions are claimed part of what we want to do: that representation must always pre-suppose non–represented but intersubjectively shared anticipations. That this is an essay <u>for</u> our readers is part of its constitution. And the generalized pattern here is that meanings always anticipate responses, always contain hopes that only others could fulfill. Meanings boil down to <u>claims</u>, structured by social relationships.

The validity concept can be articulated as derivative from the model of anticip-ating the responses of others to claims: thus, validity can be articulated as a struc-ture of meaning. The concept of reflection can be related to position–taking in order to anticipate. Thus, reflection <u>and</u> validity can be articulated as structures of meaning.

Researcher Roles and Typifications

Hello readers, Laurie and Phil again. We are using a format quite organic to the nature of the reflection/validity/meaning problematic. By talking to you for periods of time, and then talking to each other about our talk towards you, we illustrate all sorts of things relevant to reflection and validity and meaning. We use the pronoun

'I' in the italicized section to refer to either one of us, talking to the other. 'We' is used when we talk directly to you. Some of the logic of this format will become more clear as the text moves on.

Anyway, let's take up some of the threads begun in our beginning. We told you that the problematic can be thought of as a pool shaped like a fractal. To begin our chapter in this way we already made an implicit jump into the pool; describing the problematic as a fractal–pool was already choosing a place from which to start swimming. Now we make another jump, into another part of this pool. We pick an example from a recent field experience of Laurie's that illustrates a sub–problematic, that of researcher roles or stances and how they effect validity.

The guiding question was at first this: 'what does it mean to write a paper about validity and reflection and meaning?' Our second guiding question is this: 'how do researcher roles affect validity?' This second guiding question, or sub–problematic, will produce a movement tracing patterns already partially traced within the first sub–problematic. And patterns discovered in both places will repeat throughout the pool.

Researcher Roles

Laurie recently conducted a longitudinal study of elementary school children. She spent much time in their classrooms and she was a regular visitor at their homes as well. In her fieldnotes, Laurie wrote about an interaction with Lauren, an elementary school child who featured in her study:

> One day when I was talking with her [Lauren], she began to ask me questions. Before I knew what was happening, I was giving answers based on some 'suppressed' value system of my middle class, protestant childhood and she was encouraging me to rethink my decision. I had tried to position myself as a moral role model, but she had quickly positioned herself as a savvy woman who would not be tricked by a man (as she thought I had been).
>
> Here is what happened. Lauren and I were having a conversation with no one else around. She asked if I was married, to which I answered, 'No.' Then she asked if I had children, and again I answered, 'No.' 'So you live alone?' 'No, I live with my boyfriend,' and then in a panic I added, 'who I really, really, love. We're going to get married'. As I stood there wondering why I had added the marriage part (which at the time was not planned), Lauren looked at me and asked, 'Are you sure?' In response, I found myself explaining how 'in love' we were.
>
> In mere minutes, I had set aside my feminist cloak and resurrected the saving value of marriage. Lauren, without missing a beat, pursued the idea of me as a woman living with a man only in the hopes of marriage. And even extended it by positioning David (my 'boyfriend') as potentially making false promises of matrimony in exchange for sex. By taking the stance of moral role model, I was also setting up my morality to be critiqued. I had not expected my sexual conduct to be an issue in attempting to be friends with the students in my study. But what I find most striking was my assumption that I should be a moral role model, that as an adult friend I needed to follow the codes I assumed she was being raised with.

Confessing: Laurie and Phil think about making identity claims when writing about research

I think readers will quickly intuit the connection of the above set of fieldnotes with forms of researcher 'confessions' that are growing increasingly common in qualitative studies. The style and content of the above fieldnote strip is recognizable. It is a confessional. The confessional style illustrates a type of reflection: becoming aware of one's own biases, through after–the–fact ruminations, and admitting them to the reader. Confession both admits to having a partial perspective and claims an identity beyond this partiality. Confession redeems the writer at the same time that it makes the writer vulnerable. The confessional is a current discourse: using it identifies the writer with an abstract subject position within this discourse, claims a valid identity for the writer as the one who is self–aware and politically sensitive, and carries the claim that readers ought to join the writer within the subject's position of the discourse: agreeing to the valid identity asserted and agreeing to the implicit epistemology averred universally true. Readers are invited to agree that researcher observations and interpretations will always be made from the biases of the researcher herself.

'Setting aside my feminist cloak' keeps it clear to the readers that feminism is a value we support, even if we don't consistently practice it. But, then, part of feminism is exactly this sort of consciousness–raising honesty that keeps feminist theory and norms in growth. We don't consistently practice feminism, but by noting where we have failed to do so, we actually do practice feminism. The confessional is a narrative style consistent with feminist principles. Writing always carries identity claims, as does acting communicatively. We are claiming to our readers that we are 'good' because we believe in feminist principles. Actors also always make identity claims, and such claims always rest upon value and moral positions that are usually more tacit than the feminist claims in Laurie's notes.

Readers, we are back and talking again directly to you. What do you think of Laurie's experience and her manner of articulating it in fieldnotes? Well, listen to our own analysis.

Laurie had established a number of research roles with her subjects of study: roles that she alternated between during the daily flows of fieldwork. At times she was in the role of uninvolved observer. At other times she was in a role of teacher with the children in this study. And Laurie also adopted the role of advocate and expert in other contexts involving school personnel and parents.

So Laurie's researcher roles were multiple and shifted according to context. A very important role Laurie often used with the children was that of 'friend', which could take on various specific articulations such as those of 'older person — younger person friends', 'peers who are friends', and 'female friends'. She played with children in the study, both one–on–one and in groups. She drew pictures with them and she talked to them about their lives as friends would talk about their lives. The interaction with Lauren described above began as one between friends who are also peers, but then shifted in interesting ways. She suddenly found herself talking to Lauren, not as a peer–friend, but as an adult who must model morality for children. This shifted again when Lauren adopted the role of an *adult* peer female who is advising a female friend on the wily ways of men. In her reflection, Laurie found herself in yet another role: a feminist who is critical of the subtle ways in which gender stereotypes are reproduced in society.

Researcher roles are relevant to the validity problematic in several ways. One such relevancy concerns the manner in which we interpret events: the issue of researcher bias. Certainly, an interpretation will affect what is written in the fieldnotes and what sorts of analysis one produces. Roles can restrict interactions in ways that restrict analysis: producing bias.

The other relevancy concerns power dynamics. Researcher roles will affect the subjects of one's study. Effects like this might have implications for the validity of one's analysis, especially if subjects feel silenced by a researcher, or if they alter their activities and their talk out of a desire to please a researcher. Power dynamics always beg moral questions for the researcher as well.

Typifications

We will now further analyse what happened with Laurie and Lauren. Laurie and Lauren began an interaction as friends but this shifted at a crucial moment. Interactions take place through *typifications* that specify a range of possible roles as well as norms, audiences, and such things as interactive rhythm and tempo. Typifications are close to what many sociologists call 'interactive settings', or the 'pragmatic infrastructures' of interaction. But the concept of 'typification' goes a little deeper: a situation is meaningful when it is recognized as such through a typification. And when a situation is meaningful, one understands how to act within it, how others might act within it, how others might expect one's self to act within it, and so on. A typification is a structure of intersubjectivity.

Thus 'settings', in traditional sociological literature, may be understood as typifications in which interaction is possible or called for. Using the term 'typification' we emphasize the primacy of meaningful interaction in our theory of understanding and meaning.

The typification of two friends talking together had been in place when Laurie suddenly felt uncomfortable. She felt uncomfortable responding to questions about her living arrangements because she suddenly realized she was sharing information with someone who was much younger in years. The interaction now appeared to her from a different typification altogether: that of an adult interacting with a child relativized to certain cultural groups, like the teachers and parents in Laurie's study and like the middle–class adults Laurie grew up around. Laurie altered the form of her acts according to this new typification: she began to act like a moral model for children.

So the new typification was constituted by an adult–child dimension. This adult–child dimension took on a specific configuration supported by norms and values: 'sexual relationships are only legitimate when there is love', and, 'adults should be responsible for the influences they exert upon children'. A tacit *theory* underlay this structure: 'children are impressionable and their moral development is easily influenced in interactions with significant others'. An abstract and absent audience helped to constitute this typification: other adults, like parents and teachers associated with this study, and like middle class adults Laurie grew up around, comprised the constituting audience.

Recollection/repetition/iteration:
I do hope that the readers have retained the fractal metaphor while reading these sections. We are introducing and elaborating terms in relation to this one example that repeat elsewhere in the validity/reflection/meaning problematic. The term 'typification' is particularly important to the whole problematic. But 'typification' is metaphorically structured. It depends, for one thing, on the contrast between 'inside and outside'. People recognize meaningful situations through typifications that facilitate intersubjective anticipations. Typifications imply normative–evaluative claims and even theories. Typifications are partially constituted by abstract audiences who share the theories and normative–evaluative claims implied by the typification. When interacting, actors move within, that is <u>inside</u>, a typification whose structures are iterated and reclaimed by each act. A reflection puts one 'outside' the original typification in order to get clear about it, question it, modify it, critique it. Feelings can drive a reflection like this. But a reflection puts one within a new typification.

Typifications are not unlike metaphors: not unlike our use of 'pool' and 'fractal' and 'swimming' earlier in this chapter. Typifications are sort of 'pragmatic metaphors'. Movement from an inside to an outside that turns out to be just another inside, is a metaphoric pattern repeated throughout this problematic. So by analysing Laurie's shift from one role to another with the concept of 'typification' we are doing something similar to what we did when comparing our writing about validity/reflection/meaning to a fractal.

Typifications and Reflections

Back to you again, readers. Laurie's discomfort with what happened in this incident involved a *reflection*. Though the term 'reflection' is often used to indicate an act of becoming discursive about something that one formerly was little aware of, we think reflections of the discursive sort are a secondary or tertiary form: derivative from more primordial reflections.

Laurie actually felt what was taking place within her, and acted from these feelings, long before she could get discursive about them. Yet a reflection had taken place. Laurie moved from an absorption within roles acted out as part of one typification into a panic about those same roles. A panic because she could suddenly understand, in pre–discursive ways, how her actions might be interpreted by different a audience. At the moment of feeling panic, Laurie identified with this new audience, and was displeased with herself. Laurie became absorbed within a different typification and role–structure. She began acting out the 'moral teacher' as a result.

Reflection, we think, is at bottom a mode of position–taking; making a position, in which one had formerly identified one's self, objectified, via taking on the perspective of another position. Reflection is always this 'movement out of', rendering one's former position objectified within awareness.

Reflection always takes place within interactive typifications, because it is identical to monitoring an act. When we act towards another within a typification we monitor ourselves to various degrees: checking our act from the possible perspective of the one addressed (second person) and from the perspective of any anonymous person occupying the implicit audience constituting our typification (third person internal–performative).

In fact, it is the internal–performative third person position constituting a typification that is employed to shift between the first and second person positions. The internal–performative third person position of a typification corresponds to the constituting audience of the typification. This is what actors attempt to share when creating an interactive infrastructure. They attempt to share an abstract audience, any anonymous member of which would find the interactive situation meaningful in the same basic way. Actors attempt to locate themselves and their counterparts with respect to a shared abstract audience. That is what produces the typification.

With a typification roughly in place, interactions procede. As each person acts towards the other(s), reflections take place routinely as 'action monitoring'. Reflections occur routinely, but with varying degrees of degree and explicitness.

(i)   Many reflections will conform to the basic shape of the typification in play. It is through reflections of this sort that actors get some idea of how well they are expressing themselves and some idea of how well others understand them; *given the assumption of the shared typification* from which the actions come.

(ii)   But it is nearly as common for an actor to sense how the typification itself might appear from the perspective of a different typification: from the perspective of an audience not included within the initial typification. This is what happened to Laurie.

Laurie began acting out a role based on norms and values constituted by one abstract audience. Her identity as a 'good person' was claimed for this audience. A reflection occurred, however, that relativized Laurie's identity claim and cast the values and norms associated with it in doubt. She moved from one typification into another typification, the second one entailing an identity she would adopt with other feminist theorists. Reflection is a movement from one identity into another one, such that the first identity and all that constitutes it (its constituting typification) become objectified within the 'gaze' offered by the second identity.

Anticipating: Laurie and Phil worry about readers' understanding of 'role' and 'identity':
I worry that readers might misunderstand us because of our use of the terms 'role' and 'identity'. I wish we had space to explain our particular and perhaps peculiar

sense of 'role': our way of casting a role as a unit of meaning understood only via the first, second, and third person internal–performative positions rather than via the functionalist, third person–absent concept of role that is in much of the litera-ture. I wish we could explain the dialectics of identity and its fusion with typifica-tion structures. The way we use these terms, however, suggests the underlying theory: many readers will hopefully understand.

As we have said readers, typifications are partially constituted by implicit audi-ences. Laurie discovered two roles in conflict with each other; both roles that she could play with equal amounts of identification. But the second role, the role to adopt when discussing a situation like this with other feminists, came out as domin-ant after her reflection occurred. So identified was she with the second typification, her body quickly registered discomfort as soon as the reflection occurred. Identifica-tions are felt in the body, and typifications grasped pre–linguistically, holistically, in bodily states.

Validity and Researcher Roles

Thus, researcher roles have everything to do with typifications, and typifications involve reflections in a fundamental way. What about the concept of validity in rela-tion to researcher roles?

The validity of qualitative data analysis is not really threatened in this incid-ent. Laurie's interactions with Lauren did not silence Lauren. Laurie was talking with Lauren through a typification that could be roughly named, ignoring nuances: 'conversation between friends'. When the issue of living with a boyfriend came up, Laurie quickly claimed a new typification and her role within it: 'adult responsible for the moral education of a child'. This did not silence Lauren nor force any state-ments from her that did not reflect her views on gender relations within other social settings. Lauren questioned the way Laurie explained her relationship with David. 'Are you sure?', she asked Laurie. Lauren did not accept the new typification Laurie offered; did not interpret Laurie's new stream of acts in the way Laurie did. She made her own offer of a conversation between two mature female friends. She was not silenced.

Modelling Moral Positions in Qualitative Research

True, there may have been some influence exerted on Lauren by Laurie that could become important later in Lauren's life. That is a moral issue for Laurie, connected to power dynamics between her and Lauren. But we now think that since Laurie does choose to construct her relationship with David in the way she described it to Lauren — i.e., that having love is important to this relationship and that love was/ is there between David and Laurie — this sort of influence is not 'bad'. Actually, Laurie and David are now married. At the time of this interaction with Lauren,

Laurie was close to 'being herself', to being authentic. She was close, but not fully there. Reflecting upon this incident results in learning and next time something similar happens to either of us, Laurie and Phil, we will probably be capable of more authentic action.

Researchers will always model moral positions when they interact with the people they study, knowingly or unknowingly. We believe one should model positions one is comfortable with: 'be one's self'. As long as the subjects of one's study are not silenced with respect to their own moral positions, and as long as the modelling foregrounds claims about one's *own* position rather than foregrounds demands upon other people (here is where Laurie's activities were perhaps most questionable), nothing bad has happened. The validity of the information gathered was not threatened by Laurie's shift in roles.

Lauren's response to Laurie actually provides good material for reconstructive analysis. She did not question the value of marriage but rather the trust Laurie had put into men, into David as a member of the category 'men'. Lauren indicates distrust in men: they can deceive women in order to get sexual favors. Lauren seems to express caring feelings for Laurie as she quite gently asks Laurie to think a little more carefully about her living arrangements with David. More talk with Lauren could clarify these interesting ideas she seems to have, and allow us to better understand how deeply she holds to them, how broadly she applies them, and to what other cultural themes they may be linked.

Researcher Roles, Typifications, and Illuminating Data

In summary, researcher stances, or roles, are not really problems for validity as long as the qualitative researcher is aware of several things.

(i)   First, it is important to understand how typifications work and how unavoidable they are. Typifications always require roles to be played, identities to be assumed. The greater the variety of roles played by a researcher in relation to those researched, the better one may relativize one's own roles in the case of specific incidents and thus produce a sharper analysis. One can and should move between the stances of observer, friend, student–wanting–to–learn, expert–giving–advice, etc. during a field project.

(ii)   Second, it is important not to rigidly impose typifications upon the subjects of a study from one's position of power, but rather let the subjects of a study have plenty of power in generating and negotiating interactive typifications. If Laurie had cut off Lauren's voice in this incident, not allowed Lauren to express her suspicions of Laurie's relationship with David, then the data would have big gaps. Laurie almost fell into this trap of silencing those we want to understand, but Lauren had enough self–assurance to prevent this from occurring. Laurie did miss an opportunity to learn more about Lauren's views of sexual behavior and morality.

But the incident did not produce an obvious silencing and did yield some interesting expressions from Lauren. Letting doubts come up within the interactions is good practice, as is treating one's subjects of study with as much respect as possible so that their voices and their own offers of interactive infrastructure are honored.

(iii) Third, researchers should be aware that they will always model moral claims when interacting with the subjects of a study. This occurs more frequently the more often that peer and friend stances are taken. It is unavoidable and, in our opinion, ethical fieldwork can be done only if one models moral positions one actually feels comfortable with. At the same time, one should model moral positions as one's own rather than as positions that every person should adhere to. The word 'comfortable' is deliberately chosen, as we are all morally contradictory and ambiguous: feeling comfortable with one moral position in some situations and uncomfortable with that position in others. One needs to feel basically authentic and honest when acting with one's subjects of study, and this does not necessarily require a hard and fast form of consistency.

Supplementing: Laurie and Phil think together about specimens and generalizability: I think readers might recognize the form of the above arguments, which generalize from a single incident observed in the field, to correspond to 'specimen' logic rather than strictly statistical logic. From a single incident we make big conclusions. We take a one example from fieldwork and present it to readers to illustrate structures involved in all fieldwork. The example is chosen for its structural relevance, like the liver of single human being might be chosen to study structures common to all human livers. This use of a 'specimen' for generalized conclusions is a legitimate strategy in qualitative research itself, when a new concept or model is derived from qualitative data. Quantitative researchers often attack qualitative researchers on the issue of generalizability — use of specimen argumentation ought to be clarified so that defenses for this sort of generalizing procedure become more at hand.

Quantitative researchers have trouble understanding how a single, often atypical, event can be used to illuminate general cultural structures and patterns. Specimens are necessary to qualitative data analysis and their validity must be argued for in terms of structural relevance rather than through quantitative arguments employing the concepts of sample and population. Because typifications and what they holistically entail in terms of roles, identity claims, subjective references, values, norms, and tacit beliefs are the focus of much qualitative data analysis: a specimen approach is often appropriate. A single, unusual, event can tell us much about a commonly employed typification or cluster of typifications.

The structural relevance of the specimen must be argued for by documenting prolonged engagement and the rough frequencies with which either similar incidents, or non–similar incidents in meaningful contrast to typical patterns, occurred during the fieldwork. The structures of a human liver will be generalizable if the specimen examined is quite like those found in all humans, or if the specimen has a recognizable peculiarity (like a tear or a blockage) that clearly throws light on other, more usual, livers.

Typifications, Validity Claims, and Reconstructive Analysis

Readers, we have used the issue of researcher roles to trace out patterned connections between validity, reflection, and meaning. Now we will explore another sub–problematic, how qualitative data can be validly analysed. In this exploration we will continue to show up general features of reflection, validity, and meaning. We will continue to develop the concept of 'interactive typification' too, and the importance of metaphors.

The validity problematic for qualitative research is not only important for guiding sound data collection methods; it is important for guiding data analysis as well. The division of validity claims into *types* aids in all of this, as does the grounding of validity in everyday communicative practice.

When taking fieldnotes, researchers are mainly concerned with objective validity claims: claims open to multiple access, claims based on what people see and hear. One will want to use multiple recording devices, develop observation schedules, use debriefers to check for biases in attention, write in a low–inference vocabulary, and other such procedures to keep the researcher's objective claims well supported.

Analysis of qualitative data, however, generally focuses on non–objective validity claim: claims made by the people one studies about what is good, bad, right, wrong, proper, inappropriate (normative–evaluative claims); and claims made by them about what their intentions are, how they feel, what they are aware of (subjective claims). In addition, actors, like writers, always make claims about who they are: they make *identity claims.*

Although there are many various ways to analyse qualitative data, attention to the validity claims made by the actors one studies is a powerful way to understand typical role and identity structures, commonly referenced norms and values, implicit theories, the significance of commonly used metaphors, and other things that make up a culture. Qualitative data analysis will usually employ an attention to word usage, to role structures, to cultural thematics, and other such components of social action, but each of these things can be broken down to an array of validity claims made with each meaningful act.

To explore the different types of validity claim and how actors themselves make them in everyday activities, we will use another example from Laurie's fieldwork. During a project different from the one in which Lauren participated, Laurie observed a dispute between Yousita and Arthur, two students in an elementary school classroom. The teacher, Tana, had a formal system for dealing with conflicts between students. The students in conflict were given a piece of paper, called an 'I have a problem sheet', and asked to fill it out. The sheet calls for a description of what happened to cause the conflict. Students were expected to cooperate in drawing a picture and writing some words to explain the conflict. Laurie recorded Yousita and Arthur's interaction as follows:

Arthur and Yousita got into an argument and were given an 'I have a problem sheet' to resolve their conflict.

> Yousita sits down and writes her name on the line. Then she begins to draw a face, alternately looking up and listening to the book that Tana is reading. She taps Arthur's arm and says,
>
> [Yousita]: *Make yourself looking at me.*
>
> Arthur responds with a direction for her:
>
> [Arthur]: *Draw yourself sticking your tongue out.*
>
> [Yousita]: *I didn't stick it out.*
>
> [Arthur]: *You did.*
>
> Arthur points to where he was sitting and where she was and goes over the incident. Yousita responds:
>
> [Yousita]: *I did not.*
>
> Silence. Arthur picks up the pencil, holds his hand up hiding the picture, begins to draw, looks up at me [Laurie]. After a couple of seconds, Yousita leans over to look but Arthur won't let her.
>
> Arthur lays down the pencil. Yousita looks closely,
>
> [Yousita]: *Did you draw my tongue?*
>
> [Arthur]: *Yeah, because you stuck your tongue out at me.*
>
> Yousita takes the pencil and begins erasing. Arthur walks towards Tana calling:
>
> [Arthur]: *Ms. Wells.*
>
> [Yousita]: *I was not sticking my tongue out at you.*
>
> Then she turns to me:
>
> [Yousita]: *Laurie, he's wrong, I'm right.*
>
> When the discussion pauses and Tana looks at Arthur he explains,
>
> [Arthur to Tana]: *She erased her tongue and stuck it out at me.*
>
> Tana tells him she'll talk to the two of them in a minute.
>
> . . .
>
> During discussion with Tana a few minutes later, Yousita holds firm to her claim that she did not stick her tongue out at Arthur. Arthur finally suggests that Yousita might have been sticking her tongue out at someone else, rather than at him.

In terms of researcher roles, Laurie was here taking an 'observer–only' role contextualized by the students' familiarity with her both as an observer and as a frequently visiting adult willing to take on other roles with them as well. Arthur does appeal to Laurie for support at one moment, but quickly realizes he won't get any support from her in this situation, thus moving on to employ other strategies in his dispute with Yousita. Laurie wrote down as many of the speech acts, verbatim, as she was able to, and glossed events when necessary. Both when glossing and when describing body movements and postures, Laurie kept her vocabulary as objective–referenced as possible. She used words to describe things others would also have access to through their senses. These are good practices for supporting objective claims: claims structured by multiple access to events.

Types of Validity Claim

Of course, Yousita and Arthur make their own validity claims, which we can reconstruct from Laurie's notes. Validity is internally connected to meaning, because communicators must make a variety of supportable claims in order to communicate. People who hear what a communicator has to say understand what claims are involved in the communication and, roughly and usually tacitly, what support the communicator would have to provide if the communication were challenged.

Validity claims fall into various categories, the three most important of which are the objective (structured by multiple access), subjective (structured by privileged access), and normative–evaluative (structured by the most rudimentary forms of intersubjectivity) claims. Arthur and Yousita construct their communicative acts from such claims. Laurie's claims, when writing her fieldnotes and analysing them, are not different in kind from the claims made by Arthur, Yousita, and all people within the contexts of daily life.

Lamentation: Laurie and Phil lament the lack of space for exploring the question of what ultimately grounds each type of validity claim.
I can't be sure that all readers will understand the structuring principles of each type of claim; especially the structuring principles of the normative–evaluative claim. The normative claim is a claim about what is good, bad, right, wrong, appropriate, inappropriate. Rudimentary forms of this claim, serving to constitute conventions, are necessary for any position–taking to occur and thus this claim is closest to intersubjectivity per se. Less rudimentary forms build up from conventions themselves into the values and explicitly formulated norms used to legitimate conventions. I think we had better not attempt to elaborate, however, for fear of writing too much and diverting from the organization of this chapter too far. Perhaps readers will examine other publications, if they are unclear about the three claims. Habermas is the author who has formulated these categories most compellingly, but other publications employ them as well. By now, most readers will be familiar with Habermas's theories, I think. It is a pity, though, that we can not provide more details on the issue of grounding validity claims.

In Laurie's record of this dispute between Arthur and Yousita we see all three validity claims in play. Moreover, we see children of elementary school age employing the distinction between objective and subjective validity claims almost explicitly, while relying upon a tacit understanding that normative–evaluative claims are yet a third category, differing from both the objective and subjective. Arthur asserts that Yousita stuck her tongue out at him. The three categories of validity claim are fused within this assertion. The foregrounded *objective* claim is that Yousita had her tongue out when facing Arthur. The foregrounded *subjective* claim is that Yousita *intended* to stick out her tongue at Arthur in order to insult him. The principal normative–evaluative claim, playing a more backgrounded and assumedly unproblematic role, is that sticking a tongue out at someone else, intentionally, is rude and thus bad: an inappropriate behavior.

Yousita contests Arthur's assertion in terms of its objective claim only . She clearly agrees, but implicitly, that sticking out a tongue at someone else, intentionally, is a rude behavior; one worthy of sanction. But she maintains she did not stick her tongue out. The 'I have a problem sheet' forces attention on the objective features of the situation: whether or not Yousita's tongue was sticking out is an objective issue, one that could be represented by a picture for all to see (multiple access). Yousita insists upon erasing her tongue, each time Arthur draws it. Eventually, Arthur offers to agree that Yousita's subjective intention may not have been to insult him, to stick her tongue out at *him*, but he does not budge on his claim that the tongue was indeed sticking out. He offers both himself and Yousita a way out by putting subjectivity (Yousita's realm of privileged access: here her intentions), rather than objectivity, into the foreground. This would allow him to save face, if Yousita accepts it, because it would mean that he was not lying or hallucinating about the tongue sticking out. It would be a very understandable mistake to interpret the projected tongue as an indicator of intentional insult. He offers Yousita a way out, because sticking out a tongue without intending to insult is not a bad thing to do.

Qualitative researchers necessarily get some understanding of the validity claims made by actors in their communicative activities, simply because they necessarily reach some understanding of the communications actors make. One can not experience understanding others without understanding their claims about objective states–of–affairs; subjective feelings, intentions, and modes of awareness; and normative–evaluative views of what is right, wrong, good, bad, proper, inappropriate. The vast bulk of such claims are made and understood tacitly, rather than explicitly, by actors and researchers. This is because of acting and understanding work holistically, through typifications.

Reconstructive Analysis of Validity Claims

To move a tacit understanding of validity claims that constituted an observed activity into explicit, discursive, formulation requires three moves:

(i)   One becomes a virtual participant in the interaction in order to understand it. This means that one grasps the typifications in play, the roles associated with these typifications, and the range of possible acts and responses that are suggested.

(ii) Then one must reflect in order to objectify the relevant typification. Reflection, however, must follow the 'logic' of the typification. That is, one must reflect, or position–take, as one's subjects do rather than as members of a different cultural group observing the interaction might do. This comes close to an art. One must reflect as one's participants would do, if they were forced to rationalize their activities in order to either defend them or explain them.

(iii) Next, one articulates tacit understandings into discursive understandings. Once again, this must follow the 'logic' of the typifications actually used. Discursive articulations of tacit validity claims should be written from the first person position of the actor.

Our discussion so far can be summarized into a few important points:

   (i)   Validity originates in communicative practice.
   (ii) The qualitative researcher will produce an effective reconstruction of a
         culture if she articulates validity claims commonly and typically made
         by members.
   (iii) Such articulations should be made, as much as possible, from the per-
         spective of the actors: reconstruction must involve the principle of tak-
         ing positions, or reflecting, as one's subjects do, following the logic of
         the typifications in play and formulated from the first person position of
         the actor.
   (iv) Validity reconstructions will become more useful and illuminating if
         they are articulated into the analytically distinct categories of objective,
         subjective, and normative–evaluative claims. Reconstructive analysis of
         the dispute between Yousita and Arthur could serve a number of pur-
         poses that might find a place within a researcher's agenda. The inter-
         action clearly displays some awareness of the distinction between types of
         validity claims on the part of Arthur. This could be important if Laurie's
         study was to address developmental theory and its relationship to ration-
         alized (i.e., culturally differentiated distinctions between objectivity, sub-
         jectivity, and normative–evaluative reason) lifeworlds. The interaction
         also reveals what can happen when adults refuse to back children in a
         dispute as authority figures but do supply a formal process for resolving
         the dispute themselves. The interaction additionally tells us about some
         of the rules for saving face and giving insults in this specific cultural
         grouping.

The Identity Claim: Validity and Human Motivation

Validity claims are internally connected to meaningful, or communicative, action.
All meaningful acts carry arrays of claims divisible into the subjective, normative,
and objective categories. But validity claims are also related to core structures of
human motivation. It is important for qualitative researchers to spot the connection
between validity claims and motivation, for this connection shows up in highly
important ways within a large variety of human interaction.

   In particular, all meaningful action not only carries claims about subjective
states, objective states, and the rightness of norms or the goodness of values; all
meaningful action also claims the actor into existence. The construction of the self,
through meaningful activity, is also type of *claim*, dependent on the responses of
others. It is an *existential* claim, associated with validity claims.

   Laurie's fieldnotes on Yousita and Arthur suggest this very clearly. Something
of both students' identities are at stake in the dispute. Arthur is determined to stand
by his claims, because his actions towards Yousita could not be easily justified, or
'rationalized', if she really didn't stick her tongue out. Why should Arthur care
whether his actions are justifiable or not? Well, rationalizing and justifying are
a chronic feature of social action. People will usually wish their actions to be

perceived as legitimate and will usually have the means of explicitly claiming legitimacy, by articulating validity claims that tacitly constitute their actions. It is the significance of an act to the identity of the actor that motivates this chronic feature of social action. To act in ways that others would not find legitimate or in any way rationalizable is to 'be' a 'bad person', and humans usually do not wish to have negative identities. In some situations, humans will act out a negative identity just to feel some recognition from others, just to feel that they exist. Better to exist as a bad person than to feel as if one does not exist at all.

Of course, identity claims are carried by acts only in relation to some audience, and this audience may not be the actual people one is interacting with. Reference group theory has captured this feature of the identity claim well. And, the degree to which an identity claim is foregrounded by an act differs enormously from act to act. Sometimes we act with our desire for acceptance and recognition as a primary concern. Sometimes we act without even noticing that we are 'claiming ourselves' at the same time.

Arthur, however, clearly takes the audience immediate to his situation as significant and wants his activities to be recognized as legitimate by others present.

Yousita also acts in ways that would preserve her sense of being a valid person. She does not want others to think she stuck her tongue out, either because she really did not do this or because she did but does not want others to know this. Why should she care? Explanations could be most fruitfully found through a deeper understanding of Yousita's typical identity constructions. This argument with Arthur threatens her sense of self to some degree and on some levels; and this motivates her to maintain her claim that she did not stick her tongue out.

In summary, qualitative researchers can strengthen their analysis of observed interaction by gaining an understanding of the cultural themes actors employ in routine efforts to construct a valid sense of self. Actors will find very threatening challenges to certain norms, values, beliefs, and implicit theories they normally hold to, if their self–constructions depend on any of these.

Another Example of Reconstructive Analysis

Here is another example of reconstructive analysis, taken from another one of Laurie's field projects. Laurie has embedded reconstructions of tacit validity claims within her fieldnotes and has used the first person position of the actor for her articulations. She has articulated only those validity claims that seemed analytically important to her when typing the notes. More reconstructions could be articulated during further analysis. Elisa and Katie are cutting out Menorah's at Jose's table. E asks K:

> [Elisa]: *Will you do these?* pointing to the candles and rubbing her hands, My
> *hands hurt.*
> [Normative–evaluative: Friends help each other when there is a reason. One should help another suffering physical problems.]

[Katie]: *Tell me how much.*

[Normative–evaluative: To help is a free choice. There should be good reasons for helping. People should help themselves unless seriously impaired. Overcoming impairment and pain in order to work is good. Subjective: I will only help you if you are not tricking me, if you really sincerely need help. I don't know how much pain you feel.]

[Elisa]: *Killing me.*

[Subjective: My hands really hurt! Honestly!]

[Katie]: *How much killing?*

[Subjective: I'm not convinced. You might be trying to get out of doing something you could do on your own. Normative–evaluative: If you can do it yourself, you should. (Maybe) you spoil people if you help them when they could do it themselves. (Maybe) you are soft if you help people who could do it themselves. Possible identity claims: 'I am like a parent or a teacher who is firm with those trying to get out of their own work. I am not soft. I am not a sucker.'

[Elisa]: *Hurts.*

[Katie]: *How much killing and hurting? How much? Like you are dying?*

. . . .

Attention to the validity claims structuring meaningful acts must always involve the articulation of *possible* interpretations. No one in an interaction is ever absolutely sure which claims are intended or recognized by others. People work with *meaning fields* when they interact; fields of possible meanings involving various degrees of uncertainty and ambiguity. For a researcher, prolonged engagement, the observation of many interactions, and interactions with the subjects of study through various roles will help to limit the possibilities to manageable fields. This basically boils down to the ability of grasping what typifications are constructed by the actors so that one becomes an insider. Articulating the structures that constitute typifications is creative work: rather like the work a poet employs to take a holistic feeling–idea into discursive representation. Insights into cultural themes are generated in this way.

Reflecting: Laurie and Phil think together about format.
I don't want readers to forget the fractal image. Best if they read our sections cognizant of the fact that what is traced out in one domain of the problematic iterates in other domains, including their own reading experience of our chapter. I think we must keep up the format of alternating sections where we talk to them with sections where we talk to ourselves.

This format is true to the ~~identity~~ of movement and image, the image here still being that of a fractal where particular patterns bear resemblance to the whole. We talk to ourselves and <u>about our readers</u> in italics. We talk directly to the reader and <u>about ourselves</u> in non–italics. We move explicitly between these positions just as anyone, by acting, monitoring action, and understanding the acts of another, must move implicitly between positions.

When we talk to the reader, in non–italics, we illustrate the fact that validity claims are made from first person positions to an audience in second person position. It is not possible to say everything there is to be said to the audience, one must assume shared, non–articulated, understandings at all times. Similarly, as we talk to our readers we can't say everything there is to be said to them, we must assume shared, non–articulated, understandings for our foregrounded claims to be grasped. We 'face' our readers in those non–italicized sections. We present ourselves to them by referring to ourselves as 'we' (first person plural) and addressing them as 'readers' (second person plural).

But our self–presentations will always cast shadows back into realms that readers do not have direct access to. So it is with all validity claims; they are constituted by the difference between the first and second person positions, which in turn requires a third person internal–performative position.

When we talk to each other, in italics, we illustrate explicitly those 'insider only' regions that always accompany the first person position. We talk to each other as if we were thinking together, putting the reader into a third person position as witness to our thoughts. Meaningful acts always imply, or reference, non–represented portions of subjectivity: intentions, feelings, degrees of self–and–other–awareness. We write these italicized sections with our readers in an 'outsider' position: we create an 'us' vs 'them'.

But of course, we write these italicized sections knowing that our readers know that we know they <u>do</u> have access to the italicized writing. Thus they are really in a third person internal–<u>included</u> position with respect to these italicized paragraphs. What we say to each other is partially constituted by our knowledge of them as a non–participating but present and understanding audience. This would help us introduce different types of third person positions later on, had we enough room to go into it. There is the third person internal–<u>included</u> position, the third person internal–<u>excluded</u> position, the third person external–absent position, and other third person positions as well.

Three main things are illustrated by this format: the relationship of validity claims to formal communicative positions (first, second and third person positions), the play between 'inside' and 'outside' that structures validity claims in the pattern of a continuum, and the relationship between reflection and position–taking.

Conclusions and Summary

Oh my gosh, we are at the end of our page limits and there was much more to say! How to end now?! Perhaps we should just end, and not bother the form of an ending? We left out clarifications of how reflection, typifications, and communicative positions have internal linkage. Left out an exploration of the 'internal/external' metaphor. Oh well, maybe in another article?

We did trace out some iterating patterns in the validity, reflection, and meaning problematic as they appear with respect to researcher stances and reconstructive analysis. Endings are often rather contrived affairs, suggesting a closure which is not really there. One always has more one could say, and reader responses always take a text beyond its ending. The fractal pool is not, after all, an object to be drawn once and for ever. It is rather an insight that we, both authors and readers, find given to us again and again as we act and reflect in ongoing living.

Note

1   One of the breaks we will make with academic traditions concerns the issue of references. We will not cite any publications in this chapter. This text was composed without any deliberate literature review; no bibliographic searches were conducted when writing this chapter.

12   Where Was I? Or Was I?

Barry Kanpol

Introduction

'Critical' education theory, research and practice faces a major dilemma. Despite the often brilliant critical theoretical analyses (Apple, 1996; Purpel and Shapiro, 1995; Giroux, 1996, 1997; Darder, 1995; McLaren, 1993 and countless others over the last two decades or so), I have over the last few years or so begun to ask these problematic questions: to what end do critical educators theorize? why is theory so devoid of personal narrative? what relationship has critical theory to the everyday life–world of those who work in the trenches, such as teachers, administrators and students? The search to the answers of these particular critical questions fuels my response to a call for this chapter. Rather than cynically theorize over what is wrong in teacher education today, or in urban schools, or construct an alternative post–modern version of partial truth, or even present another case study relating more of the same, this chapter *Where Was I? Or Was I?* calls for an immediate subjective interpretation and further analysis of my specific role in the field of critical theory as a participant in theoretical construction, but more so as a critical ethnographic researcher in the conduits of public schools.

Critically, the subjective–objective (Phillips, 1990; Guba, 1990; Roman and Apple, 1990) debate as a part of qualitative research continues, and is vitally connected to critical practice and the prior questions I posed. Given the qualitative paradigm I have embraced and the critical ethnographic approach I have adopted over all my case studies (Kanpol, 1992, 1994), one thing is certain: none of this research would have been possible without the intrusion of my own subjectivity, personal biases or political agenda. No research is innocent or devoid of a political agenda, whether overt or covert! Given this statement, as a critical ethnographic researcher (or anyone who conducts research for that matter) one may not be aware of the often times political climate or incursions one is making into the research site. No political, or counter–hegemonic invasions into schools can be made without eventually understanding one's relationship to social structures, which embraces one's personal history.

With the above in mind, the first part of this chapter is devoted to personal stories. Second, I will summarize how these micronarratives have 'subjectively' affected my critical ethnographic studies. Third, I will theorize how a better under-standing of these personal stories today have allowed me to move from the posi-tion of critical *cynicism* to critical *joy*. Finally, I will posit suggestions for critical ethnographers in their fieldwork that would tap into a 'critical' paradigm that has been historically cynical and lacking the joyful possibilities of a counter-hegemonic agenda[1]!

A Personal Journey: And There I Was — Establishing a Criticality

Probably a defining moment for any critical theorist is their personal understanding of the oppressive structures they formerly or presently live in. Perhaps my child-hood should be divided into at least two significant areas where personal under-standing of oppressive structures existed: school and religion.

School

I vividly recall attending a private Jewish day school in Melbourne, Australia. Two pronounced things happened to me during that time. School was both a bore and extremely competitive. Tracking into subject areas that were gender inflicted was predominant. Teaching methodologies were technical and thereby not conducive to creative learning. And, often, friendships were defined by who received school achievement awards.

Fear was instilled into those who didn't compete well. Both students as well as parents were excessively competitive, where it seemed that one's personal worth was based on accomplishment. Stereotypes were abundant, and I was guilty of con-forming to and reproducing them as anyone was in school. Teachers were often authoritarian. They (male teachers anyway) were also sexist. I was usually afraid of them. At best, I recall some teachers taking a personal interest in me, usually pointing out what a good sportsman I was, but not a worthy student. My principal despised me and in my mind was the sole reason I dropped out of school in the eleventh grade. I was so scared of this authoritarian regime that as one outcome, I often lied to my parents about grades I received or tests I had taken. I was a cheat-ing expert, living on the edge when it came to exam time. I was just *not* a regi-mented learner. There was no freedom of expression. Perhaps this is why I often fell asleep in class, listened to music through earplugs when I could, or build fantasy football teams.

School was a far cry from the progressive kind that Dewey envisioned. Cur-riculum was clearly not connected to personal life experiences and/or interests. Democracy was thwarted by authoritarianism and patriarchal control. There was no substantive vision for why we were to receive an eduction, only that it would land a more prestigious job one day, thus providing upward social mobility. Indeed, much of my class time was spent dodging boredom through various individual and collect-ive activities designed to get on the teachers' nerves.

As I write this, I am not proud to be a part of those eventual dropouts who for want of a more meaningful life in school made some teachers pay for the school's deficiencies. With the advent of my dropping out, I felt doomed. And, even though my parents immigrated to Israel (and I followed suit), and despite the fact that I completed an American diploma in a highly priced American international school in Israel (it seems like my parents bought my diploma as I never had enough 'correct' credits to graduate especially without one math course), I was determined, despite my basketball scholarship to Tel Aviv University, to overcome my jock stereotype and complete my BA. I did so, ironically in the subjects I failed in eleventh grade in Australia — English literature and history.

As a teacher, more of the same nonsense occurred. I was fairly incensed with a system that was similar to the one I grew up in. There was little connection of curriculum to experience, an amazing amount of competition, tracking, survival of the fittest mentality, worth based on achievement, fear of tests (now fear of the Principal holding me accountable to every syllable on the curriculum), and so on. It was all quite repetitive. There wasn't any substantive vision — especially in my teacher education program which was purely bent on producing teaching robots with a technical mastery of skills. I was totally deskilled as a teacher and not prepared to deal with the social and cultural affairs that go on in all schools[2].

Religion

Even though I grew up in a traditionally kept Jewish home, little mention or personal analysis and scrutiny was made of this impact on my life. Much like some religious schools (McLaren, 1993), religion was (as I felt at the time) forced on me through prayer and ritual. Hand in hand with an authoritarian school system, religion also represented forced authority and control.

One could read bitterness and resentment into school and religious authority. Yet, within my religious upbringing, there were some fine memories, especially around traditional Passover times, where family gatherings were the norm, Bible stories and their heroes often came to life, my introduction to Jewish manhood through a barmitzvah ritual and so on. My major problems with religion were socially oriented. Why should I atone on the Day of Atonement (only one day a year and not the other 364 days!) when I felt that a system was full of sin? In my mind, little sense was made over mandatory services. Why was I challenging these traditions — or, put more bluntly, forced attendance at both school and religious services? These questions could not be answered then, but as a part of what Sharon Welch (1985) describes as 'dangerous memories', these feelings, ideas, and experiences must be interrogated for further explanation, understanding, interpretation, and reconfiguring, so as to view personal oppression, alienation and subordination, with the intent to challenge a system that allowed what seemed to be injustices occur. This is a part of a reflection process that is a necessary condition for the critical ethnographer.

Discrimination

As a part of this reflection process, I was met with a fair amount of anti–semitism growing up. 'Dirty Jew' and 'Jew boy' were often flung at me in discriminating and humiliating ways. Playing competitive sports for non–Jewish teams was never easy because I often felt left out, different and at times 'less than' others. I would try to hide my identity. And, although I did not go out of my way to tell my non–Jewish friends who I was, everyone knew I was Jewish. Relatedly, but just as important, I grew up in a closed Jewish community who also discriminated against non–Jews. I would often hear the words 'those Goyim' (non–Jews) as a statement of Jewish retaliation to anti–semitism. And in the street where I lived from 8–17 years of age, many kids were not allowed to play with me because I was Jewish. I was some sort of disease, I guess! Until today, I *despise* both forms of discrimination! Most sadly, I grew up with both guilt and shame at being Jewish — an interesting dualism because I was taught to be proud of my heritage.

During my formative years I learned that truth was supposedly a Jewish thing. There was no mention of meaning beyond the Old Testament, for instance. There was no mention of what being Gentile or Christian was about, except that is was a dangerous thing. Joy, love and solace was supposedly a Jewish thing, which, according to my personal experiences in and out of school were remote given the realities of forced religion and authoritarianism in school.

Since those days, life's experiences have had a way of humbling me. As a struggling immigrant to Israel, I often met the discriminating forces of people. As an immigrant I was not made to feel a part of a country[3]. Dangerous memories will remind me of a failed marriage: patriarchal domination, lack of sensitivity, issues of control, and power on both sides. Dangerous memories will remind me of a career that sits entrenched in theoretical nihilism and despair, which have often rendered me quite sarcastic, hopeless and sorry in the face of social, cultural and structural nightmares — this despite my privileged social position.

My politics have often been confusing. No wonder. Despite the post–modern insistence on multiple realities and never–ending deconstruction, I have often wondered what meaning I can take from my youth and present life that makes story telling so powerful, so profound and so real that a politics of hope can rear its head. What can I learn from, for instance from both the Old and New Testament that would make stories of Moses, Abraham, David and Jesus real without being dogmatic, hopeful without being cynical, and democratic without being authoritarian? With the above in mind, the connection between this skeleton of a personal story can and must be made to past critical ethnographic studies so as to make sense of how the cynical me can present a joyful possibility and hope for ways out of the structural nightmares public schools find themselves in today.

And There I Was

From 1985 until 1990 I was officially the visitor of three public schools at places where I was located — in Columbus, Ohio where I completed my doctorate, and in Orange, California where I was on my first professorial assignment. One thing is certain. I wasn't told in graduate school that to enter a school site was both political and very personal. What I was told in my graduate qualitative research classes was how to conduct a qualitative research study. This in itself reminded me of my teacher education days, where I was to become the deskilled practitioner rather than a reskilled, thoughtful critic of who I was in the surroundings I entered. Rather than take readers now into the research sites I entered (Kanpol, 1992, 1994), perhaps a summary of how the interplay between my earlier narrative and the research venues effected me is in order, given the nature of the topic of this book and the title of this chapter.

Hillview Middle School

I entered Hillview as a conscientious graduate student bent on getting all the information needed and following correct methodological procedures to satisfy my Doctoral Committee. During the time I was researching a group of eighth grade teachers, I was heavily into Willis's *Learning to Labor* (1977). This was no doubt a significant influence on Marxist readings, particularly as it was related to the research site and past personal experiences.

Perhaps even more importantly than the connection of qualitative research to the data, was the *unconscious* interpretation of events in this middle school that were influenced by my past schooling experiences. As a naive researcher, I saw similar themes of my own past in the actions of the subjects (particularly teachers) I was researching. Unbeknownst to me at the time, I was learning a lot about myself in the process. Following this group of cynical eighth graders (and they had reasons to be cynical given the ineptness of the administration, particularly the Principal), I was viewing what I believed to be a counter–hegemonic agenda. For the main though, I described their coping strategies as *institutional political resistance*. This form of resistance had little substance to it — and was mainly concerned with breaking rules, use of oppositional language and developing survival mechanisms that would challenge authority — *all of which I as a student and a teacher would engage in on a daily level in prior years.* There is no doubt in my mind, that given my past relationship to my school Principal, and my deskilled public school teaching career, this research venue provided a locale to vent my own anger at a system that often dehumanized me through its deskilling process! To support this notion further would be to understand that in this particular research venue there was what I believe to be a true form of counter-hegemony that I named *cultural political resistance*. In this sense there were notions of female teachers struggling against discriminatory forces. Lo and behold, given the narrative section on discrimination in the first section of this chapter, so had I in my past.

Parkview Elementary School

It took two years after my dissertation to finally get back into public schools. During those years, I read much feminist literature. I also realized that in terms of a counter–hegemonic agenda, my Hillview study was theoretically weak. I often asked my students, which of the four teachers of Hillview do you identify with? What I was really commenting on was that how all four had elements of my own personality! I was determined at Parkview Elementary to be more distant and *not* be so emotionally involved — perhaps less cynical about the administration. Nevertheless, in my introduction to the school climate, the Principal commented of this 'working class' school dominated by Hispanic Americans: 'I don't know if we can give them what they want here. They are vocationally bound.' I was thunderstruck. This comment reminded me of my Principal who told my parents when I was 12 that 'your son could be a barber!' It was at that moment that I realized that qualitative research is more personal than I could ever have imagined. That, yes, despite the need to perform what my professors taught me (the need to *bracket* one's life in an effort to seek 'truth'), there would be difficulty in my own values and experiences *not* intruding on the research site. I also then realized that any research site is a political agenda, where dominant and subordinate values prevailed. Moreover, given the nature of the research I was to conduct at Parkview Elementary, it was indubitably skewed on some level by my own history!

In short, counter–hegemony was both a personal and social concern. I was to record and view how a teacher fictitiously named Betty was to challenge the Principal's stereotypical comments about students. I was also to view how Betty challenged dominant values of rampant individualism and excessive competition, etc. Perhaps most importantly, I witnessed how Betty created a counter–hegemonic platform that I had unconsciously accepted both long ago as a resistant student growing up in Australia, as a teacher in Israel, and as a researcher in her classroom. Even more importantly, I witnessed Betty resist with *love, kindness and tolerance.* Indeed, at least on an unconscious level I was now witnessing the cynical me moving to a joyful counter–hegemonic possibility, although I wasn't aware of it at the time — being caught in a poor marriage and an Education Department bent on totally deskilling its members didn't help matters either.

I had learned one thing for sure. A one time qualitative effort like my dissertation was not enough to justify 'research' expertise. As a hungry researcher, I wanted more. I wanted to go beyond Betty or even a group of disgruntled eighth grade teachers. I wanted inner–city schooling and even more action. I wanted teacher resistant struggle in its highest form and eventually an understanding of the theoretical and practical intricacies I had gotten into. These are the reasons for the next study.

Chapel High School

How ironic it is that in this study a group of ESL (English as a Second Language) teachers volunteered to participate with me in my research effort. Ironic because in Israel I was an ESL teacher in private institutions. Ironic because these teachers were teaching immigrants and I had been an immigrant in Israel and was now one in the United States. And who says the choice of research venue or the topic to be researched is devoid of past personal experience? Clearly, looking back, my subjectivity — my whole historical and thus, political being, was totally involved in this research effort as well, even if I didn't realize it at the time.

I recall teachers contending with those students who couldn't speak English — I glibly recall me not being able to speak Hebrew in Israel. I am reminded how students resisted any learning that teachers had in mind for them. I too resisted all forms of teaching authority (especially learning Hebrew) in Israel for I didn't want to be part of the dominant culture! I recollect these ESL teachers trying so urgently to challenge stereotypes. I was stereotyped a 'jock' and 'dumb' during my school years. I fondly recall an Egyptian teacher (fictitiously named Sarah) who understood her subjectivity so well, that she became a 'resistant' role model for students to view and learn from. She well understood the subordinate role of females and the discord and strife inherent in leaving an original home. I learned from Sarah too!! She taught me that I was the students and that she was me. Moreover, she taught me that counter–hegemony is a compromise between the dominant structure and an alternative and liberating vision! That said, I learned that any counter–hegemonic struggle is a form of self–reflection on the 'dangerous memories' of your own particular struggles and conflicts.

I would argue that the three studies I conducted were about this form of struggle. The studies and/or my personal struggles were not objective. These ultimate conflicts with dominant modalities were mired in one's own particular history and interrelated with others' struggles and others' histories. Indeed these counter–hegemonic clashes with structural elements of society were I believe to be inter-subjective in nature, producing what Laclau and Mouffe (1985) term, a 'democratic imaginary' — a challenge to all forms of oppression, subordination and alienation, despite the time and place of their existence.

Clearly, I have not done justice to the three case studies I conducted a few years ago. I have merely tipped the iceberg so to speak. What I have shown to date though, is the inevitable connection between my history as a student, teacher, immigrant, resistor and male, to the choice of research venue. In the following section I will travel beyond the venues themselves and theorize more about how I believe a critical theory in education must be seen in more than just a cynical light. I will also argue that this is a very personal matter as well.

And Here I Am

It is important to note that critical theorists in general, myself in particular, have carried an air of cynicism into their work for many years now. For me, cynicism, or the cynic, is one who is inclined to investigate the sincerity of people's motives, or the value of living, one who highly questions the material interests of individuals. Let me be clear here. I am *not* arguing that cynicism, as defined above is a bad or evil thing. Critical theorists in education and/or critical ethnographers have known for some time that there are good reasons to be cynical of a society whose institutions like schools claim democratic virtues, yet in the everyday life–world espouse a contradictory capitalistic market logic (Shapiro, 1990), resulting in rampant race, class and gender inequities (Kozol, 1991, 1994; Apple, 1996).

Theoretically, the cynicism I am talking about grows out of a 'catch 22' logic that educational theory has found itself historically mired in. Put differently, how does one escape the dialectic? This was highly questioned in Willis's now notorious work in education (Willis, 1997) and in my own studies, where the inevitability of cultural reproduction weighed heavily against the backdrop of the culturally productive aspects of counter–hegemony within a capitalistic framework and resultant structural inequities. In my educational foundations classes for instance, teachers are at pains to counter damning oppressive structural constraints imposed on them by the state–mandated curriculum, intensification of labor, and deskilling, etc. At the same time that they see emancipatory and counter–hegemonic hope, hegemonic forms raise their ugly heads, and thus, my in–service teachers are at once cut back by other constraints and forced into some form of oppressive conformity. Because of this one–step forward, two–step backward syndrome, they become cynical, and find little solace in ways out of the cultural and structural nightmares they find themselves in, despite the sincerity that structures their original criticisms. No less can be said of those criticalists who argue that it becomes impossible to become the 'other' — those who are marginalized and oppressed (Ellsworth, 1989). This dualistic and oppositional logic, also cynical, while sincere in intention, and often but not always correct in the everyday life world (Kanpol, 1990), denies the theoretical and practical possibility for fusion with the 'other' in an intercommunicative dialogue of emancipatory struggle and possibility. *Indeed*, as a critical ethnographer, in order to 'get at' the voices of those oppressed teachers, I had to become much more than the critical cynic. I had to reach beyond the cultural reproduction and cultural production theoretical logic in order to communicate within an intersubjective dialogue of hope and possibility OUT of the structural nightmares these teachers found themselves in. To remain the critical cynic, while a necessary but not sufficient condition for social transformation, I also had to travel beyond my own cynical historical past so that a space could be opened for what I have termed elsewhere as 'joy' to occur (Kanpol, 1997a), where I could see, feel, and be the 'other', understanding, acknowledging and accepting the connection between the 'other of the researched' and the 'other' in me.

It is within the dialectic of cynicism and joy that I as a critical ethnographer have found myself. As a politics of meaning, *joy* is politically loaded to mean alliance, commonality, and what Lerner (1994) describes in his own work as 'renewal'. He comments, more spiritually, connecting joy to ethics:

> Reclaiming a sense of celebration and joy at the wonders of creation is another sense of the Jewish renewal . . . what is unique about Judaism is that it entwines the sense of awe, wonder, amazement, and this spiritual reality that surrounds us, with a vision of God who not only created the universe but also the force that makes possible an ethically guided universe. (p. 96)

For Lerner as well as West (1993), joy connects ethically to renewal as a form of politics of meaning in which liberation from oppressive forces becomes a guiding motif — despite their absolute differences in faith. Joy, thus understood, is a healing process. The bond of commonality entered by Lerner and West, as an act of solidarity has immense philosophical connotations and is the kind of solidarity that I as a critical ethnographer entered with some of my subjects in the research venues.

The way I am using cynicism and joy should not be seen as a static dialectic but rather as a personal crusade of *here I am* in the context of being a critical ethnographer. As a process of common democratic struggle, joy must be seen within cynicism and growing out of cynicism as a necessary condition for human liberation. For example, in his book on Deleuze, philosopher Michael Hardt (1993) argues for commonality as a basic form of joy. He relates how workers in the novel by Nanni Balestrine *Vogliamo Tutto* (*We Want Everything*) is interpreted by Deleuze as an

> attack on their essence as workers. They arrive at moment when they are able to go beyond, to discover a terrain of creation and joy beyond the worker. (p. 46)

Hardt's emphasis is that workers in this novel recognize their commonality and,

> Their expression in collective action takes the form of a spatial or social synthesis, composing an expansive and coherent body of desire. As the body of workers expands, their will and power grow. The synthesis involved in the workers' collectivity is an integral return of the will . . . precisely when the workers actualize their critique, they pass into action in the factory and in the streets, they achieve the constructive moment of joy and creation. The actualization of the workers is a practice of joy. (p. 47)

Hardt's central point here, I believe, is to locate a philosophy of joy which is necessarily tied directly to a philosophy of practice, a suggestive argument linking commonness to common behavior and/or common desire to a practice of joy. Commonness can and should also be related to what Laclau and Mouffe (1985) term, a 'democratic imaginary'. Here, political struggles and/or antagonisms are connected by their commonness to dismember various forms of alienation, subordination and oppression.

Cynicism that leads to joy as commonness within solidarity is a part of what I as a critical ethnographer underwent in my personal investigation at public school sites, in the quest to understand 'otherness'. Mired in the cynicism of 'catch 22' theoretical logic, joy and affirmation were rewarded when it was realized that 'Here I Am' had become as ethic of affirmation and one of democratic political practice. This ethic of joy as critical practice becomes a fleeting moment in time that is captured by combining the researcher's history with that of the researched and the researched 'other' with my 'other'. Joy rears its head when there is a commonness of political struggle, an intersubjectivity of pain for instance, or a bond that is created by the critical ethnographer and her/his clientele. That bond seeks common oppression, alienation and subordination as a marker to challenge the critical cynic and move to a joyful position of emancipatory possibility, where the critical ethnographer and her/his clientele move unitedly with collective democratic ground, a rise beyond otherness. To me, this is a starting place for a counter–hegemonic platform!

The above short theoretical treatise has suggested that cynicism and joy are part and parcel of a critical ethnographic position, *particularly mine*. There is no doubt in my mind that my politics has been informed by my own particular history, ultimately my personal multifarious identity — my relationship to schools, parents, authoritarianism, religion and other discriminatory forces . . . How this affected my critical ethnographic studies is quite obvious to me. It *did*, only I wasn't aware of it at the time.

Conclusion – Where I'll Go

The role of critical ethnographer cannot be underestimated. Indeed, from my personal experiences, that role is multifold. Surely the critical ethnographer is to seek knowledge of the structure under investigation — in this case schools. However, what underlies that structure becomes the gut of the critical ethnographer and his/her relationship to that structure. Thus, I have contended that an additional role of the critical ethnographer is self–reflection on their relationship to structural elements of society. In my mind, without this personal investigation, there is no way to overcome the cynicism that underlies much of critical educational theory. My argument for self–reflexivity is not a new one. However, self–reflexivity has some additional components that perhaps haven't been argued before. Self–reflexivity is indubitably connected to one's history. One's history is tied into the research site on some conscious or unconscious level. The move from critical cynic to emancipatory joy becomes a moving dialectic between researcher and researched and 'our' otherness — an ongoing process of etching out common democratic threads as an intersubjective understanding.

If anything, my three case studies briefly described earlier have convinced me of the need for far more personal reflection. I have also been encouraged to pursue the blend between the deeper personal aspects of my critical personality (and the cynic in me) with the reasons as to why I pursue a research agenda. A 'critical' research agenda isn't only about attaining knowledge of the structural elements of schools, for instance. A research agenda as I am delineating it, is a committed understanding of where one fits into the structure while conducting critical ethnography. That understood, joy becomes an emnancipatory viability for the critical ethnographer *only* if the researched and the researcher can attain this type of intersubjective compromise. It is to there that I go!

Notes

1 For an in–depth theoretical treatise of the dialectic of cynicism and joy, refer to Kanpol (1997a).
2 For an in–depth description and many examples of schooling experiences as a student and teacher, please refer to Kanpol (1997b).
3 ibid.

References

APPLE, M. (1996) *Cultural Politics and Education,* New York: Teachers College Press.

DARDER, A. (1995) *Culture and Difference: Critical Perspectives on the Bicultural Experiences in the United States,* Westport, CT: Bergin Garvey.

ELLSWORTH, E. (1989) 'Why doesn't this feel empowering: Working through the repressive myths of critical pedagogy', *Harvard Educational Review,* **59,** 3, pp. 297–324

GIROUX, H. (1996) *Fugitive Cultures: Race, Violence and Youth,* New York: Routledge.

GIROUX, H. (1997) *Pedagogy and the Politics of Hope: Theory, Culture and Schooling,* Boulder, CO: Westview Press.

GUBA, E. (1990) 'Subjectivity and objectivity', in EISNER, E. and PESHKIN, A. (Eds.) *Qualitative Inquiry in Education,* New York: Teachers College Press, pp. 74–91.

HARDT, M. (1993) *Gilles Deleuze,* Minneapolis, MN: University of Minnesota Press.

KANPOL, B. (1990) 'Reply to Ellsworth', *Harvard Educational Review,* **60,** 3, pp. 363–5.

KANPOL, B. (1992) *Towards a Theory and Practice of Teacher Cultural Politics,* New Jersey: Ablex.

KANPOL, B. (1994) *Critical Pedagogy: An Introduction,* Westport, CT: Bergin and Garvey.

KANPOL, B. (1997a) *Teachers Talking Back and Breaking Bread,* New Jersey: Hampton Press.

KANPOL, B. (1997b) *Issues and Trends in Critical Pedagogy,* New Jersey: Hampton Press.

KOZOL, J. (1991) *Savage Inequalities,* New York: Crown.

KOZOL, J. (1994) *Amazing Grace,* New York: Crown.

LACLAU, E. and MOUFFE, C. (1985) *Hegemony and the Socialist Strategy,* London: Verso.

LERNER, M. (1994) *Jewish Renewal,* New York: G.P. Putnam's Sons.

McLAREN, P. (1993) *Schooling as a Ritual Performance,* London: Routledge.

PHILLIPS, D.C. (1990) 'Subjectivity and objectivity: An objective inquiry' in EISNER, E. and PESHKIN, A. (Eds.) *Qualitative Inquiry in Education,* New York: Teachers College Press, pp. 19–37.

PURPEL, D. and SHAPIRO, S. (1995) *Beyond Liberation and Excellence: Reconstructing the Public Discourse in Education,* Wesport, CT: Bergin and Garvey.

ROMAN, L. and APPLE, M. (1990) 'Is naturalism a move away from positivism? Materialist and feminist approaches to subjectivity in ethnographic research', in EISNER, E. and PESHKIN, A. (Eds.) (1990) *Qualitative Inquiry in Education,* New York: Teachers College Press, pp. 38–73.

SHAPIRO, S. (1990) *Between Capitalism and Democracy,* Westport, CT: Bergin and Garvey.

WELCH, S. (1985) *Communities of Resistance and Solidarity,* New York: Orbis.

WEST, C. (1993) *Prophetic Thought in Postmodern Times,* Monroe, MN: Common Courage Press.

WILLIS, P. (1977) *Learning to Labor,* Lexington, MA: D.C. Heath.

13 Critical Policy Scholarship: Reflections on the Integrity of Knowledge and Research

Gerald Grace

Introduction: Being Reflexive About Being Reflexive

This volume is designed to encourage researchers in education to reflect upon 'the critical intent of the wider research project' and to turn 'a reflexive lens upon their experience as researchers'.[1] There are a number of reasons why this should be done. The first is that the existing literature of reflexivity in educational research is not extensive, although Burgess (1984, 1985, 1989), Halpin and Troyna (1994) and Walford (1994) are important examples of the genre. The neglect of reflexivity is not surprising given the prevailing culture of educational research internationally which continues to cling to nineteenth century positivist notions of what it is to be 'scientific', 'objective', 'valid' and 'robust'. As Troyna argued:

> Technicist conceptions of research, which focus purely and simply on 'how to do' empirical projects, continue to dominate the research literature . . . in their determination to lay bare the allegedly logical and sequential phases of the conception, execution and dissemination of social research, these interpretations of the activity help to sanction and reproduce the myth of objectivity. (Troyna, 1994, p. 5)

There is therefore a need for more researchers to write accounts which show the limitations of technicism, the ideological and historical struggles behind 'logic' and 'sequence' and the problematics of objectivity. Educational research must abandon pretensions to be a recontextualized form of natural science by recognizing that it is preeminently a humane study with an humane intent. As such it cannot, with integrity, develop a research culture which is not in itself humane i.e. participative, methodologically catholic, critically reflexive, culturally sensitive and intent upon the enhancement of the potentiality and dignity of persons.[2] Educational research is not an instrument for more efficient human engineering. It is, at its best, a collaborative and humane enterprise to assist the fulfilment of the creative potential of people and of societies. Research students in education must avoid coming to the view that there are 'soft' humane considerations in empirical enquiry and 'hard' methodological and analytical procedures and that the latter constitutes the real business. The requirements for humane inquiry are intellectually, personally and morally demanding but not yet fully documented or codified in the research manuals. That is why the contributions to this volume provide a useful resource for those reflecting upon the nature of humane and critical research in education.

The second reason why we need more reflexivity in educational research is that the process of research itself is subject to three major transformations, each of which threatens the integrity of research activity to a greater or lesser extent. Internationally these trends may be summed up as:

(i)   greater control by state and other external agencies of the funding available for research and of the agenda of issues to be investigated by researchers;

(ii) a quickening of the rate at which research projects must be formulated, executed and reported upon ie an intensification of the research productivity process;

(iii) the commodification of research outcomes through a system of performance indicators which have funding and status consequences for institutions and for research teams.

While some of these developments may provide a competitive edge which stimulates research activity and related rates of publication and dissemination, each of them contains potential threats to the integrity of research culture. As state and other external agencies progressively colonise the relatively autonomous intellectual space of the university, the research council or the research institution, by funding and accountability controls, the culture of independent inquiry is increasingly constrained.[3] State and business agencies become the significant definers of the 'problems' to be investigated and researchers become the servicing agents of the prescribed agenda. Insofar as this expresses a trend, at least in English–speaking cultures, we have a reversion to the 'taking' rather than the 'making' of an educational research agenda, exactly the danger which Michael FD Young warned against in his seminal writings of 1971.

The concomitant intensification of the work rate for research productivity poses other problems for intellectual and analytical integrity. Time for the formulation of a research design which does justice to the complexity of the social phenomena under investigation, is at a premium. Time for a research process which is also participative, culturally and personally sensitive and appropriately triangulated is seen as an unrealistic option. Time for thoughtful and critically reflexive analysis and commentary is short.

A research culture operating under strong time discipline and report 'delivery' indicators may enhance the productivity rate but it may be doing less than justice to the complex social phenomena under investigation and less than justice to the institutions and individuals involved in the inquiry. 'Good research takes time' is not the self–interested plea of the out of touch academic. It is the sober and considered opinion of an academic and research community which understands the complexity of social and educational cultures and of the need for an appropriate research culture in which such complexity can be properly appreciated.

Given that the intensification of the research process is taking place in many societies at the same time in which public funding for universities and research institutions is being reduced, student enrolments are being increased and the bureaucratic apparatus of quality assurance is itself being intensified (with stronger expectations for 'quality' teaching and learning) the net effect is the generation of a work culture of constant 'busyness'. In these circumstances research reflexivity becomes even more essential for the integrity and the quality of educational and social research.

The commodification of research outcomes provides the third potential threat to the integrity of research culture in the social sciences. As research and pub-lication is progressively recontextualized as a production output in a competitive market place for resources, researchers are increasingly under pressure to produce 'what counts' in the market place. This situation can have important consequences for what research is undertaken, for the methodological approaches selected and for the mode of its realization.[4]

Throughout this introduction, 'reflexivity' and 'integrity' have emerged as inter-related and crucial features of humane and critical inquiry in educational research but before addressing the substantive focus of this chapter it is necessary to be more explicit about them. In noting that reflexivity is 'a diffuse concept which is used by academics in a bewildering number of ways', Troyna (1994) made the helpful suggestion that we should all be reflexive about reflexivity (p. 5). For me, reflexivity implies a making visible of the suppressed culture of research activity as opposed to the making visible of only its formal public face. By 'suppressed cul-ture' I mean the backstage reality of research life — the struggles over project selection and formulation, difficulties with access to the field, problems of methodo-logy and analysis, change of direction, ethical dilemmas, constraints upon writing–up and publishing and, perhaps most difficult of all to be honest about, 'the critical intent of the wider research project'. Reflexivity implies a process of critical self–reflection upon the natural history of the research project in its conception, execution and dissemination. It is the other side of the story from that 'presentation of self' which appears in the research report and the formal published work. In its call for subjectivity it does not articulate easily with academic conventions for third person, disembodied and 'objective' accounts. In the power relations of the re-search enterprise and in the micropolitical struggles within institutions, being re-flexive constitutes a form of intellectual vulnerability that few want to embrace. Its relatively marginal status in contemporary research culture is therefore hardly surprising. Nevertheless if educational and social research is to be a humane and critical project, reflexivity must take a central place in the agenda for research. We may say that it is an essential part of the integrity of the research process.

This leads us to the question of what is to be understood by integrity in educational and social research. There are at least three meanings of integrity which are germane to my argument: (i) an unimpaired condition (soundness); (ii) firm adherence to a code of principles (probity); and (iii) the quality or state of being complete (comprehensiveness). These qualities describe the ideal–type of the re-search enterprise. It aspires to soundness in its methodological and analytical pro-cedures and in the strength of its evidential base for any conclusions. It strives for probity in its balanced and impartial consideration of claim and counter–claim in the field and in its application of scholarly disciplines in adjudicating such claims. It tries for comprehensiveness by locating the matter under investigation in its relational matrix i.e. its historical, theoretical, cultural, social, economic and political contexts.

Educational research of integrity aspires to these characteristics, although constraints of time and resources may impede their realization. It also aspires to keep alive the real meaning of *disinterestedness as involving knowledge constructed independently of interest groups or of the prior agendas of political and funding agencies.*[5]

In the field of education policy studies I have tried to express these ideas as 'critical policy scholarship' or sometimes simply as 'policy scholarship'.[6] In the following section I will try to be reflexive about the origins, meanings and critical intent of these concepts.

Being Reflexive about Critical Policy Scholarship

I first began to use distinctions between policy science and critical scholarship in 1984 as part of a critical exegesis of the literature of urban education studies which was published as *Education and the City: Theory, History and Contemporary Practice.* My intention at that time was to assist in the construction of an urban education collection of academic readings which would be of use to teachers and students on graduate programmes concerned particularly with the 'problems' of inner city schools. My critical purpose was to illuminate the theoretical, conceptual, substantive and research limitations of the existing field of urban education studies both in the USA and in Britain and to encourage researchers, teachers and students to go beyond these limitations. For instance, the inner–city as 'problem' had an hegemonic dominance in the discourse and theorizing of the time. I sought to show that a wider range of urban social theory extending the discourse from urban problems only to a recognition of urban conflicts and of urban contradictions gave us greater theoretical resources for understanding the inner–city school 'problems and a greater possibility of finding political and policy responses to the urban school challenge.'[7]

As I reflected upon the nature of urban education writing and research in the 1960s and 1970s it became increasingly evident to me that it was a realization of what Brian Fay (1975) had defined as policy science:

> that set of procedures which enables one to determine the technically best course of action to adopt in order to implement a decision or achieve a goal . . . in this regard the policy scientist really is a type of social engineer who makes instrumental decisions on the basis of the various laws of science — in this instance, social science — which are relevant to the problem in hand. The policy engineer . . . is one who seeks the most technically correct answer to political problems. (p. 14)

This expressed exactly my own reading of the urban education field as then constituted. The conflicts and contradictions of the urban schooling matrix were being reduced to sets of technical problems for which urban education policy scientists could then prescribe technical solutions of various kinds. Urban education study was in fact a form of 'abstracted empiricism' (Wright Mills, 1973). Since my purpose was not only to provide a theoretical and substantive critique of the field but to suggest a possible reformation of it, I felt that I had an obligation to outline a new agenda for study and a new intellectual and research paradigm for future work. If policy science was a limited and reductionist approach to urban education issues, what would be a more satisfactory one? In reflecting upon that question, I came to the conclusion that it would be *critical scholarship* and these ideas were expressed in the chapter, 'Urban education: Policy science or critical scholarship?' (Grace, 1984b).

In formulating conceptions of a critical scholarship I was again strongly influenced by Fay's (1975) exposition of the characteristics of critical social science. I recommend all research students to read the whole of his chapter 5 but the sections which spoke to my concerns were the following:

- The critical social scientist is one who seeks to disclose how the historical process was such that the social order . . . was incapable of satisfying some of the wants and needs which it engendered. (p. 96)

- Its theories must not simply explain the sources and nature of discontent . . . but also must demonstrate . . . the structural contradictions which underlie it. (p. 97)

- The theory must be translatable into the ordinary language in which the experience of the actors is expressed . . . a critical social theory must be grounded in the self–understandings of the actors even as it seeks to get them to conceive of themselves and their situations differently. (p. 98)

- The critical model envisages . . . the educative role of social theory. According to this educative conception the function of the social scientist is not to provide knowledge of quasi–causal laws to a policy scientist who will determine which social conditions are to be manipulated . . . but rather to enlighten the social actors so that, coming to see themselves and their social situation in a new way, they themselves can decide to alter the conditions which they find repressive. In other words, the social scientist tries to 'raise the consciousness' of the actors whose situation he (sic) is studying. (p. 103)

With these emphases upon historical process, structural contradictions, self–understandings of the actors, the educative role of critical social science and the raising of consciousness[8] I had found a new formulation for what urban education study might be. However, I did not think that the understanding of the urban education problematic could be contained within the boundaries of a critical social science alone — something more comprehensive and inclusive was needed. I was also aware that critical social science had its own political and ideological vulnerabilities which were becoming increasingly evident in the changing sociopolitical conditions of 1980s Britain. If one was reflexive about the wider ideological, cultural and political changes which were now constraining the intellectual autonomy of the academy, some degree of strategic thinking was necessary. At this time ideological attacks upon educationists and social scientists were becoming sharper and in particular the notion of the 'critical' was being recontextualized as 'ideologically biased' (the subversion of the academy) when counterposed to 'scholarship' (the traditional probity of the academy). It seemed to me that this ideological distortion could be overcome by uniting these apparent polarities and by establishing the legitimate credentials of an approach to be called 'critical scholarship'.

I had therefore two intentions in advancing the notion of critical scholarship as an intellectual paradigm for a reformulated field of urban education studies. In the first place, critical scholarship would transcend the limitations of policy science but it would also aspire to go beyond the intellectual boundaries of critical social science *per se* to include serious engagement with forms of historical, comparative, philosophical, economic and policy analysis which focused upon urban phenomena from different perspectives. In this sense, a critical scholarship of urban education would attempt 'to bring these various elements into some sort of intellectual relation or at least dialogue' (Grace, 1984b, p. xii). I suppose that I was saying that even critical social scientists could not claim a monopoly on relevant knowledge and insight!

In the second place, a critical scholarship could unite the strengths of critical theory (with its sharp awareness of structural and ideological oppressions and policy contradictions) with the traditional disciplines of scholarship (careful delineation of evidence and argument, balanced and judicious conclusions). I was particularly concerned to try to prevent the idea of 'scholarship' from being appropriated by a conservative academic culture intent on demonstrating that there could be no such thing as a scholarship of education or a scholarship of social science. From my perspective a critical scholarship in both fields of study was not only possible but an exciting recontextualization of traditional scholarship. In being reflexive now about what might be called the archaeology of critical scholarship, I realize that I failed to give sufficient theorisation of this approach to policy study. While explicit about the limitations of policy science, the characterization of critical scholarship remained largely implicit. In later work, I tried to address these shortcomings.

Applying the Paradigm (1): Education Reform in New Zealand

New Zealand's radical education reforms in the period 1987–1990 provided me with an exceptional opportunity to attempt to apply some aspects of a policy scholarship approach to a fast–changing education policy context. The New Zealand education reform story has now been told from a number of perspectives: Middleton et al. (1990), Ramsey (1992), Dale (1992), Lauder et al. (1995). For those who were living and working in New Zealand at the time the immediate experience of the reform process was of a blitzkrieg of education reports (New Zealand Treasury, 1987; Picot Report, 1988; Hawke Report, 1988; Meade Report, 1988) all of which appeared to offer agendas for 'modernizing' New Zealand's education from early childhood care to the tertiary sector. Almost all of the reports offered, in addition to 'modernization', claims that the implementation of their recommendations would lead to an improved education service in terms of cost efficiency, effectiveness, public responsiveness and greater educational and social equity. The pace of the reform process was very rapid, partly arising from the fact that New Zealand general elections occur on a three–year cycle and partly from the fact that most reports were modified after consultation and further publications added to the reading workload of those trying to keep pace with these developments. While I was impressed by the culture of democratic consultation in New Zealand (which compared favourably with the situation in Britain at the time) it seemed to me that the culture of reform 'busyness' which had developed so rapidly posed two major dangers for New Zealand's citizens and educators. I summarize these below as:

(i) *Policy text overload*: a situation in which discourse and analysis becomes immersed in the (changing) detail of policy formulations and implementation strategies to the neglect of fundamental principles and issues in the reform process.

(ii) *Modernization ideology*: a situation in which reforms are presented as technical, neutral or common–sense changes required by 'the modern world' (generally in terms of international economic or trading conditions). It is usual to legitimate this strategy in a discourse of 'coming to terms with the real world'.

It is in situations of education reform such as these that a critical policy scholarship can illuminate the deep structure of the reform process so that citizens and educators, politicians and policymakers are more fully informed of the issues at stake.

My critical intent in writing the chapter 'Labour and education: The crisis and settlements of education policy' for a collection of papers published in New Zealand in 1990 was precisely to offer such a resource for the use of New Zealand's citizens and educators. In a subsequent version, 'Welfare labourism versus the New Right: the struggle in New Zealand's education policy' published in *International Studies in the Sociology of Education* (1991) I sought to make this analysis available to the wider community of education policy scholars. Policy text overload and modernization ideology are likely to engender policy science writing and research and therefore my first task was to make policy science and policy scholarship distinctions more explicit than in my earlier writings.

The 'Labour and education' paper of 1990 attempted this as a preface to the substantive analysis:

A policy science approach to policy study tends to exclude consideration of wider contextual relations by its sharply focussed concern with the specifics of a particular set of policy initiatives. This approach is seductive in its concreteness, its apparently value–free and objective stance and in its direct relation to action. However, what gets lost in this perspective is the examination of the politics and ideologies and interest groups of the policymaking process; the examination of the fundamental regulative principles which pattern the reforms; the making visible of internal contradictions within policy formulations, and the wider structuring and constraining effects of the social and economic relations within which policymaking is taking place. All of this is the proper concern of policy scholarship. (Grace, 1990, p. 165)

By this characterization I wanted to warn New Zealand citizens and educators of the limitations of policy science as a mode of appreciating what was happening in New Zealand's education system and why it was happening.

As an oppositional mode of thinking, analysis and discourse about these reforms I wanted to encourage a policy scholarship stance which involved, I claimed, a wider and deeper reading of what was happening in educational reform and why it was happening. Thus I characterized policy scholarship in these terms:

The perspectives of policy scholarship examine the historical processes of policy making, processes which demonstrate the centrality of concepts of conflict and struggle . . . education policy making has been caught up in the conflict of ideologies, the conflict of class, race and gender relations, the conflict of interest groups, the conflict of central state agencies with local education agencies . . . Policy scholarship brings back into the analysis an historical and contemporary sense of the power relations which shape and pattern education policy. (ibid., p. 166)

In the substantive analysis, I sought to show how the events of 1987–1990 could be historically located; how the power struggles between welfare labourism and the New Right agencies in New Zealand were shaping events; what fundamental principles of education policy were at stake; how race and gender relations were involved in the struggle; what conflicts, compromises and contradictions were apparent in the reform process and how the whole episode could be usefully interpreted within a theoretical framework involving notions of crisis and settlement in education policy. It is for those who read the 1990 and 1991 accounts to judge to what extent I achieved the aspirations for integrity in educational and social research i.e. soundness of methodology and analysis, probity of scholarship and comprehensiveness of perspective.

Written, as it was, with the constraints of being at the same time the Chairperson of the Department of Education at Victoria University, Wellington, and also of being a new Pakeha[9] arrival in the country I can, if I use the 'reflexive lens' recommended by the editors of this volume, now see its weaknesses. In reflexive relation to Fay's (1975) four imperatives for critical social science, cited earlier, the most serious omission is 'must be grounded in the self–understanding of the actors'. In fact, because of the constraints of time, the analysis was constructed largely from documentary sources and at a distance from those directly involved in or affected by the reform process. In other words, the research process was not participative and the 'voice' of those involved in the reforms was not an integral part of the analysis unless it had been mediated in written form. This must be regarded as a weakness in work which claims to be critical and humane. This deficiency is especially significant in relation to voices already marginalized in society, in this case that of the Maori people and of women. The discussion of Maori culture and of the issues at stake in Maori education needed to be informed by and legitimated by voices from the Maori community in New Zealand.[10] Similar strictures apply to the treatment of gender relations in the analysis. While I commented upon 'the influence of women in political groups, lobby groups, working parties, consultative processes and implementation processes' (Grace, 1990, pp. 186–7) as being important in the shaping of a new education settlement across all sectors, these observations have a tokenistic quality as a postscript to the main account rather than being permeated throughout the analysis. Both race and gender relations in the power struggles of education reform are relegated to the margins of the research and the writing. Reflexively, I can now see that it is not only policy science but also policy scholarship (despite claims to be critical) that remains trapped within a white and patriarchal research lens.[11]

In undertaking this research and in writing the accounts derived from it, I was conscious of the tension between the 'sociologist as partisan' and the 'sociologist as scholar.' I saw that a major struggle was taking place in New Zealand between a conception of education as a public good or as a commodity in the market place and I had already devoted my inaugural lecture at Wellington to an attack upon New Right and Treasury arguments that education was 'not in fact a "public good" ... education shares the main characteristics of other commodities traded in the market place' (New Zealand Treasury, 1987, p. 33). The privileged space of the inaugural lecture had, I believed, permitted a sharp, critical attack upon the ideological propositions of the Treasury. However, in writing a paper for a formal academic collection of policy essays I was more conscious of the imperative to do justice to an oppositional position even when you believe it to be intellectually flawed. If critical policy scholarship is to lay claim to integrity in its modes of analysis then its critical intent must be tempered by respect for evidence and even–handedness in argument. However it must also be the case that scholarly discipline should not become a means or an excuse for the construction of the bland, the boring or the inconclusive account which contributes nothing to the public debate and to the political struggle over policy issues. Whether my New Zealand writings achieved any integrity in this respect must be judged by the readers of them.

Applying the Paradigm (2): School Leadership in England

My most recent research endeavour has been to attempt to construct a socially critical account of the implications of school reform in England for the changing nature of school leadership with special reference to the position of the headteacher (school principal).[12] Thinking reflexively about why I actually chose this particular project, for which I gathered data in the period 1990–1994 and wrote the book *School Leadership: Beyond Education Management: An Essay in Policy Scholarship* (1995), I can see an interconnected set of reasons. As in New Zealand, so in England, I had a clear sense that the education reform process which was being enacted and implemented in the blitzkrieg mode was designed not simply to change the structural and curricular arrangements but more fundamentally to change the culture and the consciousness of the education sector and of those working within it or related to it. The education reform process in England from the 1988 Education Reform Act onward was, in my view, a major attempted cultural transformation of the nature of education *per se*, of the nature of educational institutions, of the power relations within institutions and with a wider network of external agencies, and of the social relations and roles of pupils, teachers, parents, governors and headteachers. From a sociohistorical perspective (i.e., from my perspective) schools, colleges and universities were being quite rapidly dislocated from a relatively autonomous space (concerned with academic, professional, aesthetic, humane and moral values) and recontextualized within an educational market place where all of those values might be not enhanced, as the reformers claimed, but in a literal sense devalued, and in another sense corrupted. How could a researcher begin to gain some insight into these large, complex and contested questions? It seemed to me that a policy scholarship approach had much to offer. Its insistence upon historical location would make it necessary for me to characterize the cultural features, social location and regulative principles of English schooling culture before the 1980s reform process. Its insistence upon conceptual and theoretical frameworks would also require me to be explicit about distinctions between leadership and management issues, notions of crisis and settlement struggles as they related to the English reform process and critical and alternative formulations about the nature of education and the nature of school leadership. The imperative for scholarship would require a clear and balanced account of the arguments for the reform process as well as the presentation of oppositional arguments. However, what also had to be heard was the voice of those caught up in the implementation of the reforms. There were many potential voices to be heard in this major, attempted cultural transformation. Limitations of time and resourcing but also an awareness of other critical work in progress[13] meant that for me the target constituency became headteachers.

I chose headteachers to be my participative coresearchers because of the strategic and symbolically powerful position which they occupied in the leadership culture of English schooling. Historically they had been the key agents for the transmission of other educational agendas and for other attempted sociocultural transformations. At various historical junctures headteachers in England had been agents for moral and religious formation, social reproducers of hierarchy, order and discipline, and prime exemplars of officially approved pedagogy. In a later period they had become potential innovators in curriculum, assessment and pedagogy and in modes of participative school leadership regarded as more appropriate for a social democratic context. Their contemporary position as the acknowledged professional school leaders and as the operative guardians of the culture, ethos and effectiveness of the schools meant that any political programme for school transformation could only be successfully realized in alliance with the headteachers. While education reform legislation had empowered school governors (as school leaders) and parents (as 'consumers'), the professional school leaders had to be won over, or no serious progress could be expected. It seemed to me therefore that a significant struggle was in progress in England in the late 1980s and early 1990s to transform the consciousness of headteachers, their professional and educational values, their view of the schooling process and their practice as school leaders. I agreed with Ball's (1994) conclusion that:

> the ethical and ideological position of the headteacher is crucial. It seems undeniable that the government intended to capture and reconstruct the headteacher as the key actor in the process of reform and redefinition. (p. 59)

This being undoubtedly the government's intention for transformation I saw my responsibilities within the ethic of policy scholarship as being two–fold. In the first place, I felt that I had an obligation to provide an analysis which located the issues in a wider and deeper cultural framework than that constituted by the increasing hegemony of education management texts and discourse. Education Management Studies (EMS) was dominating the 'training' and development courses provided by many agencies for the reconstruction of headship. Against the emergent hegemony of EMS, I wanted to assist in the construction of an alternative agenda i.e. Critical Leadership Studies (CLS). I hoped that as headteachers reflected upon the education reform process in which they were so central, they would not become the prisoners of EMS technical managerialism and executive busyness but have some space for being reflexive about the wider significance of the reforms and of their social, cultural, political and institutional consequences. In the second place, I felt that I had to honour Fay's (1975) imperative for a critical social science account, that 'it must be grounded in the self–understanding of the actors'.

However, it is one thing to have a research intention in critical social science that the fieldwork process should be participative and based upon a coresearcher ethic with those in the social world being described; it is quite another thing to realize this intention within the actual constraints of the fieldwork process. In attempting to produce 'an essay in policy scholarship' on the changing nature of school leadership in England my starting plan had been to establish a cooperative research relationship with about 200 headteachers, located in different regions in England. With such a research network formed, my intention was to conduct semi–structured interviews with these headteachers upon their perceptions and experiences of the reform process, particularly as it impinged upon the nature and practice of professional school headship. While I had starting categories for discussion in the interviews, I wanted the heads, in a coresearcher role, to suggest to me other analytical categories and features of their experienced and lived professional world, which should be included in the research account.[14]

The research rationale was therefore constituted as follows. A collaborative and participative research culture would help to minimize the danger of researcher dominance i.e. the imposition of prior categories. A mode of inquiry conducted within such a culture, by semi–structured interview approach, would elicit in–depth accounts of headteachers' consciousness on a range of issues, while at the same time contributing to the further refinement of the research activity. A research network of 200 headteachers drawn across the primary and secondary sectors and from a range of sociocultural and political contexts in England would be likely to generate a working sample which might be reasonably indicative of, although not definitive of, transformative experiences among the total national constituency of headteachers.

Taking a reflexive stance in 1997 to this research manifesto of 1990, I can now see that this ideal–type construction was unrealizable in the context of the time. The establishment of a collaborative research network of 200 headteachers distributed nationally required, in practice, an investment of time which I did not have. Appointed as Professor of Education in the University of Durham in January 1990, I was elected as Chair of the Board of Studies in Education by October 1990 and the plans for my research activity were severely constrained. It had also become clear that even if I had the time available for the realization of the original project (and I didn't have the time!) headteachers, pressed on all sides with new demands and responsibilities arising from the reform process, had even less time. The consequences of all this can be read in chapter 4 of *School Leadership*. Written with the smooth formality of the research primer as 'Fieldwork and Analytical Approaches', it should more honestly have been called 'The Desperate Struggle to Produce this Research'. Constraints of time, resources and opportunity involved a constant scaling down of the comprehensiveness of the inquiry and of its critical integrity. The original plan for a serious collaboration network of 200 headteacher coresearchers became in practice a nominal network of 88 headteachers[15] in which the notion of coresearcher was undeveloped. The original intention to proceed by interview was compromised in practice to a situation in which 21 research interviews were conducted and further research accounts were generated by various forms of survey schedules (derived from the interviews) which were returned by 67 headteachers. The participation range of the inquiry was substantially restricted to the North–East region of England and more explicitly to the counties of Durham and Cleveland and the cities of Durham, Newcastle and Sunderland for 69 of the headteachers.

The particularizing effects of this regional refocusing had significant consequences for the integrity of the research. Given the historical cultural and political traditions of the region there were no grant maintained school headteachers to provide accounts of this new and government sponsored form of school leadership. The patriarchal dominance of headship in the region resulted in only 24 research accounts from women, despite considerable effort to encourage more.

There were problems in the fieldwork therefore with the limited range of school cultures, and gender and professional cultures involved. Only the inclusion of a sample of Catholic school headteachers (15 from the North–East and 19 nationally distributed) extended the cultural context.

Thinking reflexively about the process of research and of writing the account which became the book, I can see that my attempt to be more conscious of the importance of gender relations in school leadership was not very successful. While I gave an account of the feminist critique of existing forms of school leadership in a chapter entitled 'Critical perspectives', my use of a focused chapter entitled 'Women and educational leadership', reporting fieldwork accounts, undermined the principle that gender relations, as a particular face of power relations, must be permeated throughout the research process and the research account.

Race relations are virtually absent as a serious part of the analysis.[16] I did not introduce them as a starting category for discussion in the interviews or for reflection in the survey schedules. The participatory headteachers (with the exception of two) did not mention race as relevant to the issues under investigation. There was, in short, a culture of silence about the various ways in which race and racism were implicated in the lives of schools, the consequences of the education reform process and the responsibilities of school leadership. This situation is a long way from the aspirations for integrity in knowledge and research which are entailed in a commitment to policy scholarship.[17] It demonstrates, once again, how principles of integrity articulated at a formal and theoretical level are compromised in the politics and practice of actual research.

Being Reflexive in Conclusions

What can be derived from this reflexive essay which may be of use to other researchers in the future? In one sense, and in keeping with the culture of reflexivity, every reader will derive his or her own 'conclusions' from the previous analysis. My own conclusions are that the practice of critical policy scholarship in education must be maintained against the growing influence of policy science research which, at its worst, is technicist, reductionist and domesticated to the requirements of the state and of other external funding agencies. In these circumstances, critical research will only be possible with the support of research networks operating on institutional, national and international bases. A key function of the research network (constituted by other critical researchers in the field) will be to assist the individual scholar or academic team in realizing a higher level of integrity in analysis and in reporting. In practice, this means that in the conception, execution and dissemination of research projects the widest possible consultation on draft proposals should take place with other researchers. The process of consultation is in itself generative of crucial intellectual spaces for reflection and revision and this helps to countervail the imperative demands of deadline 'delivery' of the research product. Research networking and consultation of this type can also alert the researcher and writer at an early stage to significant omissions in the social and power relations under investigation. One of the features of policy science dominance is the marginalization of class, race and gender analysis in education policy and practice. A research network acting in the role of 'critical friend' can assist the individual researcher or the research team in maintaining the integrity of comprehensive analysis of relevant power and social relations in education.

However, it is also important in the interests of integrity to circulate draft proposals and reports not only to 'critical friends' but also to 'oppositional critics' i.e. to those researchers and writers whose intellectual world view is known to be radically at odds with those of the researcher. By this means oppositional arguments can be given due attention in the analysis and alternative perspectives can be interrogated.

Research networks including critical friends and oppositional critics can therefore be of great assistance in the realization of higher levels of integrity in policy scholarship but they are only half of the story. If Fay's (1975) requirements for 'the self–understandings of the actors' and 'the educative role of social theory' are to be honoured in practice then the critical researcher must operate with another network, that of the research participants i.e. those whose social world is being analyzed and described. In the conception, execution and dissemination of the research project significant consultation with, and participation by, 'the researched' should be a feature of the best forms of policy scholarship. In other words, such scholarship should resist the power differentials and exclusions implied in the researcher–respondent model of enquiry.

It might well be asked how such research ideals can be realized in work contexts marked by workload intensification, reduced autonomy, job insecurity and financial constraints. There can be no easy answer to this. In the last resort the integrity of research and scholarship depends, as it always has, on the moral and intellectual integrity of critical scholars.

Acknowledgments

I would like to acknowledge the help of both critical friends and of oppositional critics in comments received on the first draft of this chapter.

Notes

1 As suggested in the synopsis sent by the editors of this volume to all contributors.
2 Feminist researchers have taken the lead in calling for a research culture which is participative, humane and critically reflexive. For two recent statements see Skeggs (1994) and Siraj-Blatchford (1995).
3 As Pettigrew (1994) observes, 'currently the powers that government has to control research it commissions . . . are extreme. What is at stake for researchers is the warrant for their work, its credibility . . .' (p. 58).
4 Under the present constraints of the Research Assessment Exercise (RAE) in British universities and colleges, 'quality' research must be undertaken and published on a three to four–year cycle in order to 'count' in the bureaucratic process of status and resource distribution.
5 Disinterestedness, as at least an aspiration to scholarly impartiality and neutrality, has long been an ideal of the liberal academy. However, both Marxist and Feminist writers are critical of such claims. Skeggs (1994) for instance argues that 'Feminist epistemology exposes neutrality as a myth that works for the interest of particular groups' (p. 75).
6 Policy scholarship is simply used as a shorthand form to denote critical policy scholarship.
7 See, 'Theorizing the urban: Some approaches for students of education', in Grace (1984).
8 There are problems with the intellectual arrogance implied in notions such as 'raising consciousness'. It would be more appropriate to say that critical social scientists hope to stimulate consciousness in new ways.
9 A Maori expression for a European settler in Aotearoa/New Zealand.

10 This was especially important given that Maori culture has a strong oral tradition. In practice I consulted reports about the Maori rather than entering into a dialogue with representatives of the community.

11 As Gillborn (1997) notes, 'refusal to examine race as a pertinent social category can act to disguise policies that have a racialized impact regardless of the avowed intentions of policy-makers and practitioners' (p. 83).

12 John Smyth's two edited collections, *Critical Perspectives on Educational Leadership* (1989) and *A Socially Critical View of the Self–Managing School* (1993) have been influential in demarcating this field of inquiry.

13 The critical work of Stephen Ball, Richard Bowe and Sharon Gewirtz at King's College, London was concentrating upon the effects of education reform upon parents and pupils. The critical work of Rosemary Deem and Kevin Brehony at Lancaster was examining developments in school leadership at the level of governing bodies and their changing cultures.

14 This was stated explicitly to the participating headteachers either during the introduction to the interview sessions or in the rubric of the survey schedules.

15 I have described this in the text as 'a limited opportunity sample' (p. 72) defined as 'limited opportunity refers both to the limited size of the sample and to the limited possibilities . . . The research was accomplished against the grain of work intensification among headteachers' (p. 75).

16 I am also now reflexively aware that class relations in education policy reform are present in both my New Zealand writing and in my school leadership writing only at an implicit level. This raises important issues for the ethics of research and writing and also for notions of integrity in policy scholarship. Even in a reflexive account, the irony will be noted that I am only raising these issues in the later part of the endnotes!

17 For a view which is critical of the use of policy science/policy scholarship distinctions in social and educational research see Whitty and Edwards (1994).

References

BALL, S.J. (1994) *Education Reform: A Critical and Post–structural Approach*, Milton Keynes: Open University Press.

BURGESS, R.G. (Ed.) (1984) *The Research Process in Educational Settings: Ten Case Studies*, Lewes: Falmer Press.

BURGESS, R.G. (Ed.) (1985) *Issues in Educational Research: Qualitative Methods*, Lewes: Falmer Press.

BURGESS, R.G. (Ed.) (1989) *The Ethics of Educational Research*, London: Falmer Press.

DALE, R. (1992) 'Whither the state and education policy? Recent work in Australia and New Zealand', *British Journal of Sociology of Education*, **13**, 3, pp. 387–95.

DEEM, R., BREHONY, K. and HEATH, S. (1995) *Active Citizenship and the Governing of Schools*, Buckingham: Open University Press.

FAY, B. (1975) *Social Theory and Political Practice*, London: George Allen and Unwin.

GEWIRTZ, A., BALL, S. and BOWE, R. (1995) *Markets, Choice and Equity in Education*, Buckingham: Open University Press.

GILLBORN, D. (1997) 'Young, black and failed by school: The market, education reform and black students', *International Journal of Inclusive Education*, **1**, 1, pp. 65–87.

GRACE, G.R. (Ed.) (1984a) *Education and the City: Theory, History and Contemporary Practice*, London: Routledge and Kegan Paul.

GRACE, G.R. (1984b) 'Urban education: Policy science or critical scholarship?' in GRACE, G.R. (Ed.) *Education and the City: Theory, History and Contemporary Practice*, London: Routledge and Kegan Paul.

GRACE, G.R. (1990) 'Labour and education: The crisis and settlements of education policy', in HOLLAND, M. and BOSTON, J. (Eds.) *The Fourth Labour Government: Politics and Policy in New Zealand*, Auckland: Oxford University Press.

GRACE, G.R. (1991) 'Welfare labourism versus the New Right: The struggle in New Zealand's education policy', *International Studies in the Sociology of Education*, **1**, pp. 25–42.

GRACE, G.R. (1995) *School Leadership: Beyond Educational Management: An Essay in Policy Scholarship*, London: Falmer Press.

HALPIN, D. and TROYNA, B. (Eds.) (1994) *Researching Education Policy: Ethical and Methodological Issues*, London: Falmer Press.

HAWKE, G. (1988) *Report of the Working Group on Post-Compulsory Education* (The Hawke Report), Wellington: Government Printer.

LAUDER, H. et al. (Eds.) (1995) *Trading in Futures: The Nature of Choice in Educational Markets in New Zealand*, Wellington: Ministry of Education.

MEADE, A. (1988) *Education to be More: Report of the Early Childhood Care and Education Working Group* (The Meade Report), Wellington: Government Printer.

MIDDLETON, S. et al. (Eds.) (1990) *New Zealand Education Policy Today: Critical Perspectives*, Wellington: Allen and Unwin.

NEW ZEALAND TREASURY (1987) *Government Management: Advice to the Incoming Government Vol. 2 Education Issues*, Wellington: Government Printer.

PETTIGREW, M. (1994) 'Coming to terms with research: The contract business', in HALPIN, D. and TROYNA, B. (Eds.) *Researching Education Policy: Ethical and Methodological Issues*, London: Falmer Press.

PICOT, B. (1988) *Administering for Excellence: Report of the Taskforce to Review Education Administration* (The Picot Report), Wellington: Government Printer.

RAMSEY, P. (1992) 'Picot — Vision and reality in New Zealand schools: An insider's view', in LINGARD, B. et al. (Eds.) *Schooling Reform in Hard Times*, London: Falmer Press.

SIRAJ-BLATCHFORD, I. (1995) 'Critical social research and the academy: The role of organic intellectuals in educational research', *British Journal of Sociology of Education*, **16**, 2, pp. 205–20.

SKEGGS, B. (1994) 'The constraint of neutrality: The 1988 Education Act and feminist research', in HALPIN, D. and TROYNA, B. (Eds.) *Researching Education Policy: Ethical and Methodological Issues*, London: Falmer Press.

SMYTH, J. (Ed.) (1989) *Critical Perspectives in Educational Leadership*, London: Falmer Press.

SMYTH, J. (Ed.) (1993) *A Socially Critical View of the Self–Managing School*, London: Falmer Press.

TROYNA, B. (1994) 'Reforms, research and being reflexive about being reflective', in HALPIN, D. and TROYNA, B. (Eds.) *Researching Education Policy: Ethical and Methodological Issues*, London: Falmer Press.

WALFORD, G. (Ed.) (1994) *Researching the Powerful in Education*, London: UCL Press.

WHITTY, G. and EDWARDS, T. (1994) 'Researching Thatcherite education policy', in WALFORD, G. (Ed.) *Researching the Powerful in Education*, London: UCL Press.

WRIGHT MILLS, C. (1973) *The Sociological Imagination*, Harmondsworth: Penguin Books.

YOUNG, M.F.D. (Ed.) (1971) *Knowledge and Control: New Directions for the Sociology of Education*, London: Collier Macmillan.

Notes on Contributors

Phil Francis Carspecken
Phil Francis Carspecken is Associate Professor of Cultural Studies, Educational Sociology, and Qualitative Research at the University of Houston. His scholarly work is focused on social theory and its applications to qualitative research methodology. Phil is the author of *Community Schooling and the Nature of Power*; and *Critical Ethnography in Educational Research* (both published by Routledge). A forthcoming book, *Meaning and Truth, Philosophical Explorations of a Critical Ethnographer*, will be published by Peter Lang.

Michelle Fine
Michelle Fine is a Professor of Psychology at the City University of New York, Graduate Center and the senior consultant at the Philadelphia Schools Collaborative. Her recent publications include *Chartering Urban School Reform: Reflections on Public High Schools in the Midst of Change* (1994), *Disruptive Voices: The Transgressive Possibilities of Feminist Research* (1992), and *Framing Dropouts: Notes on the Politics of an Urban High School* (1991). She has provided expert courtroom testimony and works nationally as a consultant to parents' groups, community groups, and teacher unions on issues of school reform. She was recently awarded the Janet Helms Distinguished Scholar Award 1994.

Douglas Foley
Douglas Foley is a Professor in the Departments of Anthropology and of Curriculum and Instruction at the University of Texas, Austin. He specializes in critical cultural studies and the study of race and ethnicity in education. Some of his most recent ethnographies are *From Peones to Politicos: Class and Ethnicity in a Texas Town, 1900–1989* (University of Texas Press, 1989), *Learning Capitalist Culture: Deep in the Heart of Tejas* (University of Pennsylvania Press, 1990) and *The Heartland Chronicles* (University of Pennsylvania Press, 1995). He is also the co–editor of the *International Journal of Qualitative Studies in Education*.

Noreen Garman
Noreen Garman is a Professor in the Department of Administrative and Policy Studies at the University of Pittsburgh, Pennsylvania. She teaches and publishes in the areas of instructional supervision, curriculum studies, and qualitative research. She is currently coauthoring *Cycles of Deliberation: Shaping the Qualitative Dissertation* with Maria Piantanida for Corwin Press. She is also Co-director of the Institute for International Studies in Education at the University of Pittsburgh.

Jesse Goodman
Jesse Goodman is a Professor in the School of Education, Co-director of a Master's level elementary teacher education program, and former Chair of the doctoral Curriculum Studies Program at Indiana University. He is the Co-Director of the Harmony Education Center, an organization committed to democratic school reform. His scholarly interests include the relationship between education and democracy, issues of school reform, teacher education/socialization, and research methodology. Dr. Goodman's book, *Elementary Schooling for Critical Democracy*, was published in 1992 by the State University of New York Press. He is collecting field data on issues related to changing the culture of high poverty schools which is to be published by Teachers College Press.

Gerald Grace
Gerald Grace has taught Education at King's College, University of London, the University of Cambridge, Victoria University of Wellington, New Zealand, and at the University of Durham where he was Head of the School of Education. He is currently Professorial Research Fellow at the University of London, Institute of Education. His most recent book is *School Leadership: Beyond Education Management: an Essay in Policy Scholarship* (Falmer Press, 1995).

Barry Kanpol
Barry Kanpol is an Associate Professor of Educational Foundations at Penn State Harrisburg. His primary research interests relate critical pedagogy as a social movement to broad issues both theoretically and practically. Social concerns such as race, class, gender, popular culture, curriculum, liberation theology, school leadership and critical ethnography are connected to his work on 'critical pedagogy'. He has written extensively in the educational foundations area — numerous books and articles. His most recent book, *Teachers Talking Back and Breaking Bread* will appear with Hampton Press early in 1998.

Bradley A. Levinson
Bradley A. Levinson is Assistant Professor of Anthropology of Education in the Department of Educational Leadership and Policy Studies at Indiana University. He specializes in ethnographic studies of youth identity and student culture in secondary schooling, and his research has focused on Maxico, Latin America, and the US within a comparative framework. He is co-editor (with Douglas Foley and Dorothy Holland) of *The Cultural Production of the Educated Person: Critical Ethnographies of Schooling and Local Practice* (1996, SUNY Press).

Laurie MacGillivray
Laurie MacGillivray is an Assistant Professor of Literacy in the School of Education at the University of Southern California. Her research focuses on the social interactions of emergent readers and writers across home and school and how these can inform teaching processes from a feminist post–modern perspective. Recently, her work has appeared in the *Journal of Literacy Research, Curriculum Inquiry*, and the *Journal of Research in Childhood Education*.

Stephen May

Stephen May is a lecturer in the Sociology Department, University of Bristol, England. He was previously a secondary school teacher and teacher educator in New Zealand. His principal research interests include multicultural/anti–racist education, language and education, minority language rights, and critical research methods. He is the author of *Making Multicultural Education Work* (Multilingual Matters, 1994) and editor of *Critical Multiculturalism* (Falmer Press, 1998).

Geoffrey Shacklock

Geoffrey Shacklock is Research Associate with the Flinders Insititue for the Study of Teaching at the Flinders University of South Australia. He has interests in the sociology of teachers' work and qualitative research methodologies. He is joint author with John Smyth of a book on teachers' work: *Remaking Teaching: Ideology, Policy and Practice* (Routledge).

John Smyth

John Smyth is Foundation Professor of Teacher Education at the Flinders University of South Australia, and Associate Dean (Research). He is also Director of the Flinders Institute for the Study of Teaching. He was a Senior Fulbright Research Scholar at University of Pittsburgh in 1990, Distinguished Scholar at University of British Columbia in 1991, and received the Palmer O. Johnson Award from AERA in 1993. In 1994 he was one of the judges of the ASCD Outstanding Dissertations Awards. John Smyth has authored/edited 10 books, the latest of which is entitled *Critical Discourses on Teacher Development* (Cassell). His most recent book (with Shacklock) is entitled *Remaking Teaching: Ideology, Policy and Practice* (Routledge).

Andrew Sparkes

Andrew C. Sparkes is Professor of Social Theory and is currently with the School of Education, University of Exeter, England. His research interests are eclectic and include: the lives and careers of teachers in marginal subjects; innovation and change; and interrupted body projects, identity dilemmas, and the narrative (re)construction of self. Each of these interests are framed by a desire to seek qualitative forms of understanding and an aspiration to represent experience using a variety of genres.

Annette Street

Associate Professor Annette Street is the Director of the Nursing Research Unit at La Trobe University, Melbourne, Australia. Annette has conducted research and consultancies throughout Australia, New Zealand, Thailand and in the USA. Her research interests are primarily focused on exploring the roles and practice of health care providers and the effects on health care consumers, currently in palliative care and women's health. Her research books *Inside Nursing* (SUNY Press) and *Nursing Replay* (Churchill-Livingstone), along with her other published monographs, are used in graduate programs in nursing and education in Asian and English speaking countries.

David Tripp
David Tripp is an Associate Professor at Murdoch University who specializes in qualitative research methods in action inquiry and professional development. He has pioneered a journal writing and critical incident approaches to action research, and published a widely used book on the method. Most recently he has developed and written the SCOPE Program which provides an action inquiry approach to professional workplace learning for the National Professional Development Program.

Lois Weis
Lois Weis is a Professor of Sociology of Education at the State University of New York at Buffalo. She is the author and/or editor of numerous books and articles, most recently *Beyond Silenced Voices: Class, Race, and Gender in U.S. Schools* and *Working Class Without Work: High School Students in a De-Industrialization Economy.*

Index